Karen Brown's
ENGLAND, WALES & SCOTLAND

Buckland Manor
Buckland, England

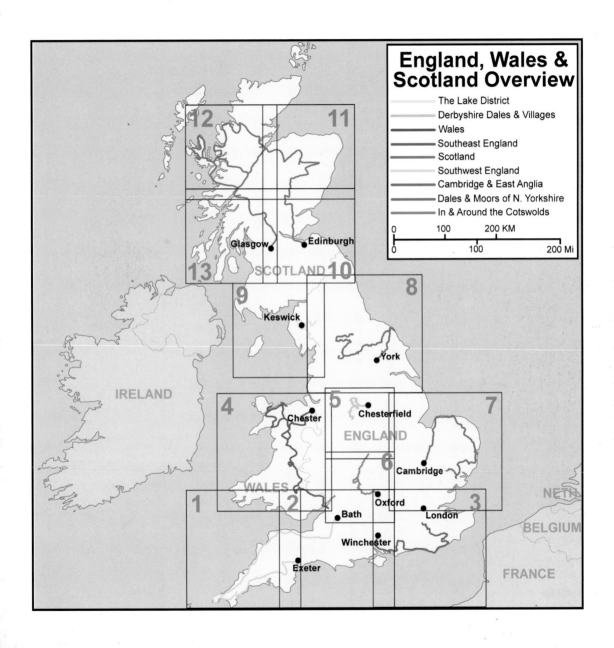

England, Wales & Scotland Overview

- The Lake District
- Derbyshire Dales & Villages
- Wales
- Southeast England
- Scotland
- Southwest England
- Cambridge & East Anglia
- Dales & Moors of N. Yorkshire
- In & Around the Cotswolds

0   100   200 KM
0   100   200 Mi

12 **11**

Glasgow Edinburgh

13 SCOTLAND **10**

9

Keswick

8

York

IRELAND

4 **5** Chesterfield **7**

Chester Chesterfield

ENGLAND

6

Cambridge

1 **2** WALES **3**

Oxford

Bath London

Winchester

Exeter

NETH

BELGIUM

FRANCE

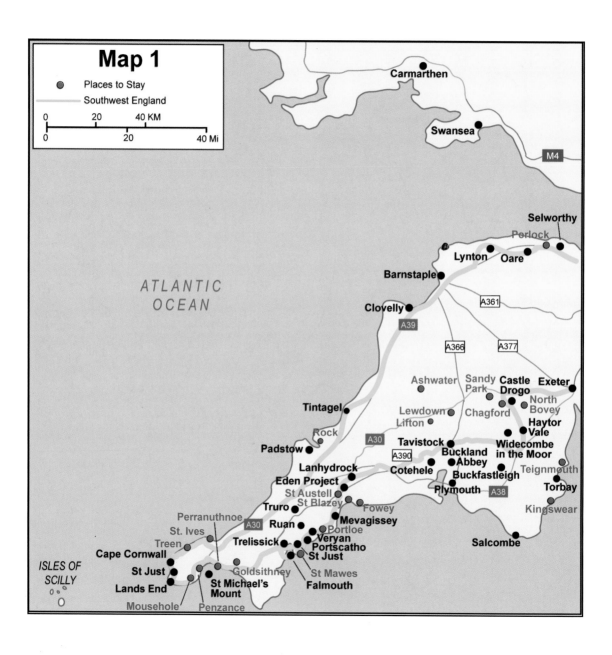

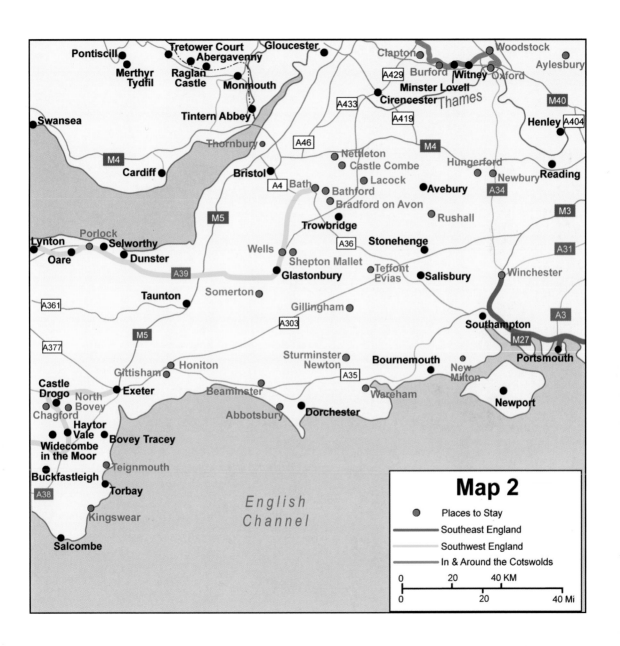

Map 2

Places to Stay
Southeast England
Southwest England
In & Around the Cotswolds

0   20   40 KM
0   20   40 Mi

English Channel

Map 3

Places to Stay

Southeast England

0   20   40 KM

0   20   40 Mi

Oxford
Aylesbury
Hertford
Chelmsford
A1
M11
A12
Henley
A404
M40
M25
London
Thames
M25
A34
M4
Reading
M3
M25
A31
A3
M23
Horley
A22
East Grinstead
Westerham
Chartwell
Hever
Penshurst
Tunbridge Wells
Scotney
M26
M2
Maidstone
M20
A229
Canterbury
A2
Ashford
Dover
Calais
Sissinghurst
Cranbrook
Strait of Dover
Midhurst
A272
Petworth
Cuckfield
Isfield
East Hoathly
Etchingham
Peasmarsh
Bodiam
Rye
Winchester
Weald & Downland Museum
Arundel
Lewes
Rushlake Green
Hartling
Hastings
M27
Brighton
Alfriston
Eastbourne
Portsmouth
Chichester
Beachy Head
Newport
English Channel
FRANCE

Map 4

- ● Places to Stay
- ── Wales

0 20 40 KM

0 20 40 Mi

Irish Sea

Holyhead

Isle of Anglesey

Beaumaris

Llanfair

Conwy Llandudno

A55

Bodnant Gardens

Chester

Huxley

A494

Caernarfon

Llanberis

Betws-y-Coed

Capel Garmon

Ruthin

A487

Blaenau Ffestiniog

A470

Llangollen

A5

Porthmadog

Portmeirion

Bala

Talsarnau

Llandrillo

Weston-under-Redcastle

Dolgellau

A494

Penmaenpool

Dinas Mawddy

Shrewsbury

M54

A458

Welshpool

Severn

Eglwysfach

Aberystwyth

Llangurig

A49

Norton

Rhayader

Elan Valley

A470

Ludlow

Leominster

Builth Wells

Hay-on-Wye

Wye

Llyswen

Hereford

Felin Fach

Newport

Fishguard

Brecon

Talybont-on-Usk

Llandeilo

Pontiscill

Tretower Court

Abergavenny

M50

Carmarthen

Merthyr Tydfil

Raglan Castle

Monmouth

Swansea

M4

Tintern Abbey

Thornbury

M5

Liverpool

M53

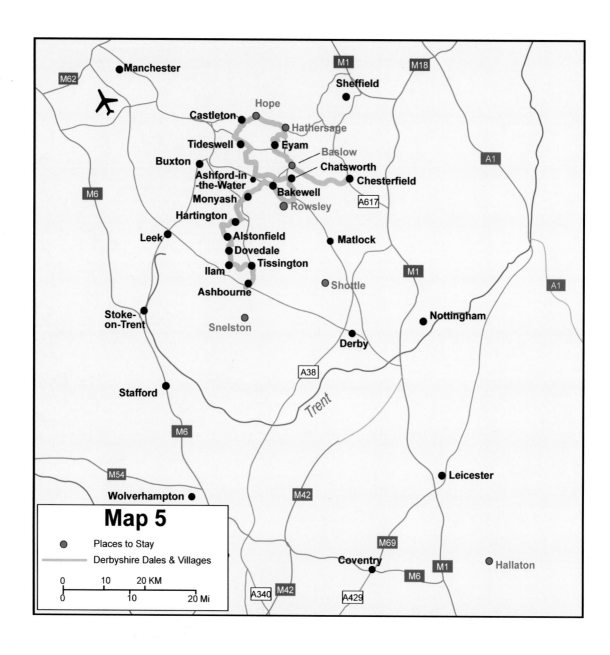

Map 5

Places to Stay
Derbyshire Dales & Villages

0   10   20 KM
0   10   20 Mi

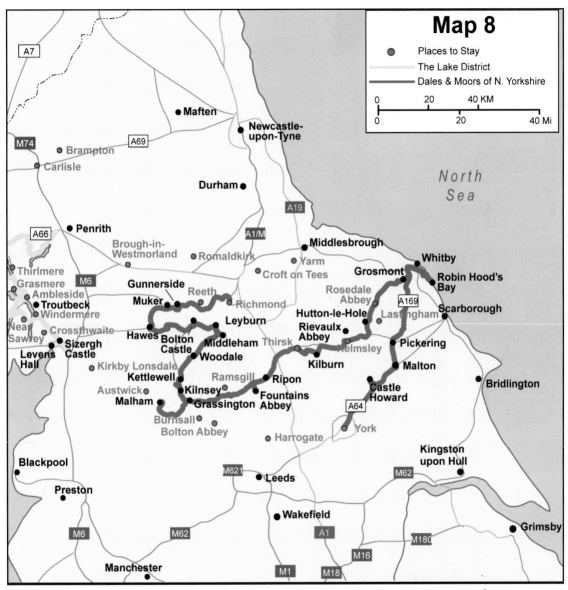

Map 8

- ● Places to Stay
- The Lake District
- Dales & Moors of N. Yorkshire

0   20   40 KM
0   20   40 Mi

A7

Maften

Newcastle-upon-Tyne

A69

M74

Brampton

Carlisle

Durham

A19

A66

Penrith

Brough-in-Westmorland

A1/M

Romaldkirk

Middlesbrough

Whitby

North Sea

Thirlmere
Grasmere
Ambleside

M6

Yarm

Croft on Tees

Grosmont

Robin Hood's Bay

Troutbeck
Windermere

Gunnerside

Reeth

Rosedale Abbey

A169

Scarborough

Near Sawrey

Crossthwaite

Muker

Richmond

Hutton-le-Hole

Lastingham

Levens Hall

Sizergh Castle

Leyburn

Rievaulx Abbey

Pickering

Hawes

Bolton Castle

Middleham

Thirsk

Helmsley

Malton

Woodale

Kirkby Lonsdale

Ramsgill

Kilburn

Bridlington

Kettlewell

Austwick

Kilnsey

Ripon

Castle Howard

Malham

Grassington

Fountains Abbey

A64

Burnsall

Bolton Abbey

Harrogate

York

Kingston upon Hull

Blackpool

M621

M62

Preston

Leeds

M6

M62

Wakefield

A1

M180

Grimsby

M16

Manchester

M1

M18

Augill Castle

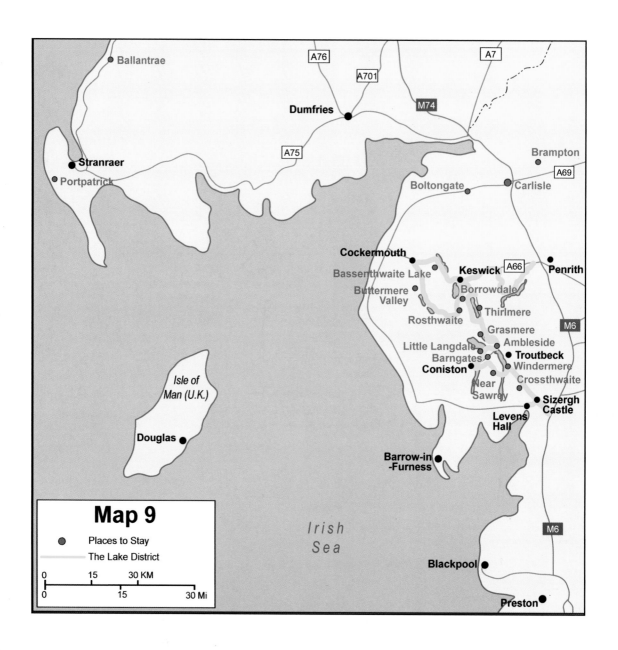

Map 9

- ● Places to Stay
- ▬ The Lake District

0   15   30 KM
0   15   30 Mi

Ballantrae

A76

A701

A7

Dumfries

M74

A75

Brampton

A69

Stranraer

Portpatrick

Boltongate

Carlisle

Cockermouth

Bassenthwaite Lake

Keswick

A66

Penrith

Buttermere Valley

Borrowdale

Thirlmere

Rosthwaite

Grasmere

M6

Little Langdale

Ambleside

Barngates

Troutbeck

Coniston

Windermere

Crossthwaite

Near Sawrey

Sizergh Castle

Levens Hall

Isle of Man (U.K.)

Douglas

Barrow-in-Furness

Irish Sea

M6

Blackpool

Preston

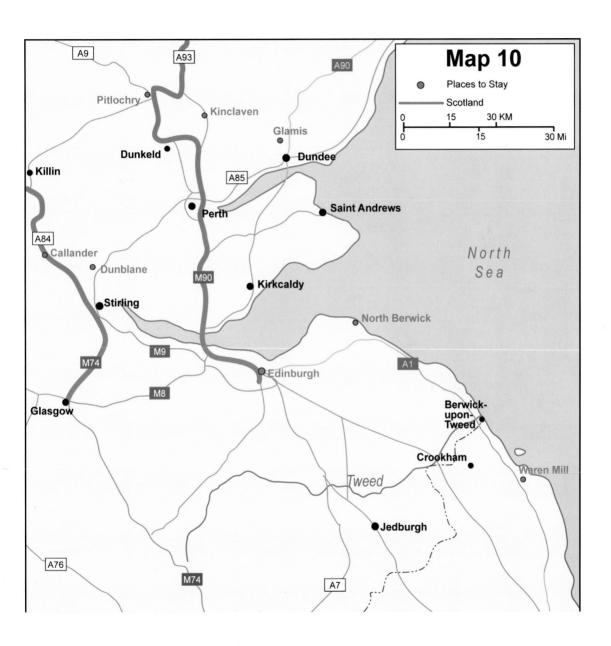

Map 10

Places to Stay
Scotland

| 0 | 15 | 30 KM |
| 0 | 15 | 30 Mi |

A9

A93

A90

Pitlochry

Kinclaven

Glamis

Dunkeld

Dundee

Killin

A85

Perth

Saint Andrews

A84

Callander

North Sea

Dunblane

M90

Stirling

Kirkcaldy

M9

North Berwick

M74

Edinburgh

A1

M8

Glasgow

Berwick-upon-Tweed

Crookham

Waren Mill

Tweed

A76

Jedburgh

M74

A7

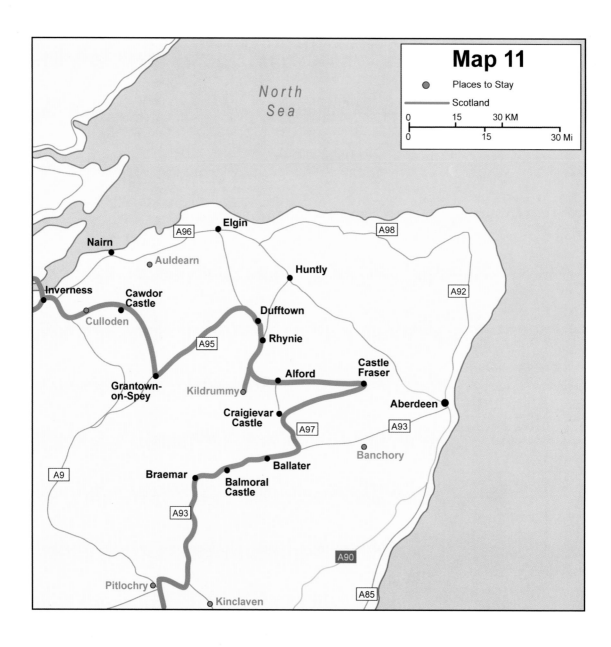

North
Sea

Map 11

● Places to Stay
— Scotland

0   15   30 KM
0   15   30 Mi

Elgin
A96   A98

Nairn
Auldearn

Huntly

Inverness   Cawdor
Castle

A92

Culloden

Dufftown

Rhynie

A95

Castle
Fraser

Alford

Aberdeen

Grantown-
on-Spey

Kildrummy

Craigievar
Castle

A97   A93

A9

Banchory

Ballater

Braemar

Balmoral
Castle

A93

A90

Pitlochry

Kinclaven

A85

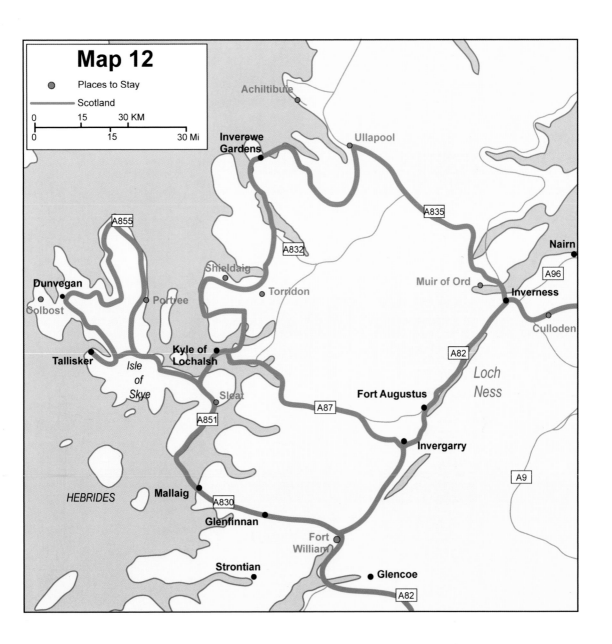

Map 12

● Places to Stay
─── Scotland

0   15   30 KM
0   15   30 Mi

Achiltibuie
Ullapool
Inverewe Gardens
A835
A832
Nairn
A96
Shieldaig
Muir of Ord
Dunvegan
Colbost
Portree
Torridon
Inverness
Culloden
Tallisker
Isle of Skye
Kyle of Lochalsh
Sleat
A87
Fort Augustus
Loch Ness
A82
A851
Invergarry
A9
HEBRIDES
Mallaig
A830
Glenfinnan
Fort William
Strontian
Glencoe
A82

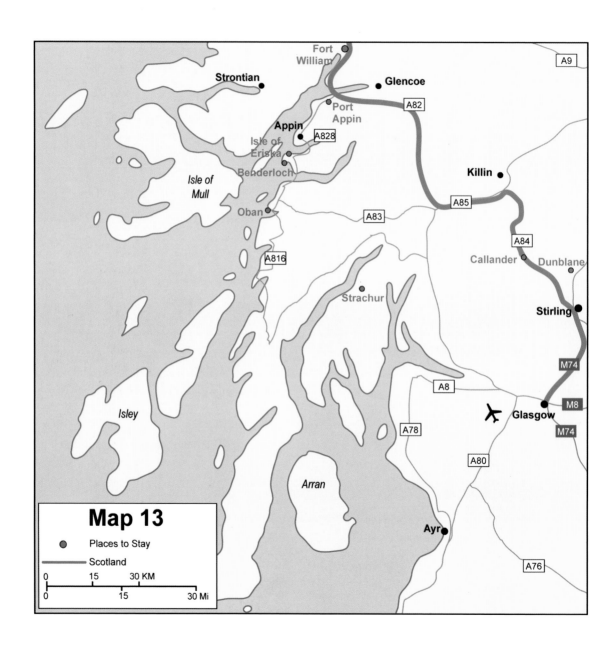

Map 13

- **Places to Stay**
- **Scotland**

0   15   30 KM
0   15   30 Mi

Fort William
Strontian
Glencoe
A82
Port Appin
Appin
A828
Isle of Eriska
Benderloch
Isle of Mull
Killin
A85
Oban
A83
A84
Callander
Dunblane
A816
Strachur
Stirling
Isley
M74
A8
Glasgow
M8
A78
M74
Arran
A80
Ayr
A76
A9

Contents

To Simon, Vanessa and Clare
in the hope that they will
discover Britain for themselves

Cover painting: Buckland Manor, Buckland

Authors: June Eveleigh Brown, Karen Brown.
Editors: Anthony Brown, Karen Brown, June Eveleigh Brown, Debbie Tokumoto.
Illustrations: Barbara Maclurcan Tapp.
Cover painting: Jann Pollard.
Maps &Technical support: Andrew Harris.

Distributed by National Book Network, 15200 NBN Way, Blue Ridge Summit, PA 17214, USA. Tel: 717-794-3800 or 1-800-462-6420, Fax: 1-800-338-4500, Email: custserv@nbnbooks.com

A catalog record for this book is available from the British Library.

ISSN 1535-7333

Introduction

This guide falls into three sections: practical information useful in planning your trip; driving itineraries that take you deep into the countryside through interesting villages full of thatched-roofed cottages and flower-filled gardens, exploring ancient castles and traversing vast purple moorlands; and lastly, but most importantly, our personal recommendations for outstanding places to stay in England, Scotland, and Wales— including an excellent selection in London. We offer accommodation in a wide range of prices from good value for money b&bs to decadent pampering resorts. Every place to stay is one that we have seen and enjoyed—our personal recommendation written with the sincere belief that where you lay your head each night makes the difference between a good and a great vacation.

About England, Wales & Scotland

The following pointers are given in alphabetical order, not in order of importance.

AIRFARE

Karen Brown's Guides have long recommended Auto Europe for their excellent car rental services. Their air travel division, Destination Europe, an airline broker working with major American and European carriers, offers deeply discounted coach- and business-class fares to over 200 European gateway cities. It also gives Karen Brown travelers an additional 5% discount off its already highly competitive prices (cannot be combined with any other offers or promotions). We recommend making reservations by phone at (800) 835-1555. When phoning, be sure to use the Karen Brown ID number 99006187 to secure your discount.

CAR RENTAL

If you are coming from overseas, it is frequently less expensive to arrange and prepay a car rental before arriving in Britain. If you plan on a visit to London, we strongly recommend that you make it either at the beginning or end of your trip. One option is to fly into London, pick your car up at the airport, tour the countryside, drop the car back at the airport, and take public transportation or a taxi into the city. If you are starting your vacation with sightseeing in London, collect your car from the airport at the end of your stay in the city. The trick is to avoid driving in London.

We always use Auto Europe—a car rental broker that works with the major car rental companies to find the lowest possible price. They also offer motor homes and chauffeur services. Auto Europe's toll-free phone service, from every European country, connects you to their U.S.-based, 24-hour reservation center (ask for the Europe Phone Numbers Card to be mailed to you). Auto Europe offers our readers a 5% discount (cannot be combined with any other offers or promotions) and, occasionally, free upgrades. Be sure to use the Karen Brown ID number 99006187 to receive your discount and any special offers. You can make your reservations online via our website, *www.karenbrown.com* (select *Auto Europe* from the home page), or, as we prefer, by phone (800-223-5555).

CURRENCY

The pound sterling (£) is the official currency of Great Britain. An increasingly popular and convenient way to obtain pounds is simply to use your bankcard at an ATM machine. You pay a fixed fee for this but, depending on the amount you withdraw, it is usually less than the percentage-based fee charged to exchange currency or travelers' checks. Be sure to check with your bank or credit card company about fees and necessary pin numbers prior to departure.

DRIVING

Just about the time overseas visitors board their return flight home, they will have adjusted to driving on the "right" side which is the left side in England. You must contend with such things as roundabouts (circular intersections); flyovers (overpasses); ring roads (peripheral roads whose purpose is to bypass city traffic); lorries (trucks); lay-bys (turn-outs); boots (trunks); and bonnets (hoods). Pedestrians are permitted to cross the road anywhere and always have the right of way. Seat belts must be worn at all times.

MOTORWAYS: The letter "M" precedes these convenient routes for covering long distances. With three or more lanes of traffic either side of a central divider, you should stay in the left-hand lane except for passing. Motorway exits are numbered and correspond to numbering on major road maps. Service areas supply petrol (gas), cafeterias, and "bathrooms" (the word "bathroom" is used in the American sense—in Britain "bathroom" means a room with a shower or bathtub, not necessarily a toilet— "loo" is the most commonly used term for an American bathroom).

"A" ROADS: The letter "A" precedes the road number. All major roads fall into this category. They vary from three lanes either side of a dividing barrier to single carriageways with an unbroken white line in the middle indicating that passing is not permitted. These roads have the rather alarming habit of changing from dual to single carriageways at a moment's notice.

"B" ROADS AND COUNTRY ROADS: The letter "B" preceding the road number, or the lack of any lettering or numbering, indicates that it belongs to the maze of country roads that crisscross Britain. These are the roads for people who have the luxury of time to enjoy the scenery en route and they require your arming yourself with a good map (although getting lost is part of the adventure). Driving these narrow roads is terrifying at first but exhilarating after a while. Meandering down these roads, you can expect to spend time crawling behind a tractor or cows being herded to the farmyard. Some lanes are so narrow that there is room for only one car.

ELECTRICITY

The power supply is usually 240 volts although most bathrooms have razor points (American style) for 110 volts. If you are coming from overseas, it is recommended that you take only dual-voltage appliances and a kit of electrical plugs. Hotel rooms come equipped with hairdryers and they are provided by most of our bed and breakfasts.

Introduction–About England, Wales & Scotland

INFORMATION

The British Tourist Authority is an invaluable source of information. You can visit their website at *www.visitbritain.com*. You'll find information centers in a great many towns and villages—always handy for local maps and sightseeing information. If you visit London before going to the countryside pick up information for your trip from the British Visitor Centre at 1 Regent Street, London SW1Y 4PQ (near Piccadilly Circus tube station) you can also reserve a coach tour or theatre tickets. It is open 9 am to 6:30 pm, Monday to Friday; 10 am to 4 pm, Saturday and Sunday, with extended hours from mid-May to September.

THE NATIONAL TRUST

The National Trust is dedicated to the preservation of places of historic interest or national beauty in England, Wales, Northern Ireland, and Scotland. Its care extends to stately homes, barns, historic houses, castles, gardens, Roman antiquities, moors, fells, woods, and even whole villages. During the course of a driving itinerary, whenever a property is under the care of the National Trust we state (NT). You can check when a property is open in the current edition of *The National Trust Handbook,* available from many National Trust shops and overseas from the British Tourist Authority, or utilize their website, *www.nationaltrust.org.uk*. If you are traveling to Scotland, you will need a copy of *The National Trust for Scotland Guide* or log on to *www.nts.org.uk*. A great many National Trust properties have excellent shops and tearooms. If you are planning on visiting several sites, consider joining the National Trust as a member, thus obtaining free entry into all properties.

SHOPPING

Visitors from non-EU countries can reclaim the VAT (Value Added Tax) that they pay on the goods they purchase. Not all stores participate in the refund scheme and there is often a minimum purchase price. Stores that do participate will ask to see your passport before completing the VAT form. This form must be presented *with the goods* to the customs officer at the point of departure from Britain within three months of purchase. The customs officer will certify the form. After having the receipts validated by customs you can receive a refund in cash from the tax-free refund counter. Alternatively, you can mail your validated receipts to the store where you bought the goods. The store will then send you a check in sterling for the refund.

WEATHER

Britain has a tendency to be moist at all times of the year. The cold in winter is rarely severe; however, the farther north you go, the greater the possibility of being snowed in. Spring can be wet but it is a lovely time to travel: the summer crowds have not descended, daffodils and bluebells fill the woodlands, and the hedgerows are filled with wildflowers. Summer offers the best chance of sunshine but also the largest crowds. Schools are usually closed the last two weeks of July and all of August—this is the time when most families take their summer holidays. Travel is especially hectic on the weekends in summer—try to avoid major routes and airports at these times. Autumn is also an ideal touring time: the weather tends to be drier than in spring and the woodlands are decked in their golden fall finery.

Overview Map of Driving Itineraries

Scotland

Edinburgh

The Dales and Moors of North Yorkshire

The Lake District

York

Derbyshire Dales and Villages

Chester

Chesterfield

Ashbourne

Cambridge and East Anglia

Wales

Coventry

Cambridge

Oxford

In and Around the Cotswolds

Bath

LONDON

Southwest England

Winchester

Exeter

Portsmouth

Southeast England

About Itineraries

Nine driving itineraries map routes through the various regions of England, Wales, and Scotland. At the beginning of each itinerary, we suggest our recommended pacing to help you decide the amount of time to allocate to each region. Often all, or a large portion, of an itinerary can be enjoyed using one hotel as a base and staying for several days.

Most sightseeing venues operate a summer and a winter opening schedule, changing over around late March/early April and late October/early November. If you happen to be visiting at the changeover times, be sure to check whether your chosen destination is open before making plans. We try to give an indication of opening times, but there is every possibility that these dates and times will have changed by the time you take your trip, so before you embark on an excursion, check the dates and hours of opening.

MAPS

Each of our driving itineraries is preceded by a map showing the route, and each hotel listing is referenced to a map at the front of the book. These are drawn by an artist and are not intended to replace commercial maps. Our suggestion is to purchase a large-scale road atlas of Britain where an inch equals 10 miles. We use the Michelin Tourist and Motoring Atlas of Great Britain–1122. To outline your trip you might want to consider the one-page map of Britain, Michelin Map 713. We sell these in our website store at *www.karenbrown.com.*

Introduction–About Itineraries

About Places to Stay

The third section of this guide contains our recommendations for outstanding places to stay in London, England, Scotland, and Wales. Each listing is very different and occasionally the owners have their eccentricities, which all adds to the allure of these special places. We have tried to be candid and honest in our appraisals and attempted to convey each property's special flavor, so that you know what to expect and will not be disappointed. All listings are places that we have inspected, or stayed in—places that we enjoy. Our recommendations cover a wide range: please do not expect the same standard of luxury at bed and breakfasts as you would at country house hotels—there is no comparison—yet each is outstanding in what it offers. We mention major sightseeing attractions near each countryside listing to encourage you to spend several nights in each location. Few countries have as much to offer as Great Britain—within a few miles of most listings there are places of interest to visit and explore: lofty cathedrals, quaint churches, museums, and grand country houses. To help you appreciate and understand what to expect the following pointers are given is alphabetical order not in order of importance.

CHILDREN

Places that welcome children have a "children welcome" icon ✼. The majority of listings in this guide do not "welcome" children but find they become tolerable at different ages over five or, more often than not, over twelve. On our website (*www.karenbrown.com*) you can put your cursor over the ✼ to see at what specific age children are welcome. These indications of children's acceptability are not cast in stone, so, for example, if you have your heart set on staying at a listing that accepts children over twelve: and you have an eight-year-old, call them, explain your situation, and they may well take you. Ideally, we would like to see all properties welcoming children and all parents doing their bit by making sure that children do not run wild.

CHRISTMAS PROGRAMS

Several listings offer Christmas getaways. If the information section indicates that the hotel is open during the Christmas season, there is a very good chance that it offers a festive Christmas package.

CREDIT CARDS

Whether or not an establishment accepts credit cards is indicated in the list of icons at the bottom of each description by the symbol ▣. We have also specified in the bottom details which cards are accepted as follows: none, AX–American Express, MC–MasterCard, VS–Visa, or simply, all major.

FINDING PLACES TO STAY

At the front of the book is a key map of Great Britain plus regional maps showing each recommended property's location. The pertinent regional map number is given at the right on the top line of each hotel's description. Also, we give concise driving directions to guide you to the listing, which is often in a more out-of-the-way place than the town or village in the address. We would be very grateful if you would let us know of cases where our directions have proved inadequate.

HANDICAP FACILITIES

If there is *at least* one guestroom that is accessible by wheelchair, it is noted with the symbol ♿. This is not the same as saying it meets full disability standards. In reality, it can be anything from a basic, ground-floor room to a fully equipped facility. Please discuss your requirements when you call your chosen place to stay to determine if they have accommodation that is suitable for you.

ICONS

We have these icons in the guidebooks and more on our website, *www.karenbrown.com*. ❄ Air conditioning in rooms, ⊥ Beach nearby, ☕ Breakfast included in room rate, 🏃 Children welcome, ♨ Cooking classes offered, 💳 Credit cards accepted, 🍲 Dinner served upon request, ☎ Direct-dial telephone in room, 🐕 Dogs by special request, 🛗 Elevator, 🏋 Exercise room, @ Internet access available for guests, 🍷 Mini-refrigerator in rooms, 🚭 Some non-smoking rooms, P Parking available (free or paid), 🍽 Restaurant, 🌿 Spa (treatments/massage etc.), 🏊 Swimming pool, 🎾 Tennis, 📺 Television with English channels in guestrooms, 💒 Wedding facilities, ♿ Wheelchair friendly, W Wireless available for guests, 🏌 Golf course nearby, 🥾 Hiking trails nearby, 🐎 Horseback riding nearby, ⛷ Skiing nearby, 🚣 Water sports nearby, 🍇 Wineries nearby. Icons allow us to provide additional information about our recommended properties. When using our website to supplement the guides, positioning the cursor over an icon will give you further details.

Introduction–About Places to Stay

MEALS

Prices quoted include breakfast, unless noted otherwise. Breakfast is most likely to be juice, a choice of porridge or cereal, followed by a plate of egg, bacon, sausage, tomatoes, and mushrooms completed by toast, marmalade, and jams—all accompanied by tea or coffee.

Quite a few bed & breakfasts offer evening meals, which should be requested at the time you make your reservation. **You cannot expect to arrive at a bed and breakfast and receive dinner if you have not made reservations for it several days in advance.** Whether or not an establishment offers dinner is indicated in the list of icons at the bottom of each description by the symbol ♨. Places that do not offer evening meals are always happy to recommend nearby pubs or restaurants.

Hotels and restaurants offer menus and wine lists, giving you more dining choices. If an establishment has a restaurant we indicate that with a ⊮ symbol. Our suggestion is that you make arrangements for dinner on the night of your arrival at the same time as you make reservations for accommodation.

RATES

Rates are those quoted to us for 2010. We have tried to keep rates uniform by quoting the 2010 range of rates for a double room. Not all places conform, so where dinner is included, we have made a note of this. Prices are usually quoted to include breakfast (except in London where breakfast is not usually included in the rate), Value Added Tax (VAT), and service (if these are applicable). Please use the figures printed as a guideline and be certain to ask what the rate is at the time of booking. Many listings offer special terms, below their normal prices, for "short breaks" of two or more nights.

RESERVATIONS

It is important to understand that once reservations for accommodation are confirmed, whether verbally, by phone or in writing, you are under contract. This means that the proprietor is obligated to provide the accommodation that was promised and that you are obligated to pay for it. If you cannot, you are liable for a portion of the accommodation charges plus your deposit. Although some proprietors do not strictly enforce a cancellation policy many, particularly the owners of the smaller properties in our book, simply cannot afford not to do so. Similarly, many airline tickets cannot be changed or refunded without penalty.

Reservations can be confining and usually must be guaranteed with a deposit. July and August are the busiest times and it is advisable to make reservations during this period. When making a reservation be specific as to what your needs are, such as a ground-floor room, en suite shower, twin beds, or family room. Check the prices, which may well have changed from the guidelines given in the book. Ask what deposit to send or give your credit card number. *Always spell out the month as the British reverse the American month/day numbering system.* Tell them about what time you intend to arrive and request dinner if you want it. Ask for a confirmation letter with brochure and map to be sent to you. There are several options for making reservations:

EMAIL: This is our preferred way of making a reservation. Every listing featured on the Karen Brown website that has email has a direct link.

FAX: If you have access to a fax machine, this is a very quick way to reach a hotel. If the place to stay has a fax, we have included the number in the listing. (See comment above about spelling out the month.)

LETTER: If you write for reservations, you will usually receive your confirmation and a map. You should then send your deposit. (Be sure to spell out the month.)

TELEPHONE: By telephoning you have your answer immediately, so if space is not available, you can then decide on an alternative. If calling from the United States, allow for the time difference (Britain is five hours ahead of New York) so that you can call during their business day. Dial 011 (the international code), 44 (Britain's code), then the city code (dropping the 0), and the telephone number.

WEBSITE

Please visit the Karen Brown website (*www.karenbrown.com*) in conjunction with this book. Our website provides trip planning assistance, new discoveries, post-press updates, feedback from you, our readers, the opportunity to purchase goods and services that we recommend (rail tickets, car rental, travel insurance, etc.), and one-stop shopping for our guides, associated maps and watercolor prints. Most of our favorite places to stay are featured with color photos and direct website and email links. Also, we invite you to participate in the Karen Brown's Readers' Choice Awards. Be sure to visit our website and vote so your favorite properties will be honored.

Warwick Castle

Southwest England

Orientation/Sightseeing

Itinerary Route

Boscastle

Tintagel

Padstow

A39

A30

Lostwithiel

A30

The Eden Project

St Austell

A390

Mevagissey

Truro

Lost Gardens
of Heligan

St Ives

Veryan

Trelissick
Gardens

Portloe

Portscatho

St Just in Roseland

Cape
Cornwall

St Just

Marazion

A394

St Mawes

Falmouth

Lands End

St Michael's
Mount

Penzance

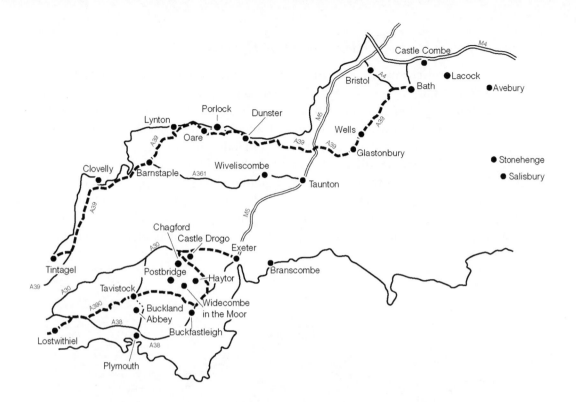

Southwest England

Scenery changes noticeably as this itinerary traverses England southwest from Bath through Somerset and along its unspoilt coast, outlining Cornwall, into the heart of Devon. Wild ponies gallop across the expanses of Exmoor. Along the northern coastline, the scenery changes dramatically from wooded inlets dropping to the sea to wild rollers crashing on granite cliffs, giving credence to old tales of wreckers luring ships onto rocky shorelines. Picturesque villages surround sheltered harbors, their quays strewn with nets and lobster pots. Southern ports present a gentler scene: bobbing yachts dot wooded estuaries and gentle waves lap the shoreline. Hedgerow-lined lanes meander inland across Dartmoor's heather-clad moorlands to picturesque towns nestling at her edge. Relax and enjoy your explorations of this westernmost spur of land jutting out into the Atlantic Ocean.

St. Michael's Mount

Recommended Pacing: Spend two full days in Bath to give you time to appreciate the flavor of this lovely city. We suggest that you select a place to stay to explore the northern coast of the peninsula, and another as a base for exploring the south of Cornwall. Add a couple of nights in south Devon to enable you to enjoy the wild beauties of Dartmoor. Complete the itinerary with a stay in or near Salisbury.

The elegant city of **Bath** with its graceful, honey-colored buildings, interesting museums, and delightful shopping area is best explored on foot over a period of several days. Bath, founded by the Romans in the 1st century around the gushing mineral hot springs, reached its peak of popularity in the early 1700s with the arrival of Beau Nash, who opened the first Pump Room where people could take the water and socialize. Architects John Wood, father and son, used the local honey-colored stone to build the elegant streets and crescents in neoclassical Palladian style.

Maps are available from the Tourist Information Centre near the abbey on York Street. Entry into the **Roman Baths** is via the **Pump Room,** which was the place to gather in the 18th and 19th centuries. The Great Bath, a large warm swimming pool built around a natural hot spring, now open to the sky, was once covered. Mosaics, monuments, and many interesting artifacts from the town can be seen in the adjacent museum.

Nearby, tucked into a narrow passageway between Abbey Green and North Parade, is **Sally Lunn's House**, a museum and a teashop. The museum, in the cellar, has the kitchen preserved much as it was in the 1680s when Sally's buns and other baked goods were the favorites of Bath society. Upstairs you can try a freshly baked Sally Lunn bun.

Eighteenth-century society came to be seen at balls and gatherings at the **Assembly Rooms** and authors such as Austen, Smolett, and Fielding captured the social importance of these events. The **Museum of Costume**, in the Assembly Rooms basement, should not be missed.

From the Museum of Costume it is an easy walk via **The Circus**, a tight circle lined with splendid houses designed by John Wood I, and Brock Street to the **Royal Crescent**, a great arc of 30 terraced houses that epitomize the Georgian elegance of Bath. **One Royal**

Crescent has been authentically restored to the 18th-century style and contains an interesting kitchen museum and a gift shop.

Bath has some wonderful restaurants and delightful shops and boutiques: whether you are in the market for antiques or high fashion, you will find shopping here a real joy.

While our itinerary takes us south and west from Bath, there are a great many interesting places to the east, listed below, that can easily be visited as day trips from this lovely city.

The village of **Avebury** (NT), made up of a church, several houses, shops, and an old pub, lies within a vast circle of standing stones surrounded by earthworks. The site covers 28 acres. Unlike Stonehenge, where the stones are larger, the site smaller and the crowds sometimes overwhelming, Avebury is a peaceful spot. Here, armed with a map, you can wander amongst the stones and wonder why 4,000 years ago Bronze Age man spent what has been estimated at 1½ million man-hours to construct such a temple. (Just off the A4 between Calne and Marlborough.)

Castle Combe is a most photogenic collection of warm, honey-stone cottages snuggled along a stream's edge. (Just south of the M4 motorway between exits 17 and 18.)

Claverton Manor is the American museum in the United Kingdom. Furniture, household equipment, and period rooms show home life in the United States from the 17th to 19th centuries. (3 miles east of Bath.)

Lacock (NT) is an exquisite village where no building dates from later than the 18th century, many dating from much earlier. Be sure to visit the **Fox Talbot Museum** of early photographs and **Lacock Abbey**. The abbey was converted to a manor house in the 16th century but retains its 13th-century cloisters. **At The Sign of The Angel** is a delightful 15th-century inn, easily distinguished by being the only black-and-white building in the village. (Between Chippenham and Melksham on the A350.)

Salisbury has been a prosperous Wiltshire market town since the 13th century. Park your car in one of the large car parks on the edge of town and wander through the bustling town center to **Salisbury Cathedral**, the only ancient English cathedral built to a single design. Completed in 1258, it sits gracefully isolated from the busy town, surrounded by a large green field.

Salisbury Cathedral

Britain's most famous ancient monument is **Stonehenge**. Built over a period of almost 1,000 years up to 1250 B.C., this circular arrangement of towering stone slabs was probably meant either to mark the seasons or to be used as a symbol of worship. It is intriguing to ponder what prompted a society thousands of years ago to drag these immense stones many miles and erect them in just such a formation, isolated in the middle of flat Salisbury Plain. Understandably, Stonehenge attracts many visitors. Your visit will be more enjoyable if you are prepared for coachloads of tourists. (On the A303 about 10 miles from Salisbury.)

When it is time to leave Bath, take the A4 following signs for Bristol until you come to the A39 Wells road. **Wells** is England's smallest cathedral city and the cathedral is glorious. Park your car in one of the well-signposted car parks on the edge of town and walk through the bustling streets to **Wells Cathedral**. The cathedral's west front is magnificently adorned with 400 statues of saints, angels, and prophets. The interior is lovely and on every hour the Great Clock comes alive as figures of four knights joust and one is unseated. From the cathedral you come to Vicars Close, a cobbled street of tall-chimneyed cottages with little cottage gardens, built over 500 years ago as housing for the clerical community. On the other side of the cathedral regal swans swim lazily in the moat beneath the Bishop's Palace where at one time they rang a bell when they wanted to be fed—now visitors' picnics provide easier meals.

Nearby **Glastonbury** is an ancient market town steeped in legends. As the story goes, Joseph of Arimathea traveled here and leaned on his staff, which rooted and flowered, a symbol that he should build a church. There may well have been a primitive church here but the ruins of **Glastonbury Abbey** that you see are those of the enormous abbey complex that was begun in the 13th century and closed by Henry VIII just as it was completed. The abbey is in the center of town. Legend also has it that Glastonbury (at that time surrounded by marshes and lakes) was the Arthurian Isle of Avalon. Arthur and Guinevere are reputedly buried here and it is said that Arthur only sleeps and will arise when England needs him.

Cross the M5 near Bridgwater, detouring around the town, and follow the A39, Minehead road, to **Dunster**, a medieval town dominated by the battlements and towers of **Dunster Castle** (NT). Constructed by a Norman baron, it has been inhabited by the Luttrell family since 1376. While much of the castle was reconstructed in the last century, it has a superb staircase, halls, and dining room. Park before you enter the town and explore the shops and ancient buildings (including a dormered Yarn Market) on the High Street. On Mill

Lane you can tour 18th-century **Dunster Watermill** (NT), which was restored to working order in 1979.

Continue your drive along the A39, watching for a sign directing you to your right to the hamlet of **Selworthy** (NT). Its pretty green, surrounded by elaborate thatched cottages, makes this a very picturesque spot. The National Trust has a small visitors' center and excellent teashop.

Porlock is a large, quaint, bustling village with narrow streets. As the road bends down to the sea, the hamlet of **Porlock Weir** appears as a few picturesque cottages, the Ship Inn facing a pebble beach and a tiny harbor dotted with boats.

Retrace your steps towards Porlock for a short distance and take the first road to the right, a private toll road that rises steeply out of Porlock Weir. It is a pretty, forested drive along a narrow lane with views of Porlock Bay. The toll road returns you to the A39, which you take for a short distance before turning left for the village of **Oare**. R. D. Blackmore who wrote about the people, moods, and landscape of Exmoor used the little church that you see in the valley below for Lorna Doone's marriage to John Ridd. Continue into the village where you can park your car near the village shop and take a 3-mile walk along the river to Badgworthy Valley, the home of the cutthroat outlaw Doone family.

Continue to Brenden where you turn right, signposted Lynton and Lynmouth, and regain the A39. A short drive through squat red and green hills brings you to the coast where the road dips steeply and you see the neighboring villages of **Lynton** and **Lynmouth**. Victorian Lynton stands at the top of the cliff and Lynmouth, a fishing village of old-style houses, nestles at its foot. Park by the harbor and take the funky old cliff railway, which connects the two villages.

Leaving Lynmouth, proceed up the hill into Lynton, and follow signs for the alternative route for light vehicles to Valley of the Rocks. Wend your way through the town and continue straight. Beyond the suburbs the road tapers and you find yourself in a narrow valley with large, rugged rock formations separating you from the sea, then in a more pastoral area with seascapes at every dip and turn.

Deposit your road toll in the honesty box and follow signs along narrow lanes for **Hunters Inn**, a lovely old pub set in a peaceful valley. From here direct yourself back towards the A39, which bends inland across the western stretches of Exmoor and south through **Barnstaple**, a market center for the area. Continue along the A39 to Bideford where a bridge sweeps you high above the old harbor.

Just beyond Bucks Cross you see a small signpost for **Clovelly**, an impossibly beautiful spot, its whitewashed cottages tumbling down cobblestone lanes to boats bobbing in the harbor far below. However, to be able to walk through this picturebook village you have to pay an entrance fee at the visitors' center, which rankles but also preserves this lovely place.

Leave the A39 at the B3263 and detour on narrow country lanes leading to the picturesque little village of **Boscastle**. Braced in a valley 400 feet above a little harbor, the town was named after the Boscastle family who once lived there, rather than an actual castle.

Nearby, **Tintagel Castle** clings to a wild headland, exposed to coastal winds, claiming the honor of being King Arthur's legendary birthplace. The sea has cut deeply into the slate cliffs, isolating the castle. Climb the steep steps to the castle and gaze down at the sea far below. Prince Charles, as Duke of Cornwall, owns the castle whose interior is more attractive than the exterior. The town itself, while it is quite touristy, has charm and the most adorable, and certainly most photographed, **Post Office** (NT) in Britain.

Leaving Tintagel, follow signs for the A39, in the direction of Truro, to the A30, which takes you around Redruth, Cambourne, and Hayle to the A3074 to **St. Ives**, about an hour-and-a-half's journey if the roads are not too busy. Stay on the A3074 until the road is signposted sharp right to the harbor. Go left and follow parking signs to the Recreation Centre. Park your car here and walk down into town. Your destination is Fore Street with its galleries, restaurants, and interesting shops. Fore Street leads you to the quaint harbor while a left on Digbey will bring you to the **Tate Gallery** on Porthmeor Beach. Whistler and Sickert discovered St. Ives while sculptress Barbara Hepworth and painter Ben Nicholson made it famous. Admission to the Tate also includes admission to Barbara Hepworth's garden filled with her sculptures. If you are not a fan of modern art, just ask for a pass to visit the rooftop café and enjoy the spectacular views.

Leaving St. Ives, follow signposts to St. Just, which brings you the most attractive, windswept stretch of Cornwall's coastline. Stone farm villages hug the bare expanse of land and are cooled by Atlantic Ocean breezes that waft up over the cliff edges. Abandoned old tin mine towers stand in ruins and regularly dot the horizon. On the western outskirts of **St. Just** lies **Cape Cornwall**. Rather than visit over-commercialized Land's End, visit here to enjoy a less crowded, more pastoral western view. Pull into **Sennen Cove** with its long, curving crescent of golden sand and the powerful Atlantic surf rolling and pounding.

The expression "from John O'Groats to Land's End" signifies the length of Britain from its northeasternmost point in Scotland to England's rocky promontory, **Land's End**, in the southwest. Many visitors to Cornwall visit Land's End, but be prepared to be disappointed—you have to pay to enter a compound of refreshment stands, exhibits, and children's rides to get to the viewpoint.

As the road rounds the peninsula from Land's End, it is exposed to the calmer Channel waters, far different from the Atlantic rollers. Mount's Bay is just around the bend from Land's End with the pretty village of **Mousehole** (pronounced "mowzle") tucked into a niche on its shores. With color-washed cottages crowded into a steep valley and multicolored fishing boats moored at its feet, this adorable village is crowded in summer but worth the aggravation endured in finding a parking spot.

Pirates from France and the Barbary Coast used to raid the flourishing port town of **Penzance** until the mid-18th century. Now it is quite a large town, a real mishmash of styles from quaint fishermen's cottages to '60s housing estates, where long, peaceful, sandy beaches contrast with the clamor and activity of dry-dock harbors.

Leave Penzance on the A30 following the graceful sweep of Mount's Bay and turn right onto a minor road that brings you to **St. Michael's Mount** (NT). Its resemblance to the more famous mount in France is not coincidental, for it was founded by monks from Mont St. Michel in 1044. A 19th-century castle and the ruins of the monastery crown the island, which is reached at low tide on foot from the town of Marazion. If you cannot coincide your arrival with low tide, do not worry—small boats ferry you to the island. The steep climb to the top of this fairy-tale mount is well worth the effort.

To the east lies **Falmouth**. Overlooking the holiday resort, yachting center, and ancient port are the ruins of **Pendennis Castle**. Built in 1540 to guard the harbor entrance, it was held during the Civil War by the Royalists and withstood six months of siege before being the last castle to surrender to Cromwell's troops in 1646. Falmouth is a bustling town whose narrow, shop-lined streets have a complex one-way system—parking is an additional problem. Unless you have shopping to do, avoid the congestion of the town center and follow signposts for Truro.

The road from Falmouth to St. Mawes winds around the river estuary by way of Truro. A faster and more scenic route is to take the **King Harry Ferry** across the river estuary. If you love wandering around gardens, you will enjoy **Trelissick Gardens** (NT), filled with subtropical plants, located on the Falmouth side of the estuary.

St. Mawes is a charming, unspoilt fishing harbor at the head of the Roseland Peninsula. Its castle was built by Henry VIII to defend the estuary. The 20 miles or so of coastline to the east of St. Mawes hide several beautiful villages located down narrow, winding country lanes. **Portscatho** is a lovely fishing village that has not been overrun with tourists. **Veryan** is a quaint village where thatched circular houses were built so that "the devil had nowhere to hide." **Portloe** is a pretty fishing hamlet. The most easterly village is **Mevagissey** whose beauty attracts writers, artists, and throngs of tourists.

Overlooking this quaint port lie the expansive estates of the Tremayne family, centered at one time on Heligan House and its vast acres of gardens and woodlands. There used to be 20 staff in the house and 22 in the garden but all this ended in the 1914–18 war when two-thirds of the gardeners died fighting in Flanders. After that the garden went into decline and when the Tremaynes sold the house, in 1970, for conversion to apartments, it simply went to sleep—a sleep from which it emerged in the 1990s when two professional gardeners hacked their way through the undergrowth and were inspired to begin the largest garden restoration project in Europe. Evoking images of *The Secret Garden,* the **Lost Gardens of Heligan** have emerged from their slumber. A magnificent complex of walled gardens, vegetable gardens, and melon yards shows how pineapples and melons were grown in Victorian times. To the south of the main garden are vast acres of palms and tree ferns know as The Jungle, which leads to the Lost Valley with its woodland walks.

Drive through St. Austell on the A390 and turn left up into the hills above the town, following signs to **The Eden Project**, set in a former china clay pit. The aim of this project is to promote the understanding and responsible management of the vital relationship between plants, people, and resources. At the bottom of the giant crater are the world's largest greenhouses clinging onto the cliffs like huge soap bubbles. In the space of a day you can walk from the scented warmth of the Mediterranean to the steaminess of a rainforest. You'll find plenty of convenient parking and enough hands-on exhibits and restaurants to make this a fun visit rather than an academic experience.

Your next destination, **Llanhydrock** (NT), lies just a short distance away. Follow signs to Bodmin and take the dual carriageway (A30) to the first exit signed Lanhydrock. Set in a vast estate and surrounded by formal gardens, Llanhydrock showcases what was the very latest in contemporary living in 1881—there's even central heating. It looks as though the family has just stepped out, leaving the dining table laid for an elaborate party, toys in the nursery waiting to be played with, the schoolroom all set for lessons, afternoon tea set up in the mistress' sitting room, and desserts all ready to be served from the kitchen.

Returning to the A30, drive northeast to **Lostwithiel**, the 13th-century capital of Cornwall. Twenty miles to the east, **Liskeard** is crowded in summer, but fortunately much of the traffic has been diverted around the town. Between Liskeard and Tavistock you find **Cotehele** (NT), built between 1485 and 1627, the home of the Edgecumbe family. The house contains original furniture, armor, and needlework. A highlight is the kitchen with all its wonderful old implements. The gardens terrace steeply down to the lovely River Tamar.

The A390 crosses the River Tay and brings you into Tavistock. Turn right at the first roundabout in town signposted B3357 Princetown (then the B3212 Mortenhampstead road), which brings you up, over a cattle grid, and into **Dartmoor National Park**. Vast expanses of moorland rise to rocky outcrops (tors and crags) where ponies and sheep graze intently among the bracken and heather, falling to picturesque wooded valleys where villages shelter beneath the moor. From Mortenhampstead it's a half-hour drive to Exeter and the motorway. But, saving the best for last, linger on Dartmoor and enjoy some of the following sights.

The view from atop **Haytor Crags** on the Bovey to Widecombe road is a spectacular one—there is a feel of *The Hound of the Baskervilles* to the place. Softer and prettier is the walk down wooded **Lydford Gorge** (NT) to White Lady Waterfall (between Tavistock and Okehampton). A cluster of cottages and a tall church steeple make up **Widecombe in the Moor**, the village made famous by the *Uncle Tom Cobbleigh* song. The famous fair is still held on the second Tuesday in September. The pretty town of **Chagford** at the edge of the moor has attractive houses and hostelries grouped round the market square. **Buckland-in-the-Moor** is full of picturesque thatched cottages. **Buckland Abbey** (NT), once a Cistercian abbey and home of Sir Francis Drake, is now a museum with scale model ships from Drake's time to today among its exhibits At **Buckfastleigh** you can take a steam train 7 miles alongside the river Dart. **Castle Drogo** (NT) is a fanciful, castlelike home designed by Edward Lutyens overlooking the moor near Drewsteignton.

Leaving Dartmoor National Park, as series of A roads quickly bring you to **Exeter**. The old town towards the River Exe has many fine old buildings including the Custom House and a maze of little streets with old inns and quaint shops. The center is a modern shopping complex. From Exeter the M5 will connect you to all parts of Britain.

Southeast England

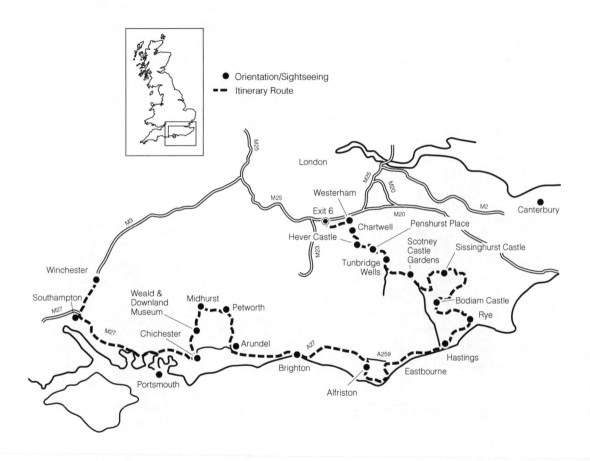

Orientation/Sightseeing
Itinerary Route

London

Westerham

Exit 6

M25

M20

M2

Canterbury

Chartwell

Penshurst Place

Hever Castle

Scotney Castle Gardens

Sissinghurst Castle

M23

Tunbridge Wells

Bodiam Castle

Winchester

Rye

Southampton

M27

Weald & Downland Museum

Midhurst

Petworth

Chichester

M27

Arundel

A27

A259

Hastings

Brighton

Eastbourne

Portsmouth

Alfriston

M3

M25

Southeast England

Southeast from London, through Kent and Sussex to England's southern coast, the land is fertile and the climate mild. Scores of narrow country lanes twist and turn among the gentle slopes of the pleasant countryside, leading you from Chartwell, Churchill's home, through castles, manors, and some of the most exquisitely beautiful gardens in England to Rye, a town full of history and rich in smugglers' tales. Along the busy, crowded coast you come to Brighton, where seaside honky-tonk contrasts with the vivid spectacle of the onion domes of the Royal Pavilion, Arundel with its mighty fortress, and Portsmouth with its historic boats.

Rye

Recommended Pacing: Spend two nights in southeast England to enable you to accomplish the first part of this itinerary. Allow a day's drive, with sightseeing, along the coast and into Winchester. Spend two nights in Winchester to give you a complete day for sightseeing.

Chartwell, your first sightseeing destination, lies 9 miles from exit 6 of the M25, through Westerham and onto country lanes. Chartwell was the home of Winston Churchill from 1924 until his death in 1965, when Lady Churchill gave the house and its contents to the nation. To visit this large home and Churchill's studio, full of his mementos and paintings, is to have a glimpse into the family life of one of Britain's most famous politicians.

Leave Chartwell to the left following the country road a short distance to **Hever Castle**, a small 13th-century moated castle that was at one time home to the Boleyn family. Anne Boleyn was Henry VIII's second wife and Elizabeth I's mother. At the turn of the last century vast amounts of money were poured into the castle's restoration by William Waldorf Astor, an extremely wealthy American who forsook his native country and became a naturalized British citizen. Because the castle was far too small to provide accommodation for his family and friends, Mr Astor built an adjacent village of snug, Tudor-style cottages and joined it to the castle. While the village is not open to the public, the restored castle, its rooms full of antiques that span the last 800 years, and the parklike grounds are open to visitors.

Leave the castle heading left in the direction of Tunbridge Wells, turning left down a small country road to **Chiddingstone**, a National Trust village, whose short main street has several 16th- and 17th-century, half-timbered houses, a church, and a teashop. Park by the old houses and follow a footpath behind the cottages to the Chiding Stone, from which the village gets its name: nagging wives were brought here to be chided by the villagers.

Just beyond the village, branch left at the oast house for Penshurst Station and **Penshurst Place**, a 14th-century manor house with an Elizabethan front surrounded by magnificent parkland and gorgeous gardens. Here Sir Philip Sidney—poet, soldier, and statesman—was born and his descendant, Viscount de l'Isle, lives today. The enormous, 14th-century great hall with its stone floor and lofty, ornate, beamed ceiling contrasts by its austerity with the sumptuously furnished state rooms. There is also a fascinating collection of old toys. The gardens are a delight, full of hedges and walls that divide them into flower-filled alleyways and rooms—each garden with a very different character.

Tunbridge Wells lies about 7 miles to the south. In its heyday Royal Tunbridge Wells rivaled Bath as a spa town. The Regency meeting place, The Pantiles, a terraced walk with shops behind a colonnade, is still there as are the elegant Regency parades and houses designed by Decimus Burton. Central parking is well signposted to the rear of the Corn Exchange, which contains an exhibit, *Day at the Wells*, which traces the town's growth from the time the spring water became fashionable for its curative powers to its popularity with wealthy Victorians.

Leave Tunbridge Wells on the A267 following signposts for Eastbourne till you are directed to the left through Bells Yew Green to cross the A21 (Hastings road) and enter **Scotney Castle Gardens** (NT), a gorgeous, romantic garden surrounding the moated ruins of a 14th-century castle.

Leave Scotney Castle Gardens to the left, taking the A21 (Hastings road) for a short distance to Flimwell where you turn left on the A268 to Hawkshurst and from here left on the A229 Maidstone road to **Cranbrook**. While it is not necessary to go through Cranbrook to get to Sissinghurst Gardens, it makes a very worthwhile detour because it is a delightful town whose High Street has many lovely, white-board houses and shops, a fine medieval church, and a huge, white-board windmill with enormous sails. On the other side of town you come to the A262 where you turn right for the short drive to Sissinghurst Castle Gardens.

Sissinghurst Castle (NT) was a jail for 3,000 French prisoners in the Seven Years' War. Its ruined remains were bought by Vita Sackville-West and her husband, Harold Nicolson, in 1930 and together they created the most gorgeous gardens with areas divided off like rooms, each with a distinctly different, beautiful garden. They also rescued part of the derelict castle where you can climb the tower in which Vita wrote her books. At the entrance to the garden an old barn has been tastefully converted into a tearoom and shop.

Scotney Castle Gardens

Continue along the A262 to Biddenden and take the A28 through **Tenterden** with its broad High Street of tiled and weather-boarded houses to the A268 (Hawkshurst road) where you turn right for the short drive to the village of Sandhurst. Here you turn left onto country lanes to **Bodiam Castle** (NT), a small, picturesque, squat fortress with crenelated turrets surrounded by a wide moat and pastoral countryside. Richard II ordered the castle built as a defensive position to secure the upper reaches of the Rother against French raiders who had ravaged nearby towns, but an attack never came.

Turn left as you leave the castle, following a country lane to Staple Cross where you turn left on the B2165, which brings you into **Rye**, a fortified seaport that was often attacked by French raiders. However, the sea has long since retreated, leaving the town marooned 2 miles inland. Find the quaintest street in Rye, **Mermaid Street**, with its weatherboard and tile-hung houses and up one cobblestoned block you find yourself on the doorstep of **The Mermaid Inn**. Opened in 1420, The Mermaid Inn is a fascinating relic of the past. As late as Georgian days, smugglers frequented this strikingly timbered inn and used to sit drinking in the pub with their pistols on the table, unchallenged by the law. Near the Norman Church is the 13th-century **Ypres Tower**—formerly a castle and prison, it is now a museum of local history. **Lamb House** (NT) (on West Street near the church) was the home of American novelist Henry James from 1898 to 1916. To learn more about Rye's fascinating history attend the sound and light show at the **Rye Town Model**.

Leave Rye on the A259, taking this fast road around Hastings and Bexhill to **Eastbourne** where you follow signs for the seafront of this old-fashioned holiday resort and continue on to the B2103, which brings you up and onto the vast chalk promontory, **Beachy Head**, rising above the town. It is a glorious, windswept place of soaring seagulls and springy turf, which ends abruptly as the earth drops away to giant chalk cliffs plummeting into the foaming sea. This is the starting point for the **South Downs Way**, a popular walking path. Passing the Belle Tout Lighthouse, you come to **Birling Gap**, a beach once popular with smugglers but now favored by bathers. The most dramatic scenery, the **Seven Sisters**, giant, white, windswept cliffs, are an invigorating walk from the visitors' center.

Your next destination is **Alfriston**, an adorable village on the South Downs Way which traces its origins back to Saxon times. Behind the main village street in a little cottage garden facing the village green sits the **Clergy House** (NT) with its deep thatched roof, the first building acquired by the National Trust, in 1896.

Either the fast A27 or the slower coastal road (A259) will bring you into **Brighton**, a onetime sleepy fishing town transformed into a fashionable resort at the beginning of the 19th century when the Prince Regent built the fanciful, extravagant **Royal Pavilion** with its onion domes and gaudy paintwork. Follow signs for the town center and park near the pavilion, an extravaganza of colorful, rather overpowering decor. Very near the Royal Pavilion are **The Lanes**, narrow streets of former fishermen's cottages now filled with restaurants and antique and gift shops. The seafront is lined by an almost 3-mile-long promenade with the beach below and gardens and tall terraces above. Many of the once-fashionable townhouses are now boarding houses and small hotels but this does not detract from the old-fashioned seaside atmosphere of the town. Stretching out into the sea, the white, wooden **Palace Pier** harks back to an earlier age. At the end is a delightful, old-fashioned funfair with a helter-skelter and carousel horses along with other rides.

Leave Brighton along the seafront in the direction of Hove to join the A27 at Shoreham-by-Sea. This section of the A27 passes through suburb after suburb and is the least interesting part of this itinerary. On the outskirts of **Arundel** the massive keep and towers of **Arundel Castle** rise above the town. Built just after the Norman Conquest to protect this area from sea pirates and raiders, the castle contains a collection of armor, tapestries, and other interesting artifacts.

From Arundel take the A284 inland towards Pulborough and then follow signs through the narrow, winding old streets of **Petworth**, proffering several antique stores, to **Petworth House** (NT), an enormous, 17th-century house in a vast deer park with landscaping by Capability Brown. The house, completed by the 6th Duke of Somerset in 1696, retains the 13th-century chapel of an earlier mansion and houses a proud art collection, which includes a series of landscapes by Turner and also paintings by Holbein, Rembrandt, Van Dyck, Gainsborough, Titian, Rubens, and Reynolds.

Retrace your route the short distance into Petworth and take the A272 through Midhurst to reach the A286 (Chichester road). **Midhurst** has some fine old houses and attractive inns. Knockhundred Row leads from North Street to Red Lion Street and the old timbered market. Curfew is faithfully rung each evening at 8 pm in the parish church. Legend has it that a rider, lost in darkness, followed the sound of the church bells and found his way to the town. To show his gratitude he purchased a piece of land in

Midhurst, now called Curfew Garden, which he presented to the town as a gift and made money available for the nightly ringing of the bells.

Across the South Downs the A286 brings you to the **Weald and Downland Museum**, an assortment of old, humble buildings such as farmhouses and barns brought to and restored on this site after their loss to demolition was inevitable. Inside several of the structures are displays showing the development of buildings through the ages.

Leaving the museum, take the A286 around Chichester to the A27 Portsmouth road, which leads you onto the M275 to the historic center of **Portsmouth** and your goal, the *H.M.S. Victory* and *Mary Rose*. The **H.M.S. Victory**, Nelson's flagship at the Battle of Trafalgar in 1805, has been restored to show what life was like on board. Nearby, the **Mary Rose**, Henry VIII's flagship, is housed in a humidified building that preserves its remains, which were raised from the seabed several years ago. The **Naval Museum** has a display of model ships, figureheads, and a panorama depicting the Battle of Trafalgar.

Retrace your steps up the M275 and onto the M27, which quickly brings you to the A33/M3 and **Winchester** where a magnificent **cathedral** stands at the center of the city. Park in one of the car parks on the edge of town and walk into the pedestrian heart of the city, which was the capital of England in King Alfred's reign during the 9th century and stayed so for 200 years. Construction of the 556-foot-long cathedral began in 1079 and finished in 1404. Treasures include a memorial window to Izaak Walton, a black marble font, seven chancery chapels for special masses, medieval wall paintings, stained glass, and tombs of ancient kings including King Canute. Close by is **Winchester College**, founded in 1382, one of the oldest public (i.e., private) schools in England. At the top of the High Street is a fascinating area that has formed an important part of the city's defenses since Roman times. Here you find the 13th-century **Great Hall**, the only surviving part of Winchester Castle and home to the legendary Round Table which has hung on the wall here for 600 years. Military history buffs will enjoy the five **military museums**, which offer guided tours by arrangement.

Leaving Winchester, the M3 will quickly take you back to London.

Cambridge & East Anglia

Holkham Hall

Morston

Wells-next-the-Sea

Holt

Caley Mill

Sandringham

Blickling Hall

King's Lynn

Norwich

A10

A146

Beccles

A145

Ely

Southwold

Walberswick

Dunwich

Framlingham

A14

Bury St Edmunds

Snape

Aldeburgh

A12

Cambridge

Lavenham

Kersey

Long Melford

Hadleigh

Ipswich

East Bergholt

Dedham

M11

To London

A12

To London

M25

● Orientation/Sightseeing

■ ■ Itinerary Route

45

Cambridge & East Anglia

Many visit the famous university town of Cambridge, but few travelers venture beyond to explore the bulge of England's eastern coastline with its sky-wide landscapes, stunning sunsets, lofty windmills, and unspoilt villages. This itinerary takes you from the vast fenlands, drained by the Dutch in the 17th century, along the pancake-flat Norfolk coastline with the sea often just out of sight beyond fields and marshes, into Norwich with its ancient streets and vast cathedral, through sleepy Suffolk villages full of quaint cottages to "Constable Country" where John Constable painted so many of his famous works. Be sure to visit Cambridge, but expand your trip to explore this quiet corner of Britain.

Kersey

Recommended Pacing: Spend one night in Norfolk, two if you have the luxury of time, and two in Suffolk, which gives you ample time to explore its quaint villages.

Leaving London, navigate yourself onto the M11 for the fast, two-hour drive to **Cambridge**, a city with much new building, but at whose heart is a fascinating university complex whose history spans over 700 years. Park your car in one of the well-marked car parks near the town center, buy a guidebook, and set out to explore, for this is a city for strolling and browsing.

At most times visitors can go into college courtyards, chapels, dining halls, and certain gardens. **King's College Chapel** is one of the finest buildings in England, with Rubens'masterpiece, the *Adoration of the Magi*, framing the altar. Be sure not to miss **Clare College**, **Trinity College**, and **St. John's College**, which backs onto the enclosed stone "Bridge of Sighs." Explore the various alleys and streets on foot, row, or punt, drifting under the willow trees that line the River Cam. **Punts** can be rented at Silver Street Bridge and Quayside.

Leaving Cambridge on the A10 towards **Ely**, you come to open countryside offering sky-wide horizons of flat farmland that are soon punctuated by the soaring mass of **Ely Cathedral**, a building so large that it seems to dwarf the little market town that surrounds it. Until the surrounding fens were drained, Ely was an island, surrounded by water, and the cathedral must have appeared even more magnificent than it does today. This awesome structure was built in 1083, awesome not only for its sheer size but because it is an amazing piece of engineering, its huge tower held up by eight massive oak timbers each more than 60 feet in length.

Leaving Ely, regain the A10, following it around Downham Market to **King's Lynn**, a large, bustling town with a well-marked historic core. A market is held every Saturday and Tuesday and the port has several fine old buildings: the **Customs House** (1683) by the harbor, now the tourist office, the **Guildhall** (1421), and the adjacent **St. Margaret's Church**. The father of George Vancouver, who explored the northwestern coast of North

America and after whom the Canadian city and island are named, was a customs officer here.

Leaving King's Lynn, follow signs for the A149 in the direction of Hunstanton. After several miles turn right for **Sandringham**, one of the Royal Family's homes, and almost immediately first left to take you on a scenic drive through the woodlands that surround it. Edward VII, at that time Prince of Wales, bought this huge Victorian house in 1861 because he did not like Osborne House on the Isle of Wight. From mid-April to the end of October from 11 am the grounds and several rooms in the house are open to the public—provided that the Royal Family is not in residence.

Leave the car park to your left, and passing the main gates (the Norwich gates, a wedding gift to Edward from the city of Norwich), go left through Dersingham to regain the A149. In summer the air is heavy with the scent of lavender and the fields surrounding **Caley Mill** are a brilliant purple for this is one of the country's centers for the cultivation of lavender. There is a gift shop selling every imaginable lavender product.

After bypassing Hunstanton, the A149 becomes narrower, pottering along through attractive villages of pebble-and-red-brick cottages (Thornham, Titchwell, Brancaster, Staithe, and Overy Staithe) as it traces the flat Norfolk coast with the sea often just out of sight beyond fields and marshes. This is not a coastline of dramatic cliffs and headlands—the land merely ends and the sea begins.

On the outskirts of **Holkham** you follow the wall surrounding **Holkham Hall** to its driveway. This magnificent, 18th-century Palladian mansion, the seat of the "modern" Earls of Leicester, contains paintings by Rubens, Van Dyck, Poussin, and Gainsborough; 17th- and 18th-century tapestry and furniture; thousands of items of bygone days, such as steam engines, kitchen equipment, smithy tools, ploughs, and fire engines; and Greek and Roman statuary. Detour into **Wells-next-the-Sea**, one of the few villages along this coast to have a waterfront. Leave the coast behind and turn inland following the B1156 into Holt then continuing in the direction of Norwich (B1354) to **Blickling Hall** (NT), a grand, 17th-century red-brick house set in acres of parkland. The house is full of fine pictures, tapestries, and gracious furniture.

Following signs for Norwich, join the A140, which takes you to the heart of this sprawling city. **Norwich** is rich in historic treasures including a beautiful Norman cathedral, topped by a 15th-century spire, with a huge close running down to the River Wensum. The castle, built by one of William the Conqueror's supporters, is now the **Castle Museum**. **Elm Hill** is a cobbled street with shops and houses from the 14th to the 18th centuries. **Colman's Mustard Shop** in Royal Arcade is a big tourist attraction. Norwich has an interesting market and some very nice shops and restaurants.

From the ring road surrounding Norwich take the A146 in the direction of Lowestoft. Turn on the A145 through Beccles to the A12 where you turn left and first right on the A1095 into **Southwold**, a quiet, sedate Victorian/Edwardian seaside resort, with most attractive houses lining the seafront and narrow rows of shops forming the town center. Across the river estuary lies **Walberswick**, a pretty little fishing/holiday village of cottages and a pub, reached by a little ferry that plies back and forth (or the longer road route that traces the estuary).

Regaining the A12, turn left, towards Ipswich, for a short distance to the village of **Blythburgh** and visit its church, so imposing in size that hereabouts it is referred to as **Blythburgh Cathedral**. The size of the church is indicative of the community's importance in years gone by when it was a thriving port, with its own mint, on the estuary of the River Blyth. Its prosperity declined and the church was neglected until it was restored this century. Carvings of the Seven Deadly Sins decorate the pew ends and the rare, wooden Jack-o'-the-Clock.

A short distance farther along the A12 you come to the left-hand turn for **Dunwich**— cross the heathlands and go through the village to the car park in front of the **Flora Tea Rooms**, (open March to October) which serves excellent fish and chips, beneath the pebbly bank which separates it from the sea. The fish comes fresh from the fishermen who draw their boats up on the beach. Along the headlands lie the few remains of the medieval port of Dunwich, which was almost completely swept out to sea in 1326 by a great storm. What was left has continued to be eroded by the sea. Local legend has it that before a storm the bells of Dunwich's 15 submerged churches can be heard ringing.

A short drive brings you to **Minsmere Nature Reserve**, a celebrated place for birdwatching, and through Westleton to **Aldeburgh**, a charming town whose streets are lined with Georgian houses and whose High Street has antique and other interesting shops. The local council still meets in the half-timbered **Moot Hall** (1512). Benjamin Britten, who directed the Aldeburgh music festival for 30 years until his death in 1976, based his opera, *Peter Grimes,* on a poem by local poet George Crabbe.

Head inland on the A1094, turning left onto the B1069 into **Snape** to arrive at **Snape Maltings**, a collection of red-brick granaries and old malthouses, which has been converted into a riverside center with interesting garden and craft shops, art galleries, tearooms, and a concert hall, home of the Aldeburgh music festival every June. From here you can take a boat trip on the River Alde, which meanders through the marshes to the sea.

Continue inland and map a quiet country route through sleepy Suffolk villages and rolling farmland to **Framlingham**, a quiet market town where Mary Tudor was proclaimed queen of England in 1553. The town is dominated by 12th-century **Framlingham Castle** with tall, gray-stone walls linking its towers.

Two miles away at **Saxtead Green** a 200-year-old **Post Mill**, one of Suffolk's few remaining windmills, stands guard over the green.

From Saxtead Green follow the A1120 towards Ipswich and the A14 as it skirts Ipswich and joins the A12 (in the Colchester direction) at a large roundabout (busy dual carriageways like these keep the small roads quiet and peaceful). Leave the A12 at the third exit, following signs to your left for **Dedham**, a pretty village settled along the banks of the lazy River Stour made famous by John Constable who painted its mill and church spire on several occasions. (Even though it is just a river bend away from East Bergholt, Constable's birthplace, today you have to go between the two villages by way of the busy A12.) Sir Alfred Munnings, the painter of horses, lived in **Castle House**, which is now a museum containing examples of his work.

Retrace your steps to the A12 and return in the direction of Ipswich, following signs for **Flatford** and **East Bergholt** where John Constable was born in 1776, the son of the miller of Flatford Mill. The little hamlet of Flatford, now a National Trust property, is signposted in East Bergholt. A one-way lane directs you to the car park above the hamlet (it is not well signposted and you may have to stop and ask the way). The collection of cottages has been restored to the way it was in Constable's time and a tearoom serves scrumptious afternoon teas and sandwiches. If the weather is fine, you can take a picnic, hire a rowing boat, or simply while away an afternoon on the river. The National Trust shop sells a packet that includes a map identifying where Constable painted some of his most famous pictures and postcards of the paintings so you can wander along the riverbank and pinpoint the very spot where he painted his father's mill, Willy Lott's cottage, or the boatbuilders at work. The scene has changed little since those times—apart from the tourists. Constable said of the area, "Those scenes made me a painter."

Leaving the Constable complex, the road returns you to East Bergholt where you turn right to go through the village and take the B1070 to **Hadleigh**, a large market town whose High Street has some lovely old houses. On the edge of the town cross the A1071 and then take the first left and first right to bring you onto the main street of **Kersey**, the most picture-book-perfect of all Suffolk villages. Its narrow main street is lined with ancient weavers' cottages, grand merchants' houses, and old pubs, all jostling one another for roadside space and each colorwashed a different color. In the middle of the village a stream runs across the road and drivers must take care to avoid the local ducks.

Join the A1141 for a short drive through **Monks Eleigh** with its thatched cottages and large craft shop selling traditional corn dollies to **Lavenham**, which in Tudor times was one of England's wealthiest towns. Now it is a sleepy village where leaning timbered houses line its quiet street. Continue into the market square with its 16th-century cross and **Guildhall** (NT), which houses displays of local history and the medieval wool industry.

Country lanes take you the 5 miles to **Long Melford** whose long, broad, tree-lined main street houses many antique shops and leads to the village green, which is overshadowed by the magnificent, 15th-century Holy Trinity Church. A short walk away, the redbrick, turreted **Melford Hall** (NT) contains a wealth of porcelain, paintings, and antiques and a display of Beatrix Potter's paintings—she was a frequent visitor here.

Leaving Long Melford, you can go south to the A12 or west to the M11, either of which quickly return you to London.

The Lake District

Carlisle

Cockermouth

Bassenthwaite Lake

Keswick

A66

A5091

Crummock Water

Derwent Water

Ullswater

Buttermere

Rosthwaite

Thirlmere

A591

Grasmere

Ambleside

Little Langdale

Troutbeck

A593

Coniston

Windermere

Hawkshead

Far Sawrey

Coniston Water

Windermere

A5074

Sizergh Castle

A590

Levens Hall

M6

● Orientation/Sightseeing

- - Itinerary Route

53

The Lake District

For generations the beauty of the Lake District has inspired poets, authors, and artists. It is a land of tranquil lakes of all shapes and sizes, quiet wooded valleys, and awesome bleak mountains, a land where much of the natural beauty is protected by the National Trust who work hard to keep this a working community of sheep farmers and to keep man in harmony with nature. One of the most determined preservers of the Lake District was Beatrix Potter, who used much of her royalties from her famous children's books to purchase vast tracts of land and donate them to the nation. It is a region to be explored not only during the summer when the roads are more heavily traveled and the towns crowded, but also in the early spring when the famous daffodils brighten the landscape and well into the autumn when the leaves turn to gold and dark storm clouds shadow the lakes.

Dove Cottage, Grasmere

Recommended Pacing: Base yourself at one of the properties we recommend in the Lake District. If you cover all of our sightseeing recommendations, you will need four nights, though three might just suffice.

From junction 36 on the M6 motorway take the A590 in the direction of Barrow then a few minutes' drive along the A591 brings you into the grounds of **Sizergh Castle** (NT), not a mighty fortress but a lovely, mostly Tudor house, the home of the Strickland family for over 700 years. The house is fully furnished—just as though the family has gone out for the day and you are a visitor to their home. There is an excellent teashop in the old cellar and a portion of the grounds presents an impressive rock garden.

Return to the A590 and in just a minute you are at another fine Tudor manor house, **Levens Hall**. The property is most famous for its topiary gardens, which have remarkably remained unchanged since 1690, when they were landscaped by a Frenchman, Guillaume Beaumont.

Join the A5074 Windermere road and on the outskirts of the town follow signs to the ferry, which takes you across the broad expanse of **Windermere** for the short drive to the tiny villages of **Near Sawrey** and **Far Sawrey**, discovered by Beatrix Potter on childhood holidays. She was so charmed by the villages that out of the royalties from *Peter Rabbit* she bought **Hill Top Farm** (NT) in Near Sawrey. It was here in a vine-covered stone cottage set among trees and a garden of flowers that she dreamed up childhood playmates such as Jemima Puddleduck, Mrs Tiggy Winkle, the Flopsy Bunnies, Cousin Ribby, and Benjamin Bunny. Because of its popularity the house is open on a very limited basis, but the National Trust shop by the roadside is open more often and you can walk through the garden to the front door.

In nearby **Hawkshead**, a pretty village with a pedestrian center, there is a delightful **Beatrix Potter Gallery** (NT) containing an exhibition of her original drawings and illustrations of her children's books, together with a display of her life as author, farmer, and preserver of her beloved Lake District. A short drive brings you to **Coniston**, a delightful village of gray-stone buildings at the head of **Coniston Water**. John Ruskin, the eloquent 19th-century scholar, lived on the east side of the lake at **Brantwood.** His home contains many mementos and pictures. You will find a small **Ruskin Museum** with drawings and manuscripts in the village.

Travel a short distance along the A593 Ambleside road and turn left to wind along a country lane up into a quiet, less touristy part of the Lake District. Stop for refreshment in **Little Langdale** at the **Three Shires**, a delightful walkers' pub that also offers accommodation. Leaving the village, you enter a wild, bleak, and beautiful area. The lane brings you to Blea Tarn and just as you think you are in the absolute midst of nowhere and contemplate turning around, you come to a cattle grid and a fork in the road. Take the right-hand fork signposted Great Langdale and follow the narrow road through wild and lonely countryside, down a steep pass, and through a lush valley into **Great Langdale**, another off-the-beaten-path village popular with walkers. Leaving the village, the road winds you up onto the moor and drops you back onto the A593 where a left-hand turn quickly brings you into Ambleside.

Ambleside is a bustling, busy town at the head of Lake Windermere with lots of shops selling walking equipment and outdoor wear, and gray Victorian row houses huddling along its streets. Leave town in the direction of Keswick (A591), watching for a right-hand turn to **Rydal Mount**, the home of William Wordsworth, the poet, from 1813 to his death in 1850. The house is furnished and contains many family portraits and possessions. A keen gardener, Wordsworth laid out the 4½ acres of informal gardens.

Wordsworth fans will also want to stop at **Dove Cottage** where Wordsworth lived from 1799 to 1808 and the adjacent **Wordsworth Museum**. Park by the tearoom on the main road and walk up to the museum to buy your ticket. Try to visit early in the day as they restrict a tour to the number of people who can comfortably fit into Wordsworth's tiny living room. As you tour the few meager rooms, which housed six adults and three children, it is hard to believe that this was home to one of the leading poets of the era. Poet laureates write poems on royal events, but not Wordsworth: he was the only poet laureate to write not a word on such occasions—but he relished the royal stipend. Just off the busy main road, the adjacent village of **Grasmere** is full of charming shops and galleries.

The A591 is a delightful drive into Keswick through in turn wild, rugged, and pastoral scenery. Take small roads to the west of **Thirlmere** as the views from the west of the lake are much better than from the A591. The lively market town of **Keswick**, cozily placed at the northern end of **Derwent Water**, is full of bakeries, sweet shops (selling fudge and Kendal mint cake), pubs, restaurants, and outdoor equipment suppliers. There are plenty of car parks near the town center, though on a busy summer afternoon you may have to drive around for a while before you secure a spot. The **Moot** (meeting) **Hall** at the center of the square is now the National Park Information Centre—full of maps, books, and good advice.

Returning to your car, head towards Derwent Water, taking the B5289 to Borrowdale for a spectacular drive between Keswick and Cockermouth, a journey not to be undertaken in bad weather. Follow Derwent Water to **Grange** where inviting woodlands beckon you to tarry awhile and walk, but desist because the most spectacular walking country lies ahead. Passing through the village of Rosthwaite, the narrow road begins to climb, curving you upwards alongside a tumbling stream to the high, treeless fells before suddenly tipping you over the crest of the mountain and snaking you down into the valley to **Buttermere** and **Crummock Water** whose placid surfaces mirror the jagged peaks surrounding this wooded, green valley. The mountains here are over 500 million years old—among the oldest in the world. Walking paths beckon in every direction—though these are not paths to be trod without equipment and maps, for the fickle weather can turn from sun to storm in just a short while. Leaving this lovely spot, the narrow road quickly brings you into the center of bustling **Cockermouth** where Wordsworthians have the opportunity to visit **Wordsworth House**, his birthplace on Main Street.

From Cockermouth follow signs for the A66 and Keswick along a country road that parallels the A66 to the head of **Bassenthwaite Lake**. At the junction cross the busy A66 onto a quiet country road to visit **The Pheasant**, a superb example of the very best of traditional pubs. From here the A66 quickly speeds you alongside Bassenthwaite Lake, around Keswick, and to the M6 motorway. However, if you have time for one more idyllic lake, take the A5091 through Troutbeck to **Ullswater** where you turn left to trace the lake to **Aira Force** (NT), a landscaped Victorian park with dramatic waterfalls, arboretum, and rock gardens (there is also a café). After a walk along the shores of Ullswater Wordsworth wrote his poem *Daffodils*. The dramatic scenery is still very much as it was in his day. Leaving Ullswater, return to the A66 and join the M6 at junction 40, with convenient connections to all parts of Britain.

The Lake District

Derbyshire Dales
& Villages

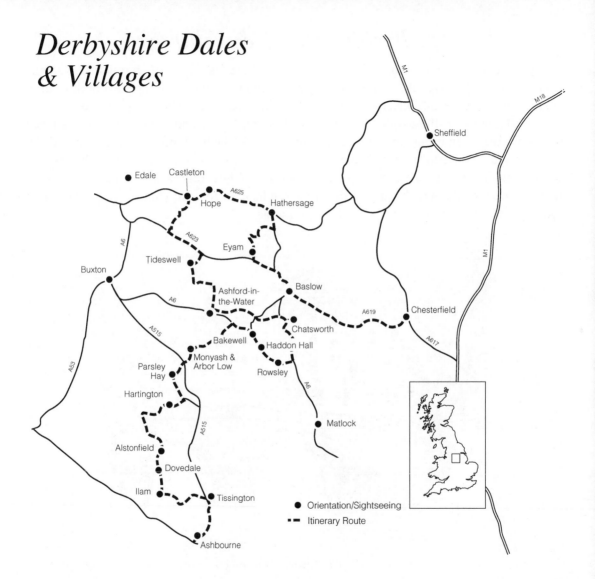

- Edale
- Castleton
- Hope
- A625
- Hathersage
- A623
- Eyam
- Tideswell
- A6
- Buxton
- Ashford-in-the-Water
- Baslow
- A619
- Chesterfield
- A617
- Chatsworth
- Bakewell
- Haddon Hall
- Monyash & Arbor Low
- Rowsley
- A515
- Parsley Hay
- A53
- A6
- Hartington
- A515
- Alstonfield
- Dovedale
- Matlock
- Ilam
- Tissington
- Ashbourne
- Sheffield
- M1
- M18

● Orientation/Sightseeing
-- Itinerary Route

Derbyshire Dales & Villages

Every structure in this itinerary—manor houses, churches, cottages, farmhouses, shops, even the walls that edge the fields, making a patchwork of the landscape—is built of gray stone. This is the Peak District, a National Park, where you can enjoy the beauty of a wild landscape of rolling rocky pastures, sheltered valleys, and windswept moors laced by swift rivers tumbling through deep dales—Monks Dale, Monsal Dale, Miller Dale, and, the most beautiful of all, Dovedale where the River Dove flows through a rocky, wooded ravine and is crossed by stepping stones. While this is a driving itinerary, to really appreciate the wild beauty of this area you have to forsake your car and proceed on foot—on the many miles of well-marked footpaths.

Chatsworth House
Derbyshire Dales & Villages

Recommended Pacing: Select a base for this itinerary. To cover all our sightseeing suggestions will take two full days.

This itinerary begins in **Ashbourne**, a small market town just south of the Peak District National Park where on Thursdays and Saturdays market stalls crowd the town square. Close by, on St. John Street, visit the **Gingerbread Shop**, which sells aromatic Ashbourne gingerbread and baked goods from a restored 15th-century timber-framed shop that gives you a glimpse of how beautiful Ashbourne must have been during its heyday.

Leave Ashbourne on the A515, Buxton road, and watch for a discreetly signposted right-hand turn that brings you through a broad avenue of trees to **Tissington** with its Jacobean manor house, Norman church, limestone cottages, and ducks swimming on the village pond. Tissington is reputedly the birthplace of the Derbyshire village tradition of well dressing, giving thanks for the unfailing supply of fresh water that the village wells provided by creating intricate, large mosaic pictures from flower petals and placing them beside the village wells. These spectacular displays are very interesting to visit, so in the course of this itinerary, the dates that villages dress their wells is mentioned in parentheses, for example, "Tissington (*wells dressed for Ascension day*)." If you carry on through the village and across open farmland, you come to a ford where the road splashes through a brook.

Retrace your steps to the A515 and cross it, heading through **Thorpe** village and down into **Dovedale**. Dr. Johnston gave it a glowing testimonial: "He who has seen Dovedale has no need to visit the Highlands." Cars can go no farther than the car park whence you walk into the dale, cross the River Dove on stepping stones and enter a rocky ravine. The farther you walk into the dale the more you are tempted to continue as round each river bend beautiful scenery unfolds—fantastic rock formations, steeply wooded hillsides, and the noisy, tumbling water. The length of the dale is a delightful 4-mile walk. Walkers can be dropped at the car park and picked up in Milldale by Viators Bridge.

At a bend in the road sits **Ilam** (pronounced "I lamb"), a picture-postcard estate village, built to house the workers on what was once a shipping magnate's vast holdings. On to

Alstonfield (pronounced "Alstonfeld") and the **Post Office Teashop**, which serves scrumptious scones and cream. (Turn right here if you are picking walkers up in nearby Milldale.)

Well Dressing

Drive into **Hartington** (*wells dressed on second Saturday in September*) with its white limestone cottages, shops, and pubs. Admire the mallards waddling by the village pond and visit the **cheese shop**, an outlet for the last of Derbyshire's cheese factories producing Hartington Stilton and Buxton Blue.

Leave Hartington on the B5054, Ashbourne road, and take the first left, signposted Crowdicote, following the narrow dale. As the dale widens, turn right to **Parsley Hay**. From here you can cycle the **Tissington Trail** towards Ashbourne or the **High Peak Trail** to Cromford. At the main road turn left (towards Buxton) and immediately right towards Monyash then right again following discreet signposts for **Arbor Low**, Derbyshire's answer to Stonehenge. The huge monoliths have all fallen to the ground and you will probably be one of only a few visitors. The stones are set atop a bare hill, swept by cold winds, and reached by tramping across fields from a lonely farm. Pause and wonder why man built here 4,000 years ago.

Retrace your path to the Monyash road, turning right in the village onto the B5055, which leads you into **Bakewell** (*wells dressed on last Saturday in June*), a lovely market town ringed by wooded hills where a picturesque, 700-year-old arched and buttressed bridge spans the swiftly flowing River Wye. The Tourist Information Centre in the splendid, 17th-century **market hall** has displays on the Peak District and information pamphlets. Behind it are set the market stalls where every Monday a farmers' market is held—offering everything from lengths of dress fabric to underwear and pigs. You can buy the original Bakewell tarts (known as puddings in Bakewell) from **Ye Olde Original Pudding Shop** and the splendid **Bakewell Pudding Factory** on Granby Arcade. The town has some excellent shops (china, antiques, clothing, and hardware). Up the hill, just behind the church, is **The Old House Museum**, a folk museum displaying kitchen and farm equipment.

Three miles along the A6 in the direction of Matlock lies **Haddon Hall**, a 14th-century manor, home of the Duke of Rutland. In my opinion, this house is more interesting to tour than the opulent Chatsworth House (your next stop) because it lacks the vastness and grandeur of Chatsworth and you can really imagine people living in these aged rooms hung with threadbare tapestries and decorated with magnificent woodcarvings. Parts of the chapel walls are covered with barely discernible frescos that date back to the 11th century. In summer the gardens are a fragrant haven, with a profusion of climbing roses and clematis decorating the house and the stone walls of the terraces.

Continue along the A6 to **Rowsley** where you can tour **Caudwell's Mill**, a water-powered flour mill and visit the craft shops. Leaving Rowsley, take the first left (B6012). Pass the edge of Beeley, cross the River Derwent on a narrow humpbacked bridge, and enter the vast Chatsworth estate. Immediately on your left is the **Chatsworth Garden**

Centre, which, in addition to an expansive array of all things garden, has a gift and coffee shop. The road leads you through rolling green parkland to **Chatsworth House**, the enormous home (the roof alone covers 1.3 acres) of the Duke and Duchess of Devonshire. While the Duke and Duchess occupy a portion of the house, you can walk through the opulent halls admiring priceless paintings, furnishings, silver plate, and china. Best of all, though, are the acres and acres of landscaped gardens: vast lawns laid down in 1760 and groomed ever since (except in wartime); the maze; the gardens (rock, kitchen, rose, cottage, and sensory). Water pours down the steps of the 1st Duke's water cascade (take off your shoes and climb its broad steps to the fountains at the top of the hill), shoots from the willow tree (known as the squirting tree), and spills from Revelation, the water-operated sculpture. There are 5 miles of walks with trees, shrubs, fountains, and ponds. There is also access to the excavated coal tunnel. The gift and teashop are a must. If you are traveling with children, they will enjoy a visit to the farm and the adventure playground.

The picturesque village of **Edensor** (pronounced "Ensor"), mentioned in the Doomsday Book of 1086, was much rebuilt and moved here in the 19th century by a duke who did not want to see it from his park. Kathleen Kennedy, JFK's sister, lies buried near the handsome old church.

Leave the estate in the direction of Baslow and take the first left, B6048, to **Pilsley** where the farm shop sells an interesting variety of nifty gifts and produce from the Chatsworth estate. As the B6048 merges with the main road take the first right on the A6020 (Ashford) following it to **Ashford-in-the-Water** and cross the river into this picturesque village strung along the River Wye. "Sheepwash" is the oldest and quaintest of the village's bridges. Built for packhorses and now closed to traffic, it gets its name from the adjacent stone enclosure in which sheep used to be washed.

Follow the narrow lanes upwards to **Monsal Head** where the ground seemingly falls away and opens up to a magnificent vista of the River Wye running through **Monsal Dale**. Go straight across, alongside the Monsal Head car park, and follow the road as it winds down into and along the dale to **Cressbrook Mill**, where the road climbs steeply past the terraces of mill cottages clinging precariously to the hillsides. The first terrace is where pauper apprentices lived and higher up are the more opulent foremen's houses. Emerging from the dale, the narrow road skirts stone-walled fields to **Litton** (*wells dressed in June*), a delightful stone village round a green where you turn left for Tideswell.

The magnificent, spacious, 14th-century church at **Tideswell** (*wells dressed on Saturday nearest John the Baptist day, June 24th*) is so impressive that it is often described as "the cathedral of the Peak." It was built between 1300 and 1370 when Tideswell was an affluent place and it is fortunate that Tideswell fell upon hard times so that parishioners could not afford to update their church as ecclesiastical fashions changed.

Leaving Tideswell, you come to the A623 and turn left in the direction of Chapel-en-le-Frith to Sparrowpit where you turn right at the Wanted Inn. Passing an enormous quarry, you see that half the mountain is missing—gone to build all the lovely stone houses and cottages. When you come to a brown-and-white country sign stating "Castleton Caverns, Peveril Castle, light traffic only," turn right into Winnats Pass, which drops you down a steep ravine between high limestone cliffs.

As the ravine opens up to the valley, **Speedwell Cavern** presents itself. This is one of several famous caverns (mixtures of natural cavities and lead-mine workings resplendent with stalagmites and stalactites) found around Castleton. Speedwell is reached by a 105-step descent to a motorboat that takes you along an underground canal to a cavern which was the working face of the former Speedwell Mine. Blue John (a corruption of the French *bleue-jaune,* blue-yellow), a translucent blue variety of fluorspar found only in this area, was mined here.

Before you head off to explore other nearby caves (Blue John, Treak Cliff, and Peak), head into **Castleton**, a village huddled far below the brooding ruins of Norman **Peveril Castle** where Henry II accepted the submission of Malcolm of Scotland in 1157.

Castleton

Below the castle is the huge mouth of **Peak Cavern**, an enormous cave that once sheltered ropemakers' cottages. The soot from the chimneys of this subterranean village can be seen on the cave's roof. Regrettably, the entrance to the cave has been marred by the erection of a high wooden barrier giving access to the cave only to those willing to pay an entrance fee. In the village's streets you will find cafés, pubs, and several shops selling the polished Blue John set into bracelets, rings, and the like.

Derbyshire Dales & Villages

This is walking country and you might consider walking up **Mam Tor (**the big bulky mountain beside Winnats Pass) known hereabouts as "Shivering Mountain" because its layers of soft shale set between harder beds of rock are constantly crumbling. Those in search of a longer walk may wish to go to nearby **Edale** where the **Pennine Way** starts its 250-mile path north.

Leave Castleton on the A625 traveling along the broad Hope valley through **Hope** (*wells dressed last Saturday in June*) and Bamford to **Hathersage**, a thriving, non-traditional Derbyshire village strung out along the main road. Its tourist attractions center on its 14th-century church, St. Michael and All Angels, built by a knight named Robert Eyre. Memorial brasses to the Eyre family are in the church and Charlotte Brontë used the village as "Morton" in *Jane Eyre*. In the graveyard is the reputed grave of Little John, the friend and lieutenant of Robin Hood.

Leaving the churchyard, backtrack on the A625 for a short distance, taking the first left (B6001), signposted Bakewell, beyond the village where you turn right, opposite The Plough, up a narrow country lane signposted "Gliding Club." This country lane takes you through the hamlet of **Abney** past the gliding club and the historic **Barrel Inn** (offering views of the valley, good pub food, and refreshing ale) and brings you, via Foolow, into **Eyam** (pronounced "Eem") (*wells dressed last Saturday in August*).

This large mining and quarrying village was made famous by its self-imposed quarantine when plague hit the village in 1665. It was thought that the virus arrived in a box of cloth from London brought by a visiting tailor. The rector persuaded the community to quarantine themselves to prevent the plague spreading to outlying villages. For over a year the village was supplied by neighboring villagers who left food and supplies at outlying points. Tragically 259 people from 76 families perished—little plaques on Eyam's cottages give the names of the victims who lived there. The church has a plague register and just inside the door is the letter written by the young rector when his wife succumbed (Katherine Mompesson is buried near the Saxon cross in the churchyard). The most poignant reminder of these grim days lies in a field about ½ mile from the village where within a solitary little enclosure, known as the **Riley Graves**, are the memorials to a father and his six children, all of whom died within eight days of each other.

Leave Eyam in the direction of Bakewell, traveling down a steeply wooded gorge that brings you to the A623. Following signs for Chesterfield, you drive down narrow **Middleton Dale**, whose limestone cliffs are so sheer they almost block the sunlight from the road, to **Stoney Middleton**, an appropriately named village huddling beneath the cliffs. It does not look at all inviting from the main road but its quiet side streets and pretty church are full of character.

Driving a few miles farther along the A623 brings you to the winding lanes of **Baslow** where the River Derwent flows past tidy houses on the northern edge of the Chatsworth estate. From here fast roads will bring you to **Chesterfield** (visit the leaning spire and if it is a Monday, Friday, or Saturday, you will enjoy the interesting open-air market) where you can join the M1 at junction 29.

The Dales & Moors of
North Yorkshire

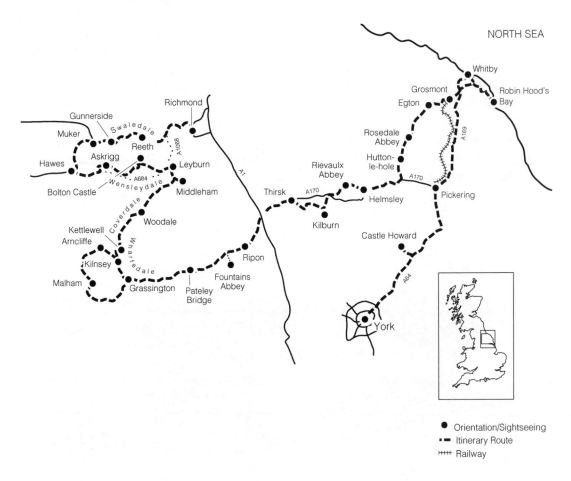

NORTH SEA

Whitby

Robin Hood's
Bay

Grosmont

Egton

Richmond

Gunnerside

Muker

Swaledale

Reeth

Rosedale
Abbey

Rievaulx
Abbey

Hutton-
le-hole

Askrigg

Leyburn

Hawes

A1068

A169

Bolton Castle

Wensleydale

A684

Pickering

Middleham

Thirsk

A170

A170

Helmsley

Coverdale

Woodale

Kilburn

Kettlewell

Castle Howard

Arncliffe

Wharfedale

Kilnsey

Ripon

Malham

Grassington

Fountains
Abbey

Pateley
Bridge

A64

York

● Orientation/Sightseeing
■-■ Itinerary Route
┼┼┼┼ Railway

69

The Dales & Moors of North Yorkshire

After exploring historic York, this itinerary samples the wild and beautiful countryside of two National Parks: the North York Moors and the Yorkshire Dales. This is an area of rugged, untamed, harsh beauty in its landscape and its stout stone villages. With seemingly endless miles of heather-covered moorlands, few roads, and even fewer sturdy villages sheltering in green valleys, the North York Moors appear vast and untamed, dipping to the sea to embrace the villages and towns of the east coast. Across the flat expanse of the Vale of York lie the Yorkshire Dales, characterized by sleepy rivers weaving through peaceful valleys and by gray-stone walls bounding the fields and tracing patterns on the countryside to the moorlands above. Here every valley has a name and a very different character—Swaledale, Littondale, Coverdale, and Wharfedale. Scattered throughout Yorkshire are small gray-stoned villages with a cluster of stone houses, a hump-backed bridge, a friendly pub, and an ancient church.

The Dales & Moors of North Yorkshire

Recommended Pacing: Spend two nights in York to appreciate the flavor of this historic city. Follow this with a minimum of one night on or near the North York Moors and two nights in the Yorkshire Dales.

If you delight in historic towns, you will love **York**, a compact city brimful of history, encircled by 700-year-old walls with great imposing gates known as "bars." There has been a settlement here since Roman times and by the time of the Norman Conquest it was, after London, the principal city of England.

Your first stop in York should be the Visitors Information Centre at York Railway Station. Avail yourself of a detailed city map and ask about walking tours that will, in the space of several hours, orient you to this historic city.

Walk the narrow, cobblestoned streets with appealing names such as The Shambles, Stonegate, and Goodramgate past timbered buildings whose upper stories lean out, almost forming a bridge over the streets. While interesting shops abound, the **National Trust Shop** on Goodramgate, **Little Bettys** (teashop) on Stonegate and **Betty's Cafe and Tearooms** on St. Helen's Square are ones to target.

York's magnificent cathedral is known simply as **The Minster**, a huge structure that towers above the skyline and dwarfs everything else around it. It was begun in 1220 and you can quickly appreciate why it took over 250 years to complete. Entering through the Great West Door, you see the vast nave stretching out in front of you and fluted pillars rising to flying buttresses reaching high above. There are more than 100 stained-glass windows and the huge east window is almost the size of a tennis court. Guided tours leave at regular intervals. Nearby the **Treasurer's House** (NT), a 17th/18th-century townhouse on the site of the former residence of the Treasurers of York Minster, has a fine collection of beautiful furniture.

The **Jorvik Viking Centre**, Coppergate, is set below ground amidst the most complete Viking dig in England. Electric cars take you on a Disneyland ride backwards through history to a re-created Viking village—complete with sounds and smells of Viking

Jorvik. Then they move you forward to the dig itself and a display of the artifacts that have been recovered.

Enjoy another trip back in time at York's outstanding **Castle Museum**. One section of the museum is a reconstructed Victorian cobbled street, with houses, shops, jail, and a hansom cab in recognition of inventor Joseph Hansom who was born in Mickelgate. Opposite the museum you can climb to the ramparts of **Clifford's Tower**, a stubby, 13th-century keep set high on a mound. From its ramparts you have a panoramic view of York.

Located beyond York's walls, just a short walk from the magnificent Victorian railway station, is the **National Railway Museum**, on Leeman Road, crammed with famous steam locomotives including the world's fastest (202 mph), *Mallard*, and a wealth of railway items.

Depart York on the A64 Scarborough road for the fast drive to **Castle Howard**, which is well signposted to your left just 4 miles from Malton. Designed by Sir John Vanbrugh for the 3rd Earl of Carlisle, a member of the Howard family, Castle Howard was built between 1699 and 1726—one glimpse of this majestic building and you understand why it took 27 years to complete. Its immense façade reflects in a broad lake and it is surrounded by a vast parkland and approached down a long, tree-lined avenue. It isn't really a castle at all but one of England's grandest homes, as impressive inside as out, full of fine furniture and paintings. This grand setting is better known to many visitors as "Brideshead" from the television dramatization of Evelyn Waugh's *Brideshead Revisited*. It is still owned by the Howard family.

From nearby Malton take the A169 through Pickering and across the vast expanse of the North York moors to **Robin Hood's Bay**, the most picturesque of villages situated beneath a cliff top, a maze of huddled houses clinging to the precipitous cliff. Park in the large car park above the village and follow the long, steep street down to the shoreline, peeping into little alleyways and following narrow byways until you emerge at the slipway. Pieces of Robin Hood's Bay have been washed away, and in an attempt to minimize further damage to this little fishing village, much of the cliff has been reinforced by a large sea wall.

The ruins of **Whitby Abbey** face the cold North Sea and the old seaside town of **Whitby**, built on either side of the River Esk. It's a lovely sight: majestic ruins high on a bleak, windy headland; rows of cottages climbing up the hillsides; and, gazing over the scene, a statue of the town's most famous mariner, Captain Cook. Cook circled the world twice, explored the coasts of Australia and New Zealand, and charted Newfoundland and the North American Pacific coast before being killed by natives in Hawaii. His home on Grape Lane is a small museum. Near Cook's statue is a whalebone arch commemorating this photogenic old town's importance as a whaling port. The whaling ships are a thing of the distant past: now just a few fishing boats bob in this large, sheltered harbor. Explore the area of the town that lies below the abbey, for this is the quaintest, most historic portion of Whitby. During the summer the town is filled with holidaymakers.

The Dales & Moors of North Yorkshire

Leave Whitby on the A169, Pickering road, and follow signs to the right for the **North Yorkshire Moors Railway**, a road that winds you to **Grosmont**, the terminus of a glorious, 18-mile steam railway that runs to and from Pickering. The railway opened in 1863 with horse-drawn carriages—steam engines came 11 years later. The line was closed by British Rail in 1965 and reopened by train enthusiasts. The railway shed is full of steam locomotives of all colors. You can see engines being prepared for their daily shift and watch restoration from the viewing gallery.

From nearby Egton a narrow road leads you up from a lush valley and onto acres of gently rolling moorland, with a mass of purple heather stretching into the distance, a dramatically empty, isolated spot. It then drops you into another green valley where stone walls separate a patchwork of fields around the tiny village of Rosedale Abbey. Go straight across the crossroads, up the steep bank, and across another stretch of vast moorland. Keep to your right at the fork in the road, and you arrive in the most picturesque village on the North York Moors, **Hutton-le-Hole**. A tumbling stream cuts through the village and children play on close-cropped grassy banks between the sturdy stone houses. At the heart of the village lies **Ryedale Folk Museum** where paths lead from a museum of domestic bygones through a collection of ancient Yorkshire buildings (from simple cottages to an elaborate cruck-framed house) rescued from demise and restored on this site.

Farther on from Hutton-le-Hole you join the A170, which brings you to **Helmsley**, a pretty market town beneath the southern rim of the moors. Around the market square (*market day Friday*) are interesting shops and the lovely **Black Swan** hotel. At the edge of town sits a ruined castle enclosed by Norman earthworks.

About 4 miles beyond Helmsley (take the B1257 towards Stokesley) lie the ruins of **Rievaulx Abbey** (pronounced "Ree-voh"), the delicate and beautiful remnants of York's first Cistercian abbey, standing quietly beside a picturesque group of thatched cottages. The abbey fell into debt and declined until Henry VIII ordered its dissolution. Today it is a graceful, ghostly ruin, often shrouded in mist. Follow the narrow lane beside the cottages, turn right over the little humpbacked bridge, proceed through Scrawton, and turn right on the A170 (Thirsk road) for a short distance to a left-hand turn that zigzags you down **Sutton Bank**. On a clear day park in the car park at the top and enjoy the sky-wide view of the Vale of York before descending down the Hambleton Hills escarpment.

A delightful side trip can by taken by turning left at the bottom of the escarpment and following the narrow lane that brings you to **Kilburn**, a village known for its fine oak furniture. Quality oak furniture found all over the world can easily be traced back here to the workshop of Robert Thompson. He died in 1955, but craftsmen he trained still use his carved signature, a small church mouse, signifying "poor as a church mouse" to identify their work. It is fun to tour the workshops and watch skilled craftsmen quietly hand-carving beautiful oaken objects with a wavy, adzed surface.

Returning to the main road, you soon come to **Thirsk**, its very pleasant cobbled market square overlooked by shops (*market day Monday*). Here you can visit the **Herriot Centre**, onetime veterinary surgery of James Herriot, quiet local vet-turned-author.

From Thirsk the A61 traverses rich farmland, crosses the A1 and meanders you through **Ripon** to the market square (*market day Thursday*) where you follow well-marked signs for Fountains Abbey.

Cistercian monks arrived in sheltered **Fountains Abbey** (NT) in 1132, at about the same time they came to Rievaulx, but, unlike Rievaulx, this abbey prospered, so that by the end of the 13th century it had acquired vast estates and the abbey was home to over 500 monks. However, its prosperity did not save it from the axe of Henry VIII who sold the monastery, leaving the abbey to fall into majestic ruin. Considering that for hundreds of years it was used as a quarry for precut stone, the complex is remarkably intact. Wander over the closely cropped grass to the soaring walls of the church. Examine the few remaining floor tiles, gaze at the flying buttresses soaring high above, wander through the cloisters, and wonder at the glory that was Fountains Abbey so many years ago. Walking paths abound: a particularly pretty path leads you across grassy meadows to the adjacent National Trust property of **Studley Royal**, an 18th-century deer park and water garden.

Turn west (B6265) through Pateley Bridge and climb higher and higher onto bleak moorlands through Greenhow and down the fellside through fields trimmed with white stone walls to Hebden and into **Grassington**, a neat village of narrow streets and cobbled squares full of shops and cafés. It's this itinerary's introduction to the Dales National Park which is very crowded in summer, so you may want to park at the National Park Information Centre (useful for maps and information) and walk into town.

To experience some magnificent scenery, take a breathtaking circular drive from Grassington and back again through Littondale, over the fells to Malham Cove, and back to the B6160 on the outskirts of town. Leave Grassington on the B6265, cross the River Wharfe, and turn right onto the B6160, which leads you up **Wharfedale** towards Kettlewell. Just after passing the huge crags that hang above Kilnsey, turn left up a narrow lane for Arncliffe. The road meanders deep into **Littondale**, a narrow, steep-sided, very pretty dale. At the cluster of cottages that make up Arncliffe turn left for Malham and follow the narrow road as it zigzags you up the side of the dale. As the road reaches the top, there is a spectacular view back into Littondale. The high, bleak moorland suddenly ends and to your left lie immense curving cliffs that drop 240 feet into a green valley. This is **Malham Cove**, one of Yorkshire's most celebrated natural features. Huddled in the valley below lies the village of **Malham**. Country lanes take you through Kirby Malham, Airton, Winterburn, Hetton, and Threshfield to rejoin the B6160, which takes you back into Wharfedale.

Retrace your steps and head north to **Kettlewell**, a pretty village at the foot of Great Whernside. In the 8th century this was an Anglican settlement, then after the Norman Conquest formed part of the estates of the powerful Percy family. A small road leads you to the right over Great Whernside and into quiet **Coverdale** through **Woodale**, **Horsehouse**, and **Carlton**, little villages that shelter in this pretty valley with the moors looming above. Horses are a feature of **Middleham** for there are many famous racing stables in this attractive town of gray-stone houses beneath the ruins of Middleham Castle.

Cross the River Ure and follow the A6108 into Leyburn then turn left on the A648 and right on country lanes through Redmire to the crumbling ruins of **Bolton Castle**, which stands grim and square, dwarfing the adjacent village, overlooking distant Wensleydale. You can tour several restored rooms. The castle's most famous visitor was Mary, Queen of Scots, who was held prisoner here for six months in 1568.

Minor roads take you up Wharfedale through Carperby (detour into **Aysgarth** if you would like to walk to **Aysgarth Falls**, a series of spectacular waterfalls where the River Ure cascades down a rocky gorge) and Woodhall to the picturesque Dales village of Askrigg. Cross the river to Bainbridge and take the A648 into **Hawes**, a bustling village whose narrow streets abound with interesting shops, good pubs, and cafés. You can visit the **Wensleydale Creamery** to watch cheese being produced. After exploring, leave town in the direction of Muker. As the road climbs from the valley go right, following signs for Muker via **Buttertubs**. This is one of the highest mountain passes in England (1,682 feet), rising steeply from Wensleydale, crossing dramatic high moorlands, and depositing you in narrower, wilder **Swaledale**. The road gets its name "Buttertubs" from the deep, limestone pits some distance from the road near the summit.

At the T-junction follow the road to the right and cross the little bridge into **Muker**, the most charming of Swaledale's little villages—just the place to stop for a refreshing cuppa.

As you travel down Swaledale, there's a feeling of remoteness: sturdy, gray-stone barns dot the stone-walled fields that checker the valley floor and rise to the green fells. **Gunnerside**, Norse for "Gunner's pasture," where a Viking chieftain herded his cattle long ago, is now an appealing village.

Through Low Row, Feetham, and Healaugh the enchantment of being in a narrow, secluded valley continues till at **Reeth** the landscape opens up and the feeling of being in a wild and lonely place is gone. You continue on to Richmond through pretty countryside.

Richmond sits at the foot of Swaledale, a network of cobbled alleys and streets stretching from its cobbled square. At its center sits an ancient church with shops set into its walls. Overhanging the River Swale, **Richmond Castle** was built by Norman lords within 20 years of the Norman Conquest. Over the years only a few Scottish raiders tested the defenses of this guardian of North Yorkshire. Sweeping views across dales down to the Vale of York can be enjoyed from the top of its 11th-century ruins.

The nearby A1 will quickly guide you north into Scotland or return you south towards York.

Scotland

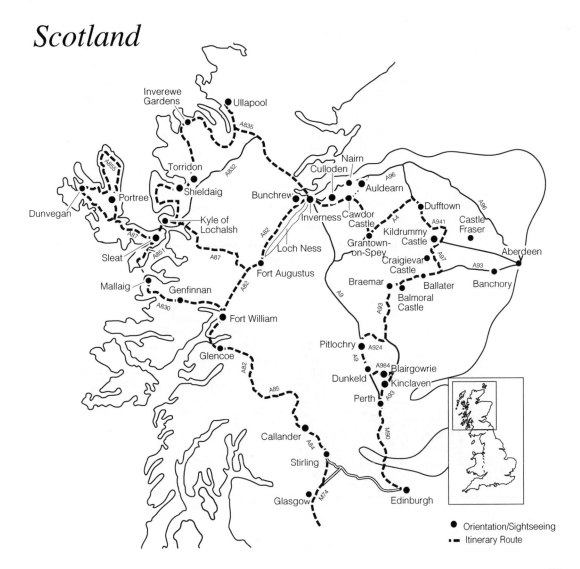

Inverewe Gardens
Ullapool
A835
A855
A832
Torridon
Shieldaig
Bunchrew
Nairn
Culloden
Auldearn
A96
Portree
Dunvegan
Kyle of Lochalsh
Inverness
Cawdor Castle
Dufftown
A96
A87
Sleat
A851
A82
Loch Ness
Grantown-on-Spey
Kildrummy Castle
A941
A4
Castle Fraser
A87
Craigievar Castle
A97
Aberdeen
Fort Augustus
A82
Braemar
Ballater
A93
Banchory
Mallaig
Genfinnan
A9
Balmoral Castle
A830
Fort William
A82
Pitlochry
A924
A9
A93
Glencoe
A82
A984
Blairgowrie
Dunkeld
Kinclaven
A85
Perth
A93
Callander
A84
M90
Stirling
Glasgow
M74
Edinburgh

● Orientation/Sightseeing
▪▬ Itinerary Route

79

Scotland

This itinerary begins in Scotland's capital, Edinburgh, journeys to Inverness via Pitlochry, samples magnificent castles and portions of "The Whisky Trail," traces the shore of Scotland's most famous lake, Loch Ness, wends through the glens, and travels over the sea to Skye. It then takes you up into the beauties of Wester Ross where the gardens at Inverewe blossom in a harsh landscape then on to Fort William, Callander, and Glasgow with its magnificent Burrell Collection. At every turn there are echoes of history and romance—Nessie the legendary monster of Loch Ness, homes that sheltered Bonnie Prince Charlie and Flora Macdonald, and the lands where Rob Roy MacGregor roamed. The roads are few and often narrow and the long distances between villages and small towns add to the feeling of isolation. The fickle Scottish weather offers no guarantee that the dramatic scenery will be revealed, but what you can be assured of is a warm, friendly welcome from the hospitable Scots.

Edinburgh Castle

Scotland

Recommended Pacing: Spend two full days sightseeing in Edinburgh. With an early-morning start you will find yourself at Kildrummy Castle by nightfall (skip Perth sightseeing). If you prefer a more leisurely pace, also include an overnight in Pitlochry. Stay overnight around Inverness because it's an all-day drive from Inverness to the Isle of Skye, then spend two nights on Skye—more if you prefer a more leisurely pace. If you are venturing up Wester Ross, plan on spending two nights there. A day-long drive from Skye will find you in Glasgow by nightfall. If you are not a cities person, skip Glasgow and stay instead in or around Callander.

Edinburgh is Scotland's beautiful capital, dominated by Edinburgh Castle sitting high above the city. Before the castle lies the long green band of gardens that separates Edinburgh's Old Town, with its narrow streets crowded with ancient buildings, and New Town where Edinburgh's shopping street, Princes Street, is backed by wide roads of elegant Georgian houses. The city's principal sights are easily explored on foot, but as an introduction to Edinburgh take one of the double-decker sightseeing buses from Waverley Bridge opposite the Tourist Information Office and railway station. The tours run every ten minutes and wind a circular route through the city with a commentary on the significance of the buildings along the route. Your ticket is valid for twenty-four hours and the bus makes frequent stops so you can take the entire tour for an overview of what there is to see and then later use it as transportation between the sights, hopping on and off to visit the places that interest you. Several guided walking tours are offered, some exploring the city's ancient underground chambers—purported to be haunted!

The most popular time to visit Scotland's capital is during the **Edinburgh Festival**. Actually the name applies to a collection of festivals that take place between the end of July and the end of August. The Jazz and Blues Festival kicks off the event followed by the Edinburgh Festival Fringe in the last three weeks of August. The Fringe offers everything from the avant-garde to the eccentric along with jugglers, mimes, and buskers, making this the most comprehensive international arts festival in the world. Pipers dance down the streets and kilts are worn almost as a uniform. The hum of bagpipes sets the stage with parades, flags, presentations, floodlights, and color appearing everywhere. The

Military Tattoo provides tradition with massed pipes and drums from Scottish regiments alongside other military participants. It's an outdoor spectacle that culminates in a fireworks display. Tickets go on sale the previous December and sell out early.

Some of Edinburgh's major sights are:

Princes Street, the elegant main thoroughfare, its north side lined by shops and its south side bordered by gardens.

Majestically perched on the edge of the city atop an extinct volcanic outcrop, **Edinburgh Castle** looms against the skyline. There has been a castle here throughout the city's history, with today's comprising a collection of buildings from the little 11th-century St. Margaret's chapel, through medieval apartments to more modern army barracks and the Scottish United Services Museum. A dramatically staged exhibition tells the tale of the Scottish Crown Jewels, the "Honours of Scotland," which dazzle the visitor from their glass case. From the castle ramparts the view over Edinburgh is spectacular.

From the castle gates you enter a famous sequence of ancient streets, referred to as The Royal Mile. A short walk finds you at **Gladstone's Land** (NT), a building which typifies the more pleasant side of what life must have been like in the crowded tenements of Old Town Edinburgh. The house is arranged as a 17th-century merchant's house with the ground floor set up as a cloth merchant's booth and the upstairs as a home.

Just a short distance off the Royal Mile on Chambers Street you find The **Museum of Scotland** which chronicles the variety and richness of Scotland's long and exciting history, bringing it all to life with the fascinating stories each object and every gallery has to tell. An added bonus is the spectacular view from its rooftop garden.

On the High Street is the great **St. Giles' Cathedral**, founded in the 1100s, whose role has been so important in the history of the Presbyterian Church. John Knox preached from its pulpit from 1561 until his death in 1572, hurling attacks at the "idolatry" of the Catholic Church.

The **Museum of Childhood** (free) is reputedly the noisiest museum in the city. Find out how children were raised, dressed and educated in times gone by, and try some of the games they played.

John Knox's home is just a little farther down the High Street.

Further down the Royal Mile in the **Museum of Edinburgh** the People's Story tells the tales of the lives, work and leisure of the ordinary people of Edinburgh.

At the end of The Royal Mile lies **The Palace of Holyroodhouse**, the historic home of the Stuarts, to which Mary, Queen of Scots came from France at the age of 18. The six years of her reign and stay at Holyrood made a tragic impact on her life. Shortly after marriage to a meek Lord Darnley, the happiness of the couple dissolved and their quarrels became bitter. Lord Darnley was jealous of Mary's secretary and constant companion, David Rizzio, and conspired to have him stabbed at Holyrood in the presence of the queen. Just a year later, Lord Darnley himself was mysteriously murdered and gossip blamed the Earl of Bothwell. Mary, however, married the Earl promptly after Lord Darnley's death and rumors still question the queen's personal involvement in the murder. Conspiracies continued and Scotland's young queen fled to the safety of the English court. However, considering her a threat to the English Crown, Queen Elizabeth I welcomed her with imprisonment and had her beheaded 19 years later. Bonnie Prince Charlie was the last Stuart king to hold court at Holyrood in 1745. Today Holyrood, whose apartments are lavishly furnished with French and Flemish tapestries and fine works of art from the Royal Collection, is used by the British monarch as an official residence in Scotland.

Just across the way is the **Scottish Parliament Building** which opened in 2004. It's a magnificent modern building that cost a small fortune to build. Admissions and tours are free and what you see depends on whether parliament is sitting or not.

The adjacent modern building is **Our Dynamic Earth** where you can take a fantastic journey of discovery from the very beginning of time to the unknown future of Planet Earth. The special effects and dioramas are amazing.

The Georgian House (NT), at 7 Charlotte Square, is typical of the elegant Georgian homes found in New Town. From the kitchen through the drawing room to the bedrooms, the house is furnished and decorated much as it would have been when it was first occupied in 1796 and gives you an insight into the way the family and servants of the house lived.

Just outside the city, at the historic port of Leith, you can visit the royal yacht *Britannia*, which traveled to every corner of the globe as a floating residence for the royal family. A visitors' center and audio-visual presentation introduce you to the yacht's history then you can take a self-guided tour to every part of the ship. If you are driving, follow signs to Leith (North Edinburgh) and *Britannia*. There is a direct bus service from Waverley Bridge, next to the railway station.

Leaving Edinburgh, follow signs for the **Firth of Forth Bridge** and Perth. After crossing the Firth of Forth, the M90 takes you through hilly farmland to the outskirts of Perth where you take the A93 following signs for Scone Palace.

Before reaching the palace you can detour off the main road to visit the city of **Perth**, known as the "Fair City," which straddles the banks of the Tay. A lovely city, it was the capital of Scotland until 1437 and the murder of James I. Following his death, his widow and young son, James II, moved the court to Edinburgh. One of Perth's most important historic buildings is **St. John's Kirk**, a fine medieval church that has been attended by many members of English and Scottish royalty. Also of interest are the **Perth Museum and Art Gallery** and the **Museum of the Black Watch**, which is housed in **Ballhousie Castle**.

Scone Palace is a 19th-century mansion that stands on the site of the Abbey of Scone, the coronation palace of all Scottish kings up to James I. By tradition, the kings were crowned on a stone that was taken from the abbey in 1297 and placed under the Coronation Chair in Westminster Abbey. This token of conquest did nothing to improve relations between Scotland and England. The present mansion is the home of the Earl of Mansfield and houses a collection of china and ivory statuettes.

Continuing along the A93, shortly after leaving the abbey you pass through **Old Scone**. This was once a thriving village but was removed in 1805 by the Earl of Mansfield to improve the landscape and only the village cross and graveyard remain to mark the site.

Continue through Guildtown to **Stobhall**, a picturesque group of buildings grouped round a courtyard. Once the home of the Drummond family, much of the structure dates back to the 15th century.

Cross the River Isla and continue alongside the enormous beech hedge that was planted in 1746 as the boundary of the Meikleour estate. At the end of the hedge turn left to the village of **Meikleour**. The focal point of the village is the 1698 mercat cross, opposite which is an old place of punishment known as the Jougs Stone. Driving through the village you join the A984 Dunkeld road.

Continue through Caputh to **Dunkeld**. Telford spanned the Tay with a fine bridge in 1809, but this picturesque town is best known for the lovely ruins of its ancient cathedral. Founded in the 9th century, it was desecrated in 1560 and further damaged in the 17th-century Battle of Dunkeld. The choir has been restored. Stroll to **Dunkeld Cathedral** by way of Cathedral Street where the National Trust has restored the little 17th- and 18th-century houses.

Leaving the town, cross Telford's bridge and take the A9 for the 11-mile drive to **Pitlochry** where the Highlands meet the Lowlands of Scotland. The town owes its ornate Victorian appearance to its popularity in the 19th century as a Highland health resort. Now it is better known for its **Festival Theatre** whose season lasts from May to October and attracts some 70,000 theatergoers each year.

In the 1940s the local electricity company built a hydroelectric station and dam across the salmon-rich River Tummel on the outskirts of town. It is hard to imagine a power station being an asset to the town but this is certainly the case here. From the observation room at the dam you can watch fish as they climb the 1,000-foot **fish ladder** around the dam and fight their way upstream to spawn in the upper reaches of the river. A special exhibition is devoted to their life cycle and the efforts being made to conserve them.

Leaving Pitlochry the A924 winds up out of town towards Braemar. After passing through the village of Moulin look for a sign indicating a left hand turn to Edradour, the smallest and most picturesque distillery in Scotland. After a wee dram, your guide will talk you through the whisky-makers art and show you round the distillery to see Edradour being made today as it was in Victorian times.

Leaving the distillery the A924 winds up to the moorlands. Alternating lush green fields and heather-clad hills give way to heather-carpeted mountains as you approach the glorious Highland scenery of **Glen Shee** (A93). At the edge of the village of **Spittal of Glenshee** large orange gates are swung across the road when it is closed by winter storms. The road begins its steep climb across the heather up the Devil's Elbow to the ski resort at the summit and drops down to the green lush valley of the River Dee and **Braemar**.

Here in this picturesque valley the clans gather for Scotland's most famous Highland games, the **Braemar Gathering,** a brilliant spectacle of pipe bands, traditional Scottish sports, and Highland dancing. The event is usually attended by the Queen and her family. Also in the village of Braemar is the cottage in which Robert Louis Stevenson lived the year he wrote *Treasure Island*.

Following the River Dee, a short drive brings you to **Braemar Castle**, a doll-sized castle on a little knoll surrounded by conifers—a hint of the magnificent castles that wait you. Following the rushing River Dee, a turn in the road offers a splendid view of **Balmoral Castle**, the Royal summer residence. It's a very overrated Victorian pile of a building built in 1853 in the Scottish baronial style at the request of Queen Victoria and Prince Albert. When the Royal Family are not in residence, you can visit the gardens and view the exhibition in the castle ballroom.

Craigievar Castle

Coming into the tiny hamlet of **Craithe**, park in the riverside car park and stroll up to **Craithe Church** whose foundation stone was laid by Queen Victoria in 1895. The Royal Family attend services here when in residence at Balmoral just across the river.

Continue into **Ballater**, an attractive, small town internationally famous for its Highland games held in August. These include many old Scottish sports and the arduous hill race to the summit of Craig Cailleach. Continue along the A93, watching for the signpost that directs you left for a drive of several miles to **Craigievar Castle** (NT). This single-turret, pink-washed fortress surrounded by farmland is the most appealing of fairy-tale castles. Up the narrow spiral staircase the rooms are small and familial and furnished as though the laird and his family are still in residence. Willie Forbes, better known as Danzig

Willie because he made his money trading with Danzig, bought an incomplete castle here in 1610. He wanted the best that money could buy and gave the master mason free reign with the castle's beautiful design. The best plasterers were busy, so Danzig Willie waited many years for the magnificent molded plasterwork ceilings that were completed the year before his death in 1627.

Twenty miles away lies **Castle Fraser** (NT), a grander, more elaborate version of Craigievar set in parklike grounds with a formal walled garden. Begun in 1575, the castle stayed in Fraser hands until the early part of this century. It contains a splendid Great Hall and what remains of an alleged eavesdropping device known as the "Laird's Lug."

Regain the A944, which takes you through Alford and on towards Rhynie. Detour from the main road to visit the romantic ruins of **Kildrummy Castle** (A97). Overlooking the ruins and surrounded by acres and acres of beautiful gardens is **Kildrummy Castle Hotel**.

The road from Kildrummy to **Dufftown** via the little Highland villages of Lumsden, Rhynie (where you leave A97 and turn left on A941), and Cabrach takes you across broad expanses of moorland. James Duff, the 4th Earl of Fife, laid out Dufftown in the form of a right-angled cross in 1817. Turn right at the Tolbooth tower in the center of the square and you come to the **Glenfiddich Distillery**, the only distillery in the Highlands where you can see the complete whisky-making process from barley to bottling.

Malt whisky is to Scotland what wine is to France. The rules for production are strict: It must be made from Highland barley dried over peat fires. Water is gathered from streams that have run through peat and over granite. Distillation is carried out in onion-shaped copper stills with the final product aged and stored in oak vats before bottling. A map is available from the tourist office in Dufftown that gives details of which distilleries are open and when.

Once a Highland fortress but now sadly in ruins, **Ballathie Castle** stands on the hill overlooking the distillery.

Four miles down the A941 you come to **Craigellachie** village and distillery (the home of White Horse Whisky). Turn left on the A95 for Grantown-on-Spey and follow the Spey valley through pleasant countryside to **Ballindalloch Castle**, the beautiful home of the Macpherson-Grants. An interesting selection of tastefully furnished rooms and a teashop are open to the public. This elegant home with its lovely gardens shows the transition from the tower house of Craigievar to the country mansion so idealized by the Victorians in the Highlands.

A short distance brings you to the **Glenlivet Distillery**.

Cross the River Spey at Advie and continue into Grantown-on-Spey on the narrow road that follows the north bank of the river. From Grantown-on-Spey the A939 leads towards the holiday resort of Nairn. After about 15 miles take a small road to the left signposted for **Cawdor Castle**. This was the castle Shakespeare had in mind when he set the scene of Duncan's death in *Macbeth*. The present-day Thane of Cawdor shares his family home and gardens with the public. Portraits, tapestries, lovely furniture, and, of course, tales of romance and mystery blend to make this an interesting tour.

An 8-mile drive brings you to the cairn that marks the site of the battle of **Culloden** (NT) where on a wet day in 1746 Bonnie Prince Charlie marched his tired, rain-soaked Highlanders into hopeless battle with the English: 1,200 Highlanders were killed. This was the last battle fought on British soil and Charles's defeat led to the decline of the Highlands and the destruction of the clan system. After the battle the British hunted Charles for five months before he escaped to France. A museum documents this sad incident and on the surrounding moorland red flags outline the Scots battle plan while yellow flags denote the English.

Nearby **Inverness** is known as the "Capital of the Highlands." Straddling the River Ness, the town takes its name from the river and the Gaelic word "inver" meaning river mouth. Leave the town on the A82 (Fort William road) and after a mile you come to the Caledonian Canal, which links the lochs of the Great Glen together to provide passage between the Irish and the North Seas. The canal splits Scotland in two and without it boats would have to risk the dangerous passage around the northernmost stretches of Scotland.

The road then follows the northern shore of Scotland's deepest (700 feet), longest (24 miles), and most famous lake, **Loch Ness**. This is the legendary home of the Loch Ness Monster or "Nessie," as she is affectionately known. So, keep an eye on the muddy gray waters of the lake and you may see more than the wind ruffling its surface. If she doesn't happen to surface for you, visit the **Loch Ness Monster Exhibition** at **Drumnadrochit**, which documents sightings that go back to the 7th century. Photographs of eel-like loops and black heads swimming give credence to the legends.

Monster spotting is a favorite pastime around Loch Ness and visitors gaze from the ramparts of **Urquhart Castle** because some of the best sightings have been made from here. The ruined castle dates from the 14th century and has a long and violent history.

Following the shores of Loch Ness, a 19-mile drive brings you to **Fort Augustus**, a village that stands at the southwestern end of the loch. Park your car by the **Caledonian Canal** and wander along its banks to see the pleasure craft being lowered and raised through the locks. Thomas Telford, the famous engineer, spent from 1803 to 1847 building the sections of this canal that connects the North Sea and the Atlantic without boats having to navigate around the treacherous Cape Wrath.

A few miles to the southwest, the little village of **Invergarry** is framed by spectacular mountain scenery. The village was burnt to the ground after the battle of Culloden because it had sheltered Bonnie Prince Charlie before and after the battle. Turn west in the village and follow the A87, through breathtaking Highland scenery, for 50 miles to Kyle of Lochalsh. The wild, rugged scenery changes with every bend in the road as you drive high above the lochs across empty moorlands then descend into glens to follow the shores of lochs whose crystal-clear, icy waters reflect the rugged mountain peaks. Habitations are few and far between yet, until the Highland chiefs decided in the 18th century that sheep were more profitable than tenants, the hillsides held crofts, schools, and chapels.

As you trace the shore of **Loch Duich**, on the last lap of the journey to Skye, **Eilean Donan Castle** appears, linked to the rocky shore by a bridge. The castle is named for a saint who lived here in the 7th century. It is a massive, walled keep that during subsequent centuries defended the coast against Danish and Norse invaders. More recently it has been restored and it is fascinating to go into rooms with 14-foot-thick walls and to climb to the battlements to see the loch spread out before you.

Eilean Donan Castle

From the busy fishing port of **Kyle of Lochalsh** the toll road bridge takes you "over the sea to Skye." There is an exhilarating feel to the often mist-shrouded shores of the **Isle of Skye** where mystery and legends intermingle with dramatic scenery. Islanders still make a living crofting and fishing, though tourism is becoming ever more important. This is the home of the Scottish heroine Flora Macdonald who disguised Bonnie Prince Charlie as her maid and brought him safely to Skye after his defeat by the English at the battle of Culloden.

Set out to explore Skye's coastline where magnificent mountains rise from the rocky shore and sea lochs provide scenic sheltered harbors. Skye has very good roads, although often quite narrow, making it easy to tour portions of the island in a day. (A trip from Portree—around the northern end of Skye, west to Dunvegan, and back to Portree by the hill road from Struan—is all that you could expect to do comfortably in one day.) If the weather is inclement and mist veils the island, content yourself with a good book by the fireside, for what appears stunningly beautiful on a fine day can appear dreary when sheathed in fog.

Follow the A87 (signposted Portree) through the scattered village of Broadford set along a broad, sheltered bay. Skirting the shoreline, you pass the island of Scalpay before tracing the southern shoreline of Loch Ainort. The surrounding humped peaks of the Cullin Hills are spectacular as you follow the road through Sconser and Sligachan to Portree.

Portree, the capital of Skye, is its most attractive town. Pastel-painted houses step down to the water's edge, fishing boats bob in the harbor, and small boats arrive and depart from its pier. Climbing away from the harbor, the town's streets are lined with attractive shops. If you have not booked your ferry passage from Armadale to Mallaig, you can do so at the Caledonian MacBrayne ferry office behind the bus station. The town derives its name from *Port an Righ*, meaning "King's Haven," following the visit in 1540 of James V who made a vain attempt to reconcile the feuding MacLeod and Macdonald clans

Leaving the town, turn right onto the A850, a narrow, single-lane road with passing places, which takes you north. As you approach the shores of Lochs Fada and Leathan, the jagged, craggy peaks of **The Storr** (mountains) come into view. Standing amongst them is the **Old Man of Storr**, one of the most challenging pinnacles for mountain climbers.

Around the island's northernmost headland the crumbling ruins of the Macdonalds' **Duntulm Castle** stand on a clifftop promontory overlooking the rocky shores of Duntulm Bay. A short drive brings you to the **Skye Croft Museum** where four traditional Highland crofts have been restored and appropriately furnished to show a family home, a smithy, a weaver's house, and a small museum. These little cottages with their thick stone walls topped by a thick straw thatch were the traditional island dwellings—very few good examples remain though, as you travel around the island, if you look very carefully, you can see several traditional cottages in various states of ruin. Flora Macdonald is buried in a nearby graveyard.

Returning to the main coastal route (A850), a short drive takes you through Kilmuir and down a steep hill into the scattered hamlet of **Uig** whose pier is used by ferries to the Outer Hebrides. It is here that Bonnie Prince Charlie and Flora Macdonald landed after fleeing the Outer Hebrides. Continue to Kensaleyre and half a mile beyond the village turn right onto the B8036. When this road meets a T-junction, turn right onto the A87 for the 22-mile drive to the village of **Dunvegan**.

Just to the north of the village is **Dunvegan Castle**, the oldest inhabited castle in Scotland and the home of the MacLeod family for over 700 years. It stands amidst hills and moorlands guarding the entrance to a sheltered bay. After parking your car walk through rhododendron-filled gardens to the fortress. The castle's 15th-century section is known as the Fairy Tower after the threadbare Fairy Flag that hangs in one of the chambers. Legend has it that this yellow silk flag with crimson spots is the consecrated banner of the Knights Templar, taken as a battle prize from the Saracens. It is said to have the magical properties to produce victory in battle, the birth of sons, and plentiful harvests. Other relics include items relating to Bonnie Prince Charlie. During the summer you can take boat excursions to view the nearby seal colonies.

The A863 winds you down the western side of Skye. If you wish to visit the island's only distillery, take the B8009 to **Talisker** where the **Talisker Distillery** offers guided tours and a tasting.

Follow the road (A851) across open moorland to **Sleat** (pronounced "Slate"), which refers to the complete southern peninsula of Skye where most of the land is divided into two estates: Clan Donald lands to the south and those of Sir Iain Noble to the north. Sir Iain is a great promoter of Gaelic, which is undergoing a revival in the western Highlands. On a rocky spit of land almost surrounded by water, the whitewashed **Eilean Iarmain** hotel, a shop, and a huddle of cottages face **Isle Ornsay**—a postage-stamp-sized island whose lighthouse was built by Robert Louis Stephenson's grandfather. (The lighthouse cottage's most famous occupant was Gavin Maxwell.) Across the sound mountains tumble directly into the sea adding a wild, end-of-the-earth feel to this hamlet.

A few more miles of narrow roads bring you to the **Clan Donald Centre** where the stable block serves as a tearoom and gift shop whence you walk through the wooded **Armadale Castle** grounds to an exhibition on the Lords of the Isles and Gaelic culture.

SKYE TO FORT WILLIAM VIA MALLAIG

If time or weather prevents you from following this itinerary north into Wester Ross, you can board the ferry for **Mallaig** in nearby **Armadale**. The ferry sails five to six times a day during the summer months and reservations should be made before sailing—it is suggested that you purchase your tickets from the Caledonian MacBrayne ferry offices in Portree. The ferry company requires that cars arrive half an hour before sailing time. It takes 1½ hours to drive from Portree to the ferry, so unless you are an insomniac, do not book the 9 am ferry. Leaving Mallaig, you cannot get lost for there is only one narrow road, "The Road to the Isles," that leads you out of town (A830).

If the weather is fine, you may want to pause at the spectacular white beaches that fringe the rocky little bays near **Morar**. The narrow road twists and turns and passing places allow cars going in opposite directions to pass one another. The village of **Arisaig** shelters on the shores of **Loch Nan Ceal** with views, and ferries, to the little islands of **Rhum** and **Eigg**.

From Arisaig your route turns eastwards following the picturesque shores of **Loch Nan Uamh**, best known for its associations with Bonnie Prince Charlie and the Jacobite Rising of 1745. The clan leaders met in a house nearby and after his defeat the prince hid near here before being taken to the Outer Hebrides—a cairn marks the spot where he left Scotland.

More than 1,000 clansmen gathered at **Glenfinnan** at the head of **Loch Shiel** to begin the 1745 Jacobite Rising. A tall castellated tower marks the place where they are said to have hoisted the Stuart standard. You climb the tower stairs to the statue of a Highlander overlooking the icy waters of the mountain-ringed loch. At the adjacent visitors' center the prince's exploits are portrayed.

Leaving the monument to Bonnie Prince Charlie's lost cause, follow the A830 for the 15-mile drive through Kinlocheil and Corpach to **Fort William**. As you approach the town, the rounded summit of Britain's highest mountain, **Ben Nevis**, appears before you.

Plockton on Loch Carron

SKYE TO FORT WILLIAM OR INVERNESS VIA WESTER ROSS

If you love Skye with its magnificent seascapes and mountains, then you will adore the Wester Ross coastline that stretches from Kyle of Lochalsh to Ullapool and beyond. It is a long day's drive from Kyle to Ullapool and the scenery is so magnificent that you may want to break the journey and spend several days in the area. Traditionally, **Wester Ross** has most sunshine in May and June, it rains more in July and August, then brightens up in September. Scottish weather is very fickle in May: we went from seven days of glorious sunshine to seemingly endless days of lashing rain. A great deal of the drive from Kyle of Lochalsh to Ullapool is on single-track road—one lane of tarmac just a few inches wider than your car (with passing places).

From **Kyle of Lochalsh** turn left to **Plockton** to see the hardy yucca palms growing bravely in the harborside gardens in this pretty village that hugs a sheltered spot of the wooded bay. Leaving Plockton, the road traces Loch Carron and after passing the Stratcarron Hotel, at the head of the loch, you turn left on the A896 for Tornapress and on to Shieldaig.

If the weather is sunny, rather than continuing along the A896 from Tornapress to Shieldaig, take the coastal road around the headland following signposts for Applecross. You will be rewarded by a most challenging drive and spectacular scenery. The narrow road twists and turns as it climbs ever higher up the **Bealach-na-Bo** pass with the mountains rising closer and taller at every turn. Crest the summit, cross a boulder-strewn moorland dotted with tarns (tiny lakes), and drop down into **Applecross**—a few whitewashed houses set in a lush green valley with salmon-pink sandy beaches. Grazing sheep fill the coastal fields and the occasional whitewashed croft faces across the water to the Isle of Raasay and, beyond that, the misty mountains of Skye. Rounding the peninsula you come to **Ardehslaig**, a few white cottages set round a rocky inlet with boats bobbing in the tiny sheltered harbor. Turn into **Shieldaig** where little cottages line the waterfront facing a nearby island densely forested with Scotch pines. It's an idyllic, peaceful spot and **Tigh an Eilean** (House by the Island) with its shop, hotel, and pub makes an excellent place to break your journey.

A deceptive few yards of two-lane road quickly turn to single track as you travel along the south shore of **Loch Torridon** where the **Loch Torridon Hotel** sits on its bank and through Glen Torridon to turn left on the A832, an arrow-straight, two-lane highway. After half a mile you find a whitewashed visitors' center on the left. The road traces **Loch Maree** with tempting glimpses of the glassy loch between groves of birch trees. The soft lushness and straight road give way to wild moorland and a single-track road to **Gairloch** with its wide bay of pink sand, scattered houses, cemetery, and golf course.

Heading inland to cross the peninsula you come to **Inverewe Gardens** (NT). Osgood MacKenzie bought this little peninsula in 1862, a barren site exposed to Atlantic gales but with frosts prevented by the warmth of the Gulf Stream. He planted belts of trees for shelter, brought in soil, and began his garden, a lifetime project that was continued by his daughter who handed over Inverewe to the National Trust in 1952. The lushness of the gardens is a striking contrast to the miles of dramatic, barren scenery that surround it. The surprise is not so much what the garden contains as the fact that it exists at all on a latitude similar to that of Leningrad. The gardens, shop, and tearoom are a venue that will occupy several hours. The National Trust brochure outlines a suggested route along the garden's pathways, but you can wander at will down the twisting paths through the azaleas, rhododendrons, and woodlands. Colorful displays are to be found in most seasons: in mid-April to May, rhododendrons; May, azaleas; June, rock garden, flower borders, and roses; September, heather; and November, maples.

Leaving Inverewe, another 35 miles finds you at the head of **Loch Broom** at an impressive vantage point that offers magnificent views down the valley across lush farmland to the distant loch. Travel down the hill and turn left into the green valley for the 12-mile drive to Ullapool.

Ullapool has a beautiful setting: cottages line the quay and overlook a jumble of slipways, quays, vessels from huge international trawlers to small wooden fishing boats, fishing gear, and nets. On the distant shore heather-clad hills rise steeply from the waters of Loch Broom. The port is a bustle of freighters and foreign fishing boats and is the terminal for the car ferry to Stornoway on the Isle of Lewis. Summer visitors add to the throng. You can always find good food and a reviving cup of coffee at **The Ceilidh Place**.

North of Ullapool there's a lot of heart-stopping scenery but beyond the Summer Isles there are no good places to stay. Journey to the **Summer Isles** by boat to see the seals and seabirds. Travel to **Lochinver** with its breathtaking views of beautiful coastline and visit the **Inchnadamph Caves** and the ruin of **Ardvreck Castle**.

Leaving Ullapool, a 60-mile drive (A835) will return you to Inverness from where it's a three-hour drive down the A9 to Edinburgh. Or retrace your steps down the northern shore of Loch Ness and continue into Fort William (A82).

Bordering the shores of **Loch Linnhe**, **Fort William** is the largest town in the Western Highlands. While the town itself cannot be described as attractive, it is the economic hub of the area and it is always crowded with tourists during the busy summer months.

From Fort William the A82 takes you southwest along the southern shore of Loch Linnhe, then turns you inland over the pass of **Glen Coe**, notorious for the massacre of the Macdonalds by the Campbells in 1692. After accepting their hospitality, the Campbells issued an order—written on the nine of diamonds playing card—to kill their hosts, the Macdonalds. The pass of Glen Coe is barren and rocky and the road south travels across this seemingly empty land. A short detour to **Killin** with its craft shops and impressive waterfalls provides an enjoyable break on a long drive.

The area of low mountains and serene lakes around **Callander**, a most attractive town, is known as **The Trossachs**. This is the country of Sir Walter Scott's novel *Rob Roy* and his poem *Lady of the Lake*. Robert MacGregor, "Rob Roy," existed as a romanticized 17th-century Robin Hood, who stole from the rich and gave to the poor. However, some regarded him more realistically as a thief and rustler! Scott's "lady" was Ellen Douglas, and her "lake" was **Loch Katrine**. There are several lovely lakes to view in this area, such as **Loch Achray** and **Loch Venachar**.

A few miles distant lies **Stirling**, dominated by its imposing Renaissance castle. **Stirling Castle**, once the home of Scottish kings, is perched high on a sheer cliff overlooking the battleground of **Bannockburn** where the Scots turned the English back in their attempt to subdue the Highland clans.

From Stirling the M80 will quickly bring you to **Glasgow**, Scotland's most populous city. Its established tradition as a port and industrial center has in recent years been surpassed by its reputation as a cultural center.

As in many large cities, the best way to get an overview of the major sights is to take a tour bus. Open-top double-deckers leave every half hour on two routes from George Square, where you also find the **Tourist Information Centre**, and you can hop on and off wherever you like. This is a Victorian city with a particular pride in its architecture and architects of that time, notably Charles Rennie Mackintosh and Alexander "Greek" Thomson, whose buildings feature prominently on the tour. Be sure to visit the 13th-century **cathedral** with its open timber roof and splendid collection of stained-glass windows. Here you find the shrine of St. Mungo, patron saint of Glasgow who died in 603, which was an important medieval pilgrimage spot.

Young and old enjoy the **Glasgow Science Centre** on the banks of the River Clyde at Pacific Quay. The Science Museum brings technology to life with hundreds of hands-on exhibits in the Science Mall. Take in a live science show and go view the latest IMAX movie.

Glasgow is home to over 30 art galleries and museums including the **Kelvingrove Art Gallery and Museum**, the most popular in Scotland, **St. Mungo's Museum** of religious life and art, the only museum of its kind in the world, and **The Burrell Collection**, Scotland's most outstanding museum. The Collection is set in the delightful surroundings of Pollok Country Park, formerly the grounds of **Pollok House** (NT), and can be reached by bus, train, or car (take the M8 towards the airport to the M77). Sir William Burrell, a successful Glasgow shipping agent, amassed a magnificent collection of some 9,000 works of art, primarily in the areas of medieval European art (the tapestries are stunning), Oriental ceramics and bronzes, and European paintings. In 1944 he bequeathed his collection to the city, with the stipulation that it be housed away from the highly polluted city center and eventually, in 1983, it found the perfect setting here in a corner of the Pollok Estate in a custom-built, award-winning building.

At the other end of the social spectrum, it is fascinating to get a glimpse of what life used to be like for working-class Glaswegians, as you can in the **Tenement House Museum** (NT), a Victorian apartment re-creating the poorest living conditions in the first half of the 20th century. The **People's Palace** opened in 1898 as a cultural center for the people of the East End, one of the unhealthiest and most overcrowded parts of the city. It is now the local history museum of Glasgow, telling the story of the people from 1750 to the present. Attached to the People's Palace is the elegant Victorian glasshouse -the Winter Gardens -where you can relax among the tropical plants and enjoy the café.

Shopping is excellent in Glasgow and evenings are alive with every kind of entertainment from opera to nightclubs.

Scotland

Wales

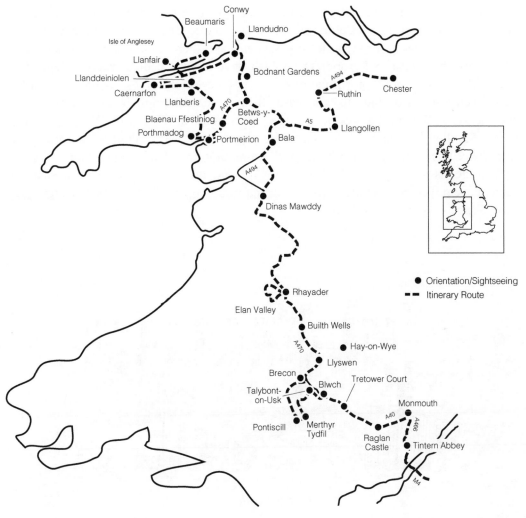

Isle of Anglesey

Beaumaris
Conwy
Llandudno

Llanfair
Bodnant Gardens
Ruthin
Chester
A494

Llanddeiniolen
Caernarfon
Llanberis
A470
Betws-y-Coed
A5
Llangollen

Blaenau Ffestiniog
Porthmadog
Portmeirion
Bala

A494

Dinas Mawddy

Rhayader

Elan Valley

Builth Wells

Hay-on-Wye
A470
Llyswen
Brecon
Blwch
Tretower Court
Talybont-on-Usk
Monmouth
A40
A466
Pontiscill
Merthyr Tydfil
Raglan Castle
Tintern Abbey
M4

● Orientation/Sightseeing
▬ ▬ Itinerary Route

103

Wales

Wales has myriad towns and villages with seemingly unpronounceable names, its own language, an ancient form of Celtic, and its own prince, Charles. Narrow-gauge steam railways puff contentedly through glorious scenery, and there are more castles per square mile than anywhere else in Europe. The Welsh have always been fiercely independent. Consequently, they built fortifications to defend themselves while Edward I commissioned a series of daunting fortresses from which the English could sally forth to subdue the fiery Welsh. Today these mighty fortresses are some of Wales's greatest treasures. Smaller but beloved treasures are the "Great Little Trains," narrow-gauge steam railway lines with hard-working "toy" trains that once hauled slate and still steam through gorgeous countryside. And at journey's end there is bound to be a steaming cuppa to be enjoyed with *bara brith*, a scrumptious currant bread. As the signs say, *Croeso i Cymru*—Welcome to Wales.

Conwy Castle

Recommended Pacing: One night in southern Wales is all you need to accomplish the sightseeing outlined in this itinerary. In our opinion, Wales's most magnificent scenery and stunning castles lie to the north in and around Snowdonia National Park, so allow at least two nights in northern Wales.

Leave England on the M4 crossing the Severn toll bridge. The first indication that you are in another country is that all road signs appear in two languages, Welsh first, English second. As you leave the bridge take the first left turnoff signed A466 Monmouth and the Wye Valley. The road winds a course up the steep-sided, wooded valley to **Tintern Abbey**, a romantic ruin adored by the sentimental Victorians. Drive alongside the ruin to the car park at the rear by the tourist office. Stretch your legs with a quick walk round the ruin or, if you would like to visit the prettiest spot on the 168-mile length of **Offa's Dyke**, the tourist office will provide you with a detailed instruction sheet called *Offa's Dyke and the Devil's Pulpit Viewpoint*. Offa's Dyke was a great earthwork built over 1,200 years ago at the direction of King Offa to divide England and Wales.

Follow the river as it winds into Monmouth and turn left on the A40 towards Abergavenny. Traveling this dual carriageway quickly brings into view the substantial ruins of **Raglan Castle** in a field to your right. Because it is on the opposite side of a divided highway you need to do an about-face at the first roundabout. Raglan Castle is the last of the medieval castles, dating from the later Middle Ages when its builders could afford to indulge in decorative touches. It was begun in 1431 and its Great Tower was rendered the ruin you see today by Oliver Cromwell's demolition engineers. A huge fireplace and the windows are all that remain of the Grand Hall but with imagination and the aid of a map you can picture what a splendid place this must have been. You can climb the battlements and picnic in the grassy grounds.

Stay on the ring road around Abergavenny and 2 miles after passing through **Crickhowell**, a one-time stagecoach stop for coach travelers on the way to Brecon, turn right on the A479 to **Tretower Court and Castle**. The castle, a sturdy keep, was usurped as a habitation in the 14th century by nearby Tretower Court, a grand mansion that was the home of the Vaughan family for three centuries. As you walk through the empty medieval hall and along the stone passageways, you can imagine how splendid a home it was.

Leaving Tretower, continue down the lane, beside the house, and turn right on the A40. If the weather is fine, you can enjoy an almost circular driving tour through the **Brecon Beacons** by turning left towards Llangynidr and, after crossing the river, taking a right turn to Cwm Cronon and Talybont-on-Usk. Here you turn left and follow a beautiful wooded valley alongside lakes and over the hills to Pontiscill. On a fine day it is a spectacular drive along a narrow paved road, but this is not a trip to be appreciated when the clouds hang low over the mountains and visibility is not good. From Pontiscill the road weaves down to the outskirts of Merthyr Tydfil where you turn right on the A470 along another lovely valley and climb the stark, bare escarpment over the pass to Brecon.

If you do not deviate through the Brecon Beacons, remain on the A40 where views of the Usk Valley and the mountains present themselves as the road climbs to the village of Blwch. Bypass the market town of Brecon and take the A470 (Buith Wells) to **Llyswen** where you can enjoy an overnight stay at **Llangoed Hall**. From Llyswen an 18-mile round-trip detour will afford you the chance to explore the many bookstores and antique shops of **Hay-on-Wye**.

It's a lovely drive to Buith Wells as the road follows the River Wye through soft, pretty countryside. Crossing the river, head to **Rhayader** where an opportunity to enjoy a beautiful (in fair weather) drive through wild, rugged moorlands rising from vast reservoirs is afforded by turning left in the village for the **Elan Valley**. Your first stop lies beneath the looming dam at the information center where a small display outlines the importance and history of clean drinking water and gives details on the vast reservoirs that provide 76 million gallons of drinking water a day. Returning to the road, follow it as it traces the reservoir through fern-covered mountains. A right-hand turn returns you to the center of Rhayader and the A470.

From Rhayader the A470 quickly takes you north. After the junction with the A458 be on the lookout for a small sign that directs you into the pretty roadside village of Dinas

Mawddy and along a narrow lane that climbs and climbs above the green fields into stark mountains. You crest the pass and wind down and around the lake to the outskirts of Bala. Here you make a right-hand turn then go immediately left on the A4212 (Trawsfyndd road) for a short distance to the B4501, which quickly brings you to Cerrigydrudion. There you turn left on the A5 to **Betws-y-Coed**, set in a narrow, densely wooded valley at the confluence of three rivers. Crowds of visitors come to admire this town, which was popularized by the Victorian painter David Cox.

From Betws-y-Coed take the A470, following the eastern bank of the River Conwy north as it winds its way to the sea. After passing through the village of Tal-y-Cafn, look for **Bodnant Gardens** (NT) on your right. Garden lovers will enjoy almost a hundred acres of camellias, rhododendrons, magnolias, and laburnum, which provide incredible displays of spring color. Above are terraces, lawns, and formal rose and flower beds; below, in a wooded valley, a stream runs through the secluded, wild garden.

The swell of **Conwy Bay** is flanked by high cliffs and the town of **Conwy** is unforgettable for its picturesque castle set on a promontory at the confluence of two rivers and for the town's wall—over ¾ mile in length with 22 towers and 3 original gateways. **Conwy Castle** was begun in the 13th century for Edward I and suffered the scars of the turbulent years of the Middle Ages and the Civil War. The defensive complex includes an exhibit on Edward I and his castles in Wales. On the top floor of the Chapel Tower is a scale model of how the castle and the town might have appeared in 1312.

Leaving the castle, cross the road to the quay to visit a tiny home that claims to be the smallest house in Britain, then turn onto the High Street and visit the oldest house in Wales, **Aberconwy House** (NT).

Leave Conwy and follow the A55 as it hugs the coast in the direction of Caernarfon. Rather than going directly to Caernarfon, follow signs for Bangor (A5122) and call in at **Penrhyn Castle** (NT), a fabulous sham castle built as a grand home by a local slate magnate in the 19th century. This impressive house of intricate masonry and woodwork is filled with stupendous furniture.

Cross over the Menai Straight to the **Isle of Anglesey** on the Menai suspension bridge, the first of its kind, built by the famous engineer Thomas Telford, then follow the road that hugs the coast to **Beaumaris** with its closely huddled houses painted in pastel shades strung along the road. **Beaumaris Castle**, the last of the castles built by Edward I in his attempt to control Wales, is a squat, moated fortress with grassy grounds inside thick walls facing a harbor full of sailboats.

Return to the Menai bridge and, if you are inclined to have your picture taken by the sign of the town with the longest name in the world, follow directions to **Llanfair**, the abbreviation (that fits on signposts) for Llanfairpwllgwyngyllgogerychwyndrobwyllllan-tysiliogogogoch. This translates as "St. Mary's Church by the white aspens over the whirlpool and St. Tysilio's Church by the red cave." The drab little town has little to recommend it but commercial opportunists have cleverly situated a large shopping complex directly next to the station.

The A5 (Bangor road) quickly returns you to the mainland via the Britannia road bridge where you pick up signs for **Caernarfon**. Edward I laid the foundations of **Caernarfon Castle** in 1283 after his armies had defeated the princes of North Wales. Many revolts against English rule took place in this imposing fortress and during the Civil War it was one of Cromwell's strongholds. The first English Prince of Wales was born here in 1284. The investitures of the Duke of Windsor in 1911 and of Prince Charles in 1969 as Prince of Wales both took place in this majestic setting. This is the most massive and best preserved of the fortifications in this itinerary. It takes several hours to clamber up the towers, peep through arrow slits in the massive walls, and visit the exhibitions on the Princes of Wales, Castles of Edward I, and the Museum of the Royal Welsh Fusiliers.

Caernarfon Castle

Leave the coast at Caernarfon with the beauty of Snowdonia ahead of you, following the A4086 Llanberis road. The **Snowdonia National Park** is a region of wild mountains which, while they cannot be compared in size to the Alps or the Rockies (Snowdon rises to 3,560 feet), are nevertheless dramatically beautiful with ravines and sheer cliffs whose sides plummet into glacier-cut valleys sparkling with wood-fringed lakes and cascading waterfalls.

The village of **Llanberis** is the starting point for the ascent of the highest mountain in Wales, **Mount Snowdon**. Easier than the rugged walking ascent is the two-hour round-trip journey on the **Snowdon Mountain Railway**, an adorable "toy" steam train that pushes its carriages up the mountainside on a rack-and-pinion railway. The little train winds you along the edges of precipices and up steep gradients to the mountain's summit. If the weather is fine (the train runs only in clear weather) and especially if it is July, August, or the weekend, arrive for your adventure early to secure a pass that entitles you to return at an appointed time. On the day we visited a 10:30 am arrival assured us of a place on the 4:30 pm return train. Remember to take warm clothing with you as it is always cold on the summit.

When you return from your mountain experience make your way to the other side of the lake to ride the **Llanberis Lake Railway** (rarely do you have to book in advance). The adorable little train that once served the slate quarries now puffs along 2 miles of track by the edge of the lake beneath the towering mountains. On fine days you have lovely views of Snowdon.

When you leave Llanberis the road climbs the pass and the scenery becomes ever more rocky and rugged: small wonder that Hillary and Hunt trained for the 1953 Everest ascent in this area. At the Pen-y-Gwryd hotel turn right on the A498 for Beddgelert. The landscape softens as you pass Lake Gwynant and, with the River Glaslyn as its guide, the road passes through a valley that is softer and more pastoral than those of Snowdonia's other lakes.

Crowding the riverbank where three valleys meet is the little village of **Beddgelert**, nestled in the foothills of Mount Snowdon. From Beddgelert, the road follows the tumbling River Glaslyn which settles into a lazy glide as it approaches **Porthmadog**, the terminus of the hard-working little **Ffestiniog Narrow-Gauge Railway**, which runs to and from nearby Ffestiniog. The train provides riders with a mobile viewpoint from which to enjoy the most spectacular scenery as it follows the coast and chugs up into rugged Snowdonia, at one point traveling almost in a circle to gain altitude, to terminate its journey at **Blaenau Ffestiniog**. Here, in summer, you can connect with a bus that takes you for a visit to the nearby slate caverns before taking you back to the station for your return journey to Porthmadog. This rugged little train for many years carried slate from the mines to the port of Porthmadog.

A short drive on the A487 brings you to Minffordd where you turn right to the extravagant fantasy village of **Portmeirion**, which looks like a little piece of Italy transported to Wales. It has a piazza, a campanile, and an eclectic mixture of cottages and buildings squeezed into a small space and surrounded by gardens full of subtropical plants and ornate pools. The village is a mass of color—the façades are terra cotta, bright pink, yellow, and cream, and the gardens full of brightly colored flowers and shrubs. Portmeirion was the realization of a dream for Sir Clough Williams-Ellis who bought this wooded hillside plot above the broad sandy river estuary and built the village to show that architecture could be fun and could enhance a beautiful site, not defile it. His architectural model was Portofino and, while there are many Italianate touches to this fantasy village, there are also lots of local recycled houses. Sir Clough rescued many old buildings and cottages from destruction (he termed Portmeirion "the home for fallen buildings"), transporting them here and erecting them on the site. Day visitors are charged an admission fee but if you really want to fully enjoy the fantasy spend the night at the hotel or in one of the rooms in the village and enjoy it after the visitors have left.

Leave the coast behind you and turn inland to Blaenau Ffestiniog where terraced houses huddle together beneath the massive, gray-slate mountain to form a village. Taking the A470 towards Betws-y-Coed, the road follows terrace upon terrace of somber gray slate up the mountainside to the **Llechwedd Slate Caverns**. Exhibits show the importance of slate mining but the most exciting part of a visit here is to travel underground into the deep mine and follow a walking tour through the caverns.

Continuing north (A470), a 15-minute drive takes you over the pass to **Dolwyddelan Castle**, a 13th-century keep built by Prince Llewyn which was captured by Edward I and subsequently restored in the 19th century.

From Betws-y-Coed take the A5 to **Llangollen**, a town that has become the famous scene of the colorful extravaganza, the international Musical Eisteddfod, the contest for folk dancers, singers, orchestras, and instrumentalists. Llangollen's 14th-century stone bridge spanning the salmon-rich River Dee is one of Wales's Seven Wonders.

Leave Llangollen on the A542 and travel over the scenic Horseshoe Pass past the ruins of the Cistercian abbey, Valle Crucis, to **Ruthin**. Nestled in the fertile valley of Clwyd and closed in by a ring of wooded hills, Ruthin is an old, once-fortified market town whose castle is now a very commercialized hotel complete with medieval banquets.

From here a fast drive on the A494 returns you to England and motorways that quickly take you to all corners of the realm. But before leaving the area, consider visiting the charming medieval city of **Chester**. The Romans settled here in 79 A.D. and made Chester a key stronghold. Much of the original Roman wall survives, although many towers and gates seen today were additions from the Middle Ages. Chester is a fascinating city with a 2-mile walk around its **battlements**—the best way to orient yourself. It's great fun to browse in **The Rows**, double-decker layers of shops—one layer of stores at street level and the other stacked on top.

London Hotel Map

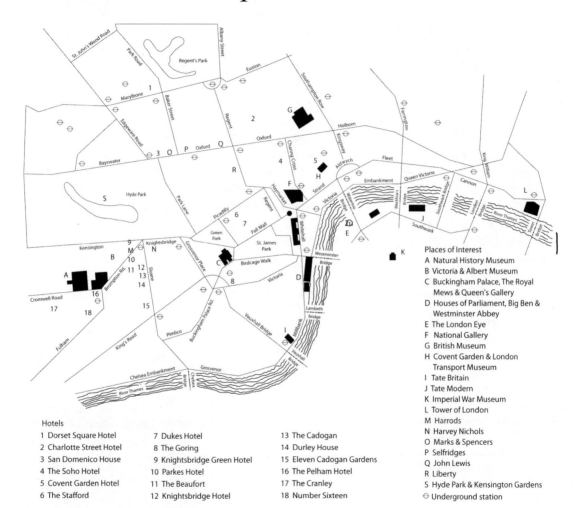

Hotels

1 Dorset Square Hotel
2 Charlotte Street Hotel
3 San Domenico House
4 The Soho Hotel
5 Covent Garden Hotel
6 The Stafford
7 Dukes Hotel
8 The Goring
9 Knightsbridge Green Hotel
10 Parkes Hotel
11 The Beaufort
12 Knightsbridge Hotel
13 The Cadogan
14 Durley House
15 Eleven Cadogan Gardens
16 The Pelham Hotel
17 The Cranley
18 Number Sixteen

Places of Interest

A Natural History Museum
B Victoria & Albert Museum
C Buckingham Palace, The Royal
   Mews & Queen's Gallery
D Houses of Parliament, Big Ben &
   Westminster Abbey
E The London Eye
F National Gallery
G British Museum
H Covent Garden & London
   Transport Museum
I Tate Britain
J Tate Modern
K Imperial War Museum
L Tower of London
M Harrods
N Harvey Nichols
O Marks & Spencers
P Selfridges
Q John Lewis
R Liberty
S Hyde Park & Kensington Gardens
⊖ Underground station

Nestled in a residential neighborhood, but conveniently located just around the corner from Harrods, the designer shops of Beauchamp Place and the museums of Natural History, Science and the Victoria and Albert, the Beaufort is an is an alluring example of a small luxury hotel that puts comfort and convenience of its guests first. The walls are hung with English watercolors and the contemporary styled sitting room exudes warmth and comfort. After a hard day sightseeing, or shopping, enjoy a cup of tea in the sitting room and tuck into sumptuous home made scones with clotted cream and strawberry jam. Drinks are served here compliments of the house, alcoholic drinks between 3 and 11 pm, soft drinks round the clock. Corporate travelers take advantage of the well-equipped business centre (which doubles as a second residents' lounge) with email access and computer and fax facilities. As you retire to your room you soon realize why the Beaufort is your home away from home. The air-conditioned rooms are equipped with state-of-the-art interactive television, choice of film channels, and CD player. There is complimentary WiFi and little extras such as mineral water, chocolates and biscuits. The Beaufort is ideally located in the tranquil tree-lined cul-de-sac of Beaufort Gardens, just of Brompton Road and a short walk from the tube station. Nearest Underground: Knightsbridge.

THE BEAUFORT
Manager: Izabella Cousens
33 Beaufort Gardens
London SW3 1PP, England
Tel: 0207 584 5252, Fax: 0207 589 2834
29 Rooms, Double: £160–£335*
*Breakfast not included: £9.50
*Tax: 15%
Open: all year, Credit cards: all major

For over a century the Cadogan Hotel has epitomised discreet distinction. Soon after it was finished in 1888, it became inextricably linked with two of the most famous people of the age—Lillie Langtry, the beautiful actress and mistress of Edward VII, and her admirer Oscar Wilde, the famous dramatist. Lillie's drawing and dining room are still to be seen in the hotel today. From the comfortable paneled drawing room to the spacious studios and elegant suites (all soundproofed and most air-conditioned), the hotel exudes quality and the staff showers its guests with personal attention. Breakfast is served in the elegant restaurant on tables set with silver and fresh flowers. The Oscar Wilde Suite with its front corner turret, his pictures on the wall, famous plays on the bookshelves, and stylish decor—in sky blue and chocolate to reflect his character and is understandably popular for its historical interest, as this is where the great man actually resided. Guests in need of exercise can avail themselves of the small gym, Cadogan Gardens across the road, a cool oasis of green in the summer, provides tennis courts in the better weather. Less vigorous pursuits include enjoying afternoon cream tea with scones and strawberry jam. The Cadogan's location is handy for museums, smart shops, Hyde Park, and restaurants. Nearest Underground: Sloane Square or Knightsbridge.

❄ 🏊 💳 ☎ 🐕 🛗 🏋 @ W ⅄ P 🍴 🚶 🔔 ⛷

THE CADOGAN
Manager: Fabio Gallo
75 Sloane Street
London SX1X 9SG, England
Tel: 0207 235 7141, Fax: 0207 245 0994
65 Rooms, Double: £275–£650*
*Breakfast not included: £20–£24.50
*Tax: 15%
Open: all year, Credit cards: all major

The stunningly stylish and luxurious Charlotte Street Hotel, situated in the bustling neighborhood of North Soho, hums with activity, particularly in the busy brasserie, a visual feast with its open-plan kitchen and original murals depicting contemporary London life. Decor throughout has a modern, English flavor with pastel colors, gorgeous fabrics, well-placed works of art, and striking flower arrangements. The drawing room, with its beige walls and carpet, pale-blue couches, and log-burning fireplace, is irresistibly comfortable and inviting. Bedrooms, like those in the sister Covent Garden Hotel, are superbly appointed with amenities such as CD players, VCRs, fax/modem points, and cellular phones. They even have color TVs in their magnificent granite-and-oak bathrooms. Particularly appealing are the four loft suites (bedrooms upstairs, sitting room with sofa bed downstairs) with their soaring ceilings and windows. For even more luxury, opt to stay in the penthouse suite. On-site facilities include a state of the art screening room (ask about the film-night/dinner package) and fully equipped gymnasium. Nearest Underground: Tottenham Court Road or Goodge Street.

CHARLOTTE STREET HOTEL
Owners: Kit & Tim Kemp
Manager: Fiona Milne
15 Charlotte Street
London W1T 1RJ, England
Tel: 0207 806 2000, Fax: 0207 806 2002
52 Rooms, Double: £220–£1150*
*Breakfast not included: £19.50
*Tax: 15%
Open: all year, Credit cards: all major

In keeping with its location at the heart of London's theatre district, the Covent Garden Hotel is dramatic and exuberant in its decor, flamboyant yet tasteful, and unabashedly luxurious. The lobby welcomes you grandly with lavish flower arrangements and Oriental carpets, then the imposing stone staircase sweeps you up to the wood-paneled, red-themed drawing room which manages to look cozy despite its grand scale and quirky furniture. Bedrooms are generously sized—even single rooms have queen beds. Individually decorated, each has air conditioning, a hand-quilted bedspread, the Kemp's trademark tailor's mannequin in matching fabric, a large writing desk, a sumptuous granite and mahogany bathroom, and every modern amenity including CD player and cellular phone. Favorite rooms include 304 with its king four-poster bed, beautiful blue drapes, huge mirror, and fireplace; 205 with its coronet-draped, king-sized bed, massive oil painting, wing chairs, and lovely desk; and 417 with its high ceilings, exposed beams, and turret dining area. The hotel also features 24-hour room service, a gym, treatment room, private screening room (ask about the film-night/dinner package) and popular brasserie. Nearest Underground: Covent Garden.

COVENT GARDEN HOTEL
Owners: Kit & Tim Kemp
Manager: Helle Jensen
10 Monmouth Street
London WC2H 9HB, England
Tel: 0207 806 1000, Fax: 0207 806 1100
58 Rooms, Double: £285–£1150*
*Breakfast not included: £19.50, Tax 15%
Open: all year, Credit cards: all major

The Cranley is a delight. A Victorian townhouse hotel on a quiet street in South Kensington, handy for museums, shopping, and exhibition areas; run by an attentive, friendly, and enthusiastic team. Its public areas and bedrooms are tastefully decorated with a superb eye for detail. The elegant drawing room is serene and inviting, with blue walls, long blue drapes, comfortable seating, antique pieces, and a lovely mirror over the fireplace. The spacious, air-conditioned guestrooms, eight with four-posters, many have half testers, all have excellent beds with attractive white spreads, soothing decor, good lighting, working desks, wireless internet, and sparkling bathrooms with traditional Victorian fixtures, stocked with plush bathrobes. Three bedrooms have views of London and the penthouse room enjoys its own terrace. Guests are spoiled with special treats such as a welcome drink, fruit basket in the bedroom, afternoon tea (warm scones and clotted cream). Baby-sitting service is available. Nearest Underground: Gloucester Road.

THE CRANLEY
Manager: John Alexander
10 Bina Gardens
London SW5 0LA, England
Tel: 0207 373 0123, Fax: 0207 373 9497
39 Rooms, Double: £235–£360*
*Breakfast not included: £12.50
*Tax: 17.5%
Open: all year, Credit cards: AX, MC, VS

Dorset Square Hotel, a beautifully restored Regency townhouse, is located in the area of London made famous by Sherlock Holmes and just down the road from Madame Tussaud's. It overlooks the tree-filled garden which was the original site of Lord's Cricket Ground. The contemporary English decor uses lots of antiques, original oils, and wonderful flower arrangements. The air-conditioned bedrooms all have marble bathrooms and the more expensive rooms are truly lovely. If you stay in one of the hotel's smallest, least expensive rooms, you find yourself enjoying the fabulous ambiance of an elegant hotel at a price that is good value for money. All are fully equipped with facilities expected by today's traveler. Below street level, The Potting Shed Restaurant, where you can hear live jazz, lives up to its name in its design, with terra cotta pots piled up against the wall, pots of flowers on the tables, and a glass ceiling over half of the room. Snuggle up in the Library with a book and a drink. There's very much a country feeling to this small hotel within easy reach of Bond Street, Regent's Park, the theaters, and the West End. Nearest Underground: Marylebone or Baker Street.

DORSET SQUARE HOTEL
Manager: Nicholas Chakmakjian
39-40 Dorset Square
London NW1 6QN, England
Tel: 0207 723 7874, Fax: 0207 724 3328
37 Rooms, Double: £160–£350*
*Breakfast not included: £13.50–£15.75
*Tax: 15%
Open: all year, Credit cards: all major

Dukes is a very special hotel—it remains one of our favorites. Conveniently located only steps from St. James's Street, a stone's throw from Piccadilly Circus, Dukes is tucked into its own little flower-filled, gas-lit courtyard. Just off the lobby is a snug lounge and beyond is a paneled cocktail bar famous for its dry martinis and selection of vintage cognacs. The airy conservatory is an excellent place to enjoy light meals, coffee, and afternoon tea. The air-conditioned guestrooms, decorated and furnished in country house style, vary in size from spacious rooms to splendid suites with large bedrooms and impressive lounges. All feature modern, marble bathroom facilities with sparkling glass and chrome fixtures and sumptuous towels and robes, and all are equipped with the necessities of today's business traveler. The Penthouse suite enjoys spectacular nighttime views across the rooftops to Green Park and Westminster Abbey. All guests have access to the luxuriously appointed health club with its high-tech exercise equipment and a wide choice of personalised beauty and body treatments. Nearest Underground: Green Park.

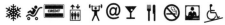

DUKES HOTEL
Manager: David Silver
35, St. James's Place
London SW1A 1NY, England
Tel: 0207 491 4840, Fax: 0207 493 1264
90 Rooms, Double: £345–£1050*
*Breakfast not included: £22
*Tax: 15%
Open: all year, Credit cards: all major

The one and two bedroom apartments at Durley House on Sloane Street are for those who want to have their own pied-à-terre in the heart of Knightsbridge. They provide all the comfort and services of a hotel coupled with the privacy and convenience of your own apartment. No expense has been spared in outfitting them in an attractive, traditional country-house style. Besides a bedroom (or two) and separate living room, all have a well-equipped kitchen. Guests intending to use the self-catering facilities can call ahead and the staff will happily arrange to purchase initial grocery supplies. Alternatively there is a kitchen on site, offering room service 24-hours a day. If requested, a waiter will bring you dinner and serve it to you in your apartment. Complete picnic catering services, right down to rugs to sit on, are available to simplify planning those occasional days out in the country. The large apartments, although expensive for two, prove a good value for a family or couples traveling together. Energetic guests have the use of tennis courts in the private gardens across the way. A short walk brings you to Sloane Street's sophisticated shops. Nearest Underground: Sloane Square.

DURLEY HOUSE
Manager: Alex Schweizer
115 Sloane Street
London SW1X 9PJ, England
Tel & Fax: 0207 235 5537
11 Rooms, Double: £380–£650*
*Breakfast not included: £13.50–£19.50
*Tax: 15%
Open: all year, Credit cards: all major

There is no sign that this Victorian townhouse in a quiet part of Chelsea is a hotel. Having successfully overcome the mysterious house-numbering system in Cadogan Gardens, you ring the doorbell, step into the paneled hall, sign the visitors' book, and are enveloped by the refined atmosphere of days gone by. It is rather like a discreet private club with Victorian wing chairs, stern portraits, dark wood paneling and doors, guests daintily sipping afternoon tea, whispered conversations, and a chauffeured Mercedes at your bidding. Larger bedrooms are very quiet, as all but one are at the back of the hotel. The suites can only be described as magnificent. Guest room décor is generally on a lighter theme compared to the public areas, marble bathrooms abound. Breakfast and light meals are served in the newly renovated dining room in the basement with its Portland-stone floor, cream paint, wood-paneled walls adorned with a display of ceramic plates, and original black iron range (discovered buried in the walls during recent construction activities). Other amenities include private gardens and a fully-equipped gymnasium. The shops and restaurants of Knightsbridge are a few minutes' walk away. Nearest Underground: Sloane Square.

ELEVEN CADOGAN GARDENS
Manager: Gabriella Davies
11 Cadogan Gardens
London SW3 2RJ, England
Tel: 0207 730 7000, Fax: 0207 730 5217
60 Rooms, Double: £250–£650*
*Breakfast not included: £15–£20
Open: all year, Credit cards: all major

Founded in the reign of King Edward VII by the present owner's great-grandfather and located on a quiet side street just around the corner from Buckingham Palace, The Goring is recognized as one of London's premier hotels. It takes great pride in offering guests a warm welcome and luxuriously appointed accommodations. Maintaining a personal touch, the current (fourth generation) Mr. Goring invites guests to his Sunday cocktail party (6–7 pm). Bedrooms and suites offer the highest level of comfort with luxurious decor and furnishings and beautiful marble bathrooms. All are air-conditioned and several overlook a peaceful garden (three have private balconies). Although elegant and polished, the decor displays a humorous theme. Comic strips from (the senior) Mr. Goring's personal memoirs are exhibited throughout and two large West-Country sheep sit either side of the drawing-room fireplace while the rest of the flock reside in several of the bedrooms. Relax over morning coffee and pastries in the lounge or sample English afternoon tea on the terrace. Later in the day the Garden Bar is a perfect venue to unwind, a stone's throw away from Buckingham Palace, a world away from the bustle of central London. Nearest Underground: Victoria.

THE GORING
Manager: David Morgan Hewitt
Beeston Place, Grosvenor Gardens
London SW1W 0JW, England
Tel: 0207 396 9000, Fax: 0207 834 4393
71 Rooms, Double: £209–£990*
*Breakfast not included: £14–£25
*Tax: 15%
Open: all year, Credit cards: all major

Close to shopping and Hyde Park and just a few yards from the Knightsbridge tube station, the Knightsbridge Green stands out as a more reasonably priced hotel with a superb location. Its unobtrusive front door is almost lost on the busy street front. It is located in a tall, narrow building where an old-fashioned lift takes you up from the street-level lobby to the six floors of air conditioned bedrooms. Double glazing effectively eliminates any traffic noise from the bustling street below. Rooms are spacious and suites have separate sitting rooms, some with a sofa bed, ideal for traveling families. The decor is sunny, with pastel-washed walls and pretty fabrics, bathrooms are nicely appointed in glass and marble with all the expected amenities. English, continental, or express breakfasts are prepared in the on-site kitchen with provisions from the food halls at Harrods (just around the corner) and served to order in the rooms. Complimentary coffee and tea are available on request. For a small extra charge guests have the use of a nearby health club with fully-equipped gymnasium and swimming pool. Broadband web access is available in the lobby. This is a very popular hotel, so it is advisable to book well ahead. Nearest Underground: Knightsbridge.

KNIGHTSBRIDGE GREEN HOTEL
Manager: Ali Farhani
159 Knightsbridge
London SW1X 7PD, England
Tel: 0207 584 6274, Fax: 0207 225 1635
30 Rooms, Double: £185–£250*
*Breakfast not included: £5.50–£14.50
Open: all year, Credit cards: all major

Another successful project by London hoteliers Tim and Kit Kemp, the Knightsbridge Hotel is situated in Beaufort Gardens, a quiet, tree-lined street in the heart of fashionable Knightsbridge. The hotel is just a walk away from Sloane Street's stylish international designer stores, Hyde Park, the Victoria and Albert, Natural History, and Science Museums, and sits in the shadow of Harrods. The Kemps' intent is to provide a "chic bed and breakfast hotel for discerning travelers spending their own money"—and they have succeeded quite nicely. Luxurious, individually-styled bedrooms are decorated in a modern English vein using a variety of eye-catching colors and sumptuous fabrics, and are equipped with every modern convenience for those conducting business during their stay. Spacious bathrooms feature granite and oak. Room service is available 24-hours a day and breakfast, ordered from an ample menu the evening before, is served in your room. Two spacious public areas are to be found downstairs. The drawing room is furnished with comfortable sofas and decorated with African overtones, offset by a collection of framed Scottie dogs on the wall and a stone fireplace whose mantel is adorned with miniature mannequins. The library, its comfy chairs and fireplace surrounded with floor-to-ceiling bookshelves, is a great place to settle down with a good book and a drink from the honor bar next door. Nearest Underground: Knightsbridge.

KNIGHTSBRIDGE HOTEL
Owners: Kit & Tim Kemp
Manager: Gisele Clark
10 Beaufort Gardens
London SW3 1PT, England
Tel: 0207 584 6300, Fax: 0207 584 6355
44 Rooms, Double: £210–£595*
*Breakfast not included: £15
*Tax: 17.5%
Open: all year, Credit cards: all major

Number Sixteen is an elegant, upscale bed and breakfast located in the heart of fashionable South Kensington. A member of the Firmdale Hotel Group, and yet another example of the Kemps' stylish approach to London living, it forms part of a white-stucco mid-Victorian terrace. There are 42 individually decorated bedrooms each featuring hand-embroidered bedspreads and exquisite Frette bed linen, and several have terraces onto the private garden at the rear, a cool green oasis on those hot London summer days. Ornate plaster ceilings and antique furniture, modern bathrooms, and all requisite creature comforts combine to provide the feel of staying in a private house. We prefer the rooms above street level to those below stairs. Guests are encouraged to treat this deluxe pension as their home-away-from-home and two drawing rooms and a sunny conservatory are provided to entertain friends, relax, and unwind. There is no restaurant but there are a great many close by. Breakfast can be served in the garden, drawing rooms, conservatory, or in your room. Wireless internet access throughout. Nearest Underground: South Kensington.

NUMBER SIXTEEN
Owners: Kit & Tim Kemp
16 Sumner Place
London SW7 3EG, England
Tel: 0207 589 5232, Fax: 0207 584 8615
42 Rooms, Double: £200–£270*
*Breakfast not included: £16.50–£17.50
*Service: 12.5%
*Tax: 15%
Open: all year, Credit cards: all major

Tucked away from the city clamor in the calm oasis of Beaufort Gardens, yet only minutes from the bustling shopper's paradise of Knightsbridge (Harrods is literally just around the corner), Parkes epitomizes the perfect small townhouse hotel. Enter the wood-paneled reception area and the attentive staff will minister to your every need. Originally three private houses, the buildings have been artfully combined to provide a wide variety of tastefully decorated accommodations, all with ample space for those who need to work. Creature comforts abound: luxurious linens, sumptuous towels, mini-bars featuring a broad variety of whiskies, marvelous marble, glass, and chrome bathrooms. There are some interesting high-tech touches, heated bathroom floors, huge shower heads with water pressure to match, heated non-misting bathroom mirrors, wireless internet, flat -screened TVs and movies on demand. Many of the suites are provided with small well-equipped kitchens—which, with a little imaginative shopping in Harrods' food halls, can provide a welcome respite from the rigors of restaurant meals. Any of the larger split-level suites would indeed provide a wonderfully spacious home-away-from-home for lengthier stays. There is a cozy oak-paneled guests' lounge and the breakfast room offers either buffet continental or cooked-to-order full English breakfast. Nearest tube station: Knightsbridge.

PARKES HOTEL
Manager: Susan Shaw
41 Beaufort Gardens
London SW3 1PW, England
Tel: 020 7581 9944, Fax: 020 7581 1999
33 Rooms, Double: £265–£525*
*Breakfast not included: £12.50
Open: all year, Credit cards: MC, VS

You might well pass by The Pelham thinking this is a private club, for with its discreet exterior, only the flag and classy brass plaque signify that a hotel is within. Inside, no expense has been spared to create an inviting, traditional atmosphere—lavish bouquets of flowers, gorgeous antiques, and original oil paintings set the mood of a fetching English country house hotel. Public areas, such as the lovely wood-paneled library and drawing room, each with an open fireplace, and Kemps, the attractive lower-ground-floor restaurant and bar invite you to linger. Sedate gray-carpeted hallways lead you to the accommodations, which range from large suites to smaller rooms with twin, queen, or king beds, equipped with every amenity including mobile phones, VCRs, and high speed internet access. All have smart bathrooms fitted out in granite and mahogany. The very friendly staff really strives to make this a home-away-from-home. The restaurant's cuisine and stylish decor attract a number of celebrities. Surrounding you are the interesting boutiques, museums, antique shops, and restaurants of South Kensington and Knightsbridge. Nearest Underground: South Kensington.

THE PELHAM HOTEL
General Manager: Ian Dick
15 Cromwell Place
London SW7 2LA, England
Tel: 0207 589 8288, Fax: 0207 584 8444
52 Rooms, Double: £180–£610*
*Breakfast not included: £15
*Tax: 17.5%
Open: all year, Credit cards: all major

The San Domenico House is located just steps from London's bustling Sloane Square in the heart of the fashionable borough of Chelsea. With easy access to both the City and the West End it appeals to business executives and leisure travelers alike. Behind the Victorian façade lies a luxurious townhouse hotel, lovingly decorated with a touch of Italy as well as beautiful antique furniture from around the world and rare 19th century European pieces of art. Across from the marbled lobby is a cozy drawing room where guests order traditional afternoon tea or enjoy an aperitif before going on to one of the many restaurants located nearby. A small elevator whisks guests to one of the sixteen rooms (of which there are nine suites), all individually decorated, air conditioned and featuring heavy tapestry fabrics, lovely antiques and ensuite bathroom. I personally liked room 403 with its black marble bathroom but my favorite is room 104, a split-level suite presided over by its grand Venetian-style canopied bed. A roof terrace with stunning views across Chelsea and the surrounding area is perfect for guests to have breakfast in the summer and enjoy pre-dinner drinks. The San Domenico House provides privacy, efficient yet unobtrusive service, luxury and comfort. Nearest Underground: Sloane Square.

SAN DOMENICO HOUSE
Manager: Aldo Melpignano
29-31 Draycott Place
London SW3 2SH, England
Tel: 0207 581 5757, Fax: 0207 584 1348
15 Rooms, Double: £235–£360*
*Breakfast not included: £14–£21
*Tax: 15%
Open: all year, Credit cards: all major

The Soho Hotel is now the latest, grandest, addition to the Kemp's impressive collection of upscale accommodations in London. From the moment you walk into the reception area, dominated by its massive Botero sculpture of a fat cat, you are aware that this is somewhere very special. Central to the attractions of Covent Garden, the British Museum, the Royal Opera House and the National Gallery, the Soho is located on a quiet cul-de-sac, a few minutes walk from the bustle of Shaftesbury Avenue and Oxford Street. Interiors mirror the renowned attention to detail of owner Kit Kemp. All the rooms are different, sleekly modern, and appointed for the sophisticated traveler featuring blond oak furnishings, massive beds, crisp linens, luxurious bath towels and robes, fabulous granite, and glass and chrome bathrooms with large walk-in showers and double basins. Soft pastels with surprising splashes of color are accented with original art. For those who simply must remain in touch with the world outside there are DVD/CD systems, flat-screen TVs, dual-line telephones with voice mail and high-speed internet access. Work out in the well-equipped "Soholistic" gym. Relax with a massage in the treatment rooms. Retire to Refuel, the chic bar and restaurant with colorful car-themed mural reflecting the hotel's prior life as a multi-story parking lot. Entertain your friends in one of the two private movie-screening rooms. Nearest tube station: Tottenham Court Road.

THE SOHO HOTEL
Owners: Kit & Tim Kemp
Manager: Carrie Wicks
4 Richmond Mews
London W1D 3DH, England
Tel: 020 7559 3000, Fax: 020 7559 3003
91 Rooms, Double: £280–£2750*
*Breakfast not included: £18.50
*Tax: 15%
Open: all year, Credit cards: all major

The bustle of London seems far away from this quiet, refined hotel in historic St. James', just a short walk from Piccadilly. Some of London's most exclusive real estate is tucked back in the privacy of this cul-de-sac. Originally built as a private residence in the mid-17th century, the Stafford maintains the air of an exclusive club. Ornate plaster ceilings grace the elegant lounge and excellent dining room. The colorful bar is worth a visit in itself. It is decorated with an eclectic collection of caps, ties, hard hats, American football helmets, and assorted pictures and memorabilia dating back to World War II when the hotel was home to (among others) the officers of the American Eagle Squadron. Outside across a cobbled courtyards lies the Stafford Mews (26 luxury suites topped by a penthouse) and the Carriage House featuring the original timber beams, supposedly reclaimed from old sailing ships during the original construction. Today it houses deluxe bedrooms and the incomparable two-story Guv'nor's Suite. Like the guestrooms located within the hotel, they are all decorated in a most luxurious manner and equipped with absolutely everything your heart could desire, including the not-to-be-forgotten sailboat in every bathtub. Nearest Underground: Green Park.

❄ ✎ 💳 ☎ 🚻 ✗ @ P ¶ 🚭 🖼 ⚗ ♿ ⛵ ⸸ 🏃 ⛷ 🏇 ⛵

THE STAFFORD HOTEL
General Manager: Stuart Proctor
16-18 St. James's Place
London SW1A 1NJ, England
Tel: 0207 493 0111, Fax: 0207 493 7121
143 Rooms, Double: £300–£1400*
*Breakfast not included: £17–£25
*Tax: 15%
Open: all year, Credit cards: AX, MC, VS

Places to Stay in England

The Benedictine monks chose a magnificent site high on a hill overlooking the sea to found their Abbey of St. Peter in 1024. Despite being sacked by Henry VIII and burned by Cromwell, a lot of the monastic settlement remains: the church, the magnificent swannery, an enormous thatched tithe barn, a ruined watermill, and, most importantly, the infirmary. Now home to the Cookes, the infirmary was originally a resting place for visitors, evolving over the years into a farmhouse and now a welcoming guesthouse and tearoom. Pink chairs and tables topped with pink cloths are set around the giant inglenook fireplace in the old kitchen. Breakfast and lunch are served here or, on warm summer days, under the vine-covered arbor or on the lawn overlooking the barn. Bedrooms range in size from a spacious suite with a sitting room and separate bedroom to a cottagey little room set beneath the eaves and reached by a narrow staircase. The adjacent tithe barn contains interesting exhibits while the farm with its array of animals is a great attraction, as is the nearby swannery with its vast colony of swans. Abbotsbury is a delightful village of thatched houses very typical of those found just a short drive away in Hardy country, a favorite destination for visitors. *Directions:* Abbotsbury is midway between Weymouth and Bridport on the B3157. In Abbotsbury turn towards the sea (signposted The Swannery) and Abbey House is on your left after 100 yards.

ABBEY HOUSE
Owner: Jonathan and Maureen Cooke
Church Street
Abbotsbury DT3 4JJ, England
Tel: 01305 871330, Fax: 01305 871088
6 Rooms, Double: £70–£100
Open: all year, Credit cards: none

Rothay Manor is an exceptionally enjoyable establishment in the very heart of the Lake District. It has the feel of a refined, old-fashioned British resort hotel where everything is done with kindness and without fuss. In the afternoon, an array of trim little sandwiches, decorated cakes, and biscuits tempts you to partake of tea. Children's "teas" are served so that youngsters can be tucked up in bed before parents go down to dinner. Your choice of a two to five course dinner is served in the dining room. Afterwards, coffee and chocolates are set out in the hall to be enjoyed in one of the comfortable sitting rooms. Premier bedrooms are those at the front with balconies. We particularly enjoyed room 6. Joined to the hotel by a glass-sided corridor, rooms in the new wing are especially attractive. Downstairs is a smaller room that features a small, private garden patio. Upstairs the airy suite has an extra bedroom for children. Room 15 and the adjacent 14 can be combined as a family suite. A downstairs bedroom is available for those who use a wheelchair or have difficulty with stairs. The weather forecast is posted in the hallway so you can be prepared for the fickle Lake District weather. Picturesque villages and stunning scenery are easily reached by car or explored on foot. *Directions:* From Ambleside, follow signs for Coniston (A593). You will find the hotel in the middle of the one-way system on the outskirts of town.

ROTHAY MANOR
Owner: Nigel Nixon
Rothay Bridge
Ambleside LA22 0EH, England
Tel: 015394 33605, Fax: 015394 33607
9 Rooms, Double: £150–£225
Closed: Jan 3 to Jan 29, Credit cards: all major

Blagdon Manor is a little gem of a hotel set in the gently undulating northwest Devon countryside. This is not a grand manor house but rather a farmhouse of comfortably proportioned rooms with little windows peeking out through thick stone walls. Built in the 17th century on the site of a farmhouse mentioned in the 1086 Domesday Book, the house is pleasantly rambling, with lots of interesting nooks and crannies—we particularly liked the cozy beamed bar. It stands in its own grounds well away from traffic with lawns that stretch out to a vista of fields and the distant hills. Owners Liz and Steve Morey are always in evidence, so you really feel that you are staying in the countryside with friends rather than at a hotel. Steve offers six choices for each of the three courses of dinner in the low, beamed dining room. The country-cozy bedrooms are decorated in sunny colors, and each is accompanied by a very nice bathroom. Ask for one of the larger rooms. Room 8 is a large luxurious suite. You can tour much of Devon and Cornwall from this peaceful countryside spot. To the west lie Boscastle Harbour and the ruins of Tintagel Castle, while to the south is Llanhydrock, a not-to-be-missed stately home. *Directions:* Leave Launceston on the A388, Holsworthy road. Pass Chapman's Well and the first sign to Ashwater. Turn right at the second Ashwater sign (8 miles from Holsworthy) and first right, signposted Blagdon. The hotel is on the right.

BLAGDON MANOR HOTEL
Owners: Liz & Steve Morey
Ashwater EX21 5DF, England
Tel: 01409 211224, Fax: 01409 211634
8 Rooms, Double: £140–£200
Open: all year, Credit cards: MC, VS

Standing in its own thirteen-acre estate with a slightly elevated position above the village, as befits its prior status as residence of the Lord of the Manor, Austwick Hall was originally constructed as a fortified pele tower to protect the local area from marauding Scots. The structure reportedly dates back to the late twelfth century and over the years has been modified and expanded by successive owners, ranging from wool merchants to Masters of the Mint, resulting in an interesting mélange of architectural style and features. Current owners Michael and Eric have decorated with a tastefully eclectic mix of oriental rugs, Asian collectibles, wall art, stained glass and local antiques to produce a comfortable country house atmosphere. The five guest rooms (Blue, Half Tester, Coronet, Four Poster and Mullioned) vary in size from extremely large to more than adequate. We were particularly taken with the Blue room, which reportedly hosted Sir Winston Churchill on one of his painting vacations. Its particularly large bathroom features a roll-top free-standing bathtub with views over the herb gardens. Breakfast is served in the formal dining room and five-course dinners are available with prior notice. *Directions:* Austwick is off the A65 midway between Skipton and Kendal. In the village, pass the post office on the right; just after the school turn left, the hall's gates are on the left after 100 yards.

AUSTWICK HALL
Owners: Eric Culley & Michael Pearson
Austwick
Settle LA2 8BS, England
Tel: 015242 51794
5 Rooms, Double: £125–£155
Open: all year, Credit cards: all major

Hartwell offers you the opportunity to stay in a National Trust stately home that was the residence of the exiled King Louis XVIII of France who lived here for five years beginning in 1809. Grand, gorgeous public rooms are yours to enjoy, including the great hall, the paneled oak bar, the morning room, the drawing room and the library. Imaginative food is enjoyed in the dining room, composed of several adjoining rooms that overlook the garden. A dramatic staircase with its Jacobean carved figures leads to thirty gracious bedrooms. First-floor bedrooms, named after the court of Louis XVIII, who occupied them, are the largest, and the corner rooms are all four-posters. The second floor bedrooms are cozier; some of them open onto a sheltered roof terrace where rabbits were reared and vegetables grown by the French émigrés. Additional lovely bedrooms are found in the stable building adjacent to the conference center and Hartwell Spa with its spacious indoor swimming pool, gym and beauty salons. A path leads into the walled garden, which houses two tennis courts. The surrounding parkland with its ruined church, pavilion, and lake is perfect for long country walks. Oxford is just 20 miles away and Heathrow airport is less than an hour's drive. *Directions:* Hartwell House is 2 miles from Aylesbury on the A418, Oxford road.

❄ ☕ ⚙ 🖼 CREDIT ☎ 🐕 👥 🏃 @ W ⬥ P 🍴 ✿ ≈ 🚶 🐾 ♿ 🎣 👥 ♉

HARTWELL HOUSE
Manager: Jonathan Thompson
Aylesbury HP17 8NL, England
Tel: 01296 747444, Fax: 01296 747450
Toll Free: (800) 260-8338
49 Rooms, Double: £260–£600
Open: all year, Credit cards: all major

The signpost to Skelwith Bridge and Hawkshead and the inn has stood at the crossroads more than 400 years. Today, the Drunken Duck offers comfortable accommodation and fine food. A range of beers, produced in their brewery on site, are named after dogs and cats who have graced the property in recent times, Cracker, Tag Lag, Chesters and Catnap. Comfy sofas, antiques, and wall art make the sitting room a great place to escape. Indulge yourself in a traditional cream tea served to residents every afternoon. Whether in the pub (mostly cute and cozy) or across the courtyard, each of the guestrooms offers a unique blend of comfort and contemporary design with bathrooms en suite. A firm favorite is the Garden room with open-beamed ceiling, floor-length windows, views across Langdale Valley, and a private balcony above the gardens and Tarn. It is hard to secure this room so know that most of the various size courtyard rooms offer fabulous views—we particularly loved our room 11. The modern British cuisine served in the romantic restaurant merits several nights stay. Overall, while deliciously modern, little has changed over the years; chalk-written menus, foaming pints of hand-pulled beer, open log fires and twinkling candlelight offer a warm welcome. *Directions:* From Ambleside take A593 (Conistone Road), turn left on the B5286 (Hawkshead Road) for 1 mile, turn right (signposted: The Duck) and the inn is on the crossroads at the top of the hill.

THE DRUNKEN DUCK
Owner: Steph Barton
Barngates
Ambleside LA22 0NG, England
Tel: 015394 36347, Fax: 015394 36781
17 Rooms, Double: £95–£275
Open: all year, Credit cards: all major

The Cavendish Hotel sits at the edge of the Chatsworth estate, which surrounds one of England's loveliest stately houses, the home of the Duke and Duchess of Devonshire. Eric Marsh, the owner, has restored and expanded what was originally an 18th-century fishing inn into a fine hotel. The Garden Room (perfect for lunch and informal dinners) frames a panoramic view of the River Derwent meandering through green fields across the estate; comfy sofas and chairs in the adjacent lounge invite you to linger and relax. The bar is a cozy gathering spot for drinks before dinner in the highly commended dining room (you can request a table for two in a corner of the kitchen if you are eager to peek at what happens behind the scenes). Bedrooms in the oldest part of the hotel have an old world ambiance and lovely views across an open countryside. We loved our stay in room 9, a spacious four-poster room. An adjoining wing of bedrooms with a more contemporary style has been built to match the original building. They're called the Mitford Rooms after their designer, the Duchess of Devonshire, and her Mitford family. A pathway leads you on a beautiful walk through the Chatsworth estate to Chatsworth House. Explorations farther afield reveal unspoiled villages set in beautiful rolling countryside of stone-walled fields, green valleys, and spectacular dales. *Directions:* Exit the M1 motorway at junction 29 and follow signs for Chatsworth through Chesterfield to Baslow.

CAVENDISH HOTEL
Owner: Eric Marsh
General Manager: Philip Joseph
Baslow DE45 1SP, England
Tel: 01246 582311, Fax: 01246 582312
24 Rooms, Double: £165–£295*
*Breakfast not included: £18.50
Open: all year, Credit cards: all major

Fischer's at Baslow Hall is a dream place for a relaxed getaway, with splendid cooking, especially friendly service, and the nearby delights of the Peak District National Park. This superb house with its lead-paned windows set in stone frames, dark-oak paneling, and wide-plank wooden floors has the feeling of a Tudor manor, yet it was built only in 1907 as a home for the Reverend Jeremiah Stockdale. It continued as a home until 1989 when Susan and Max Fischer purchased it to house their successful restaurant, Fischer's, and also provide the most tasteful of accommodation. The house is furnished and decorated with imagination and flair, with a delightful use of soft yet quite vivid colors to create a feeling of warmth. Upstairs Vernon and Haddon are especially lovely bedrooms. If you prefer even more space and contemporary decor opt for rooms 2, 3, 4 or 5 which open up onto a little courtyard garden—perfect for hiding away. Max offers traditional English dishes as well as more elaborate fare on his mouth-watering menus that range from the menu du jour (not available on Fri and Sat), to the Gourmet and Prestige menus featuring evening-long dining extravaganzas. The surrounding countryside offers plenty to keep you busy for a week—Chatsworth House, Haddon Hall, lovely villages, and glorious scenery. *Directions:* Exit M1 jct 29 (Chesterfield) and follow Chatsworth signs to Baslow. Turn right on the A623 (Manchester). Baslow Hall is on the right after 1/2 mile.

FISCHER'S AT BASLOW HALL
Owners: Susan & Max Fischer
Calver Road
Baslow DE45 1RR, England
Tel: 01246 583259, Fax: 01246 583818
11 Rooms, Double: £140–£195
Closed: Christmas & New Year, Credit cards: all major

From the moment you enter through the rustic porchway into the long, low, whitewashed Pheasant inn, you are captivated by its charms: a front parlor all decked in chintz with an old-fashioned, open fire; a dimly lit, Dickensian bar with tobacco-stained walls and ceiling, oak settles, and clusters of tables and chairs; a long, low-beamed dining room, its tables covered with crisp damask cloths; dramatic fresh and dried flower arrangements; a blazing fire in the hearth beneath a copper hood in the large, airy sitting room, and the former farmhouse kitchen dating back over 400 years. It is reputed that the legendary John Peel used to be one of the 19th-century regulars in the bar. Whether you stop in for a traditional Cumbrian afternoon tea or partake of fine dining in an evening you will find excellent food. Each spacious and inviting bedroom has a large, modern bathroom. Two lodge rooms offer peace and quiet and are handy for anyone having difficulty with stairs. Behind the inn, a garden with benches lining its pathways tumbles into the beechwoods, which belongs (as does the inn) to Lord Inglewood's estate. The Pheasant sits on a quiet country lane, just out of sight of Bassenthwaite Lake. This is a peaceful part of the Lake District with beautiful views round every corner. Sailing, boating, fishing, bird watching, and, of course, walking are available nearby. *Directions:* The Pheasant is signposted on the A66, at the head of Bassenthwaite Lake, between Keswick and Cockermouth.

THE PHEASANT
Manager: Matthew Wylie
Bassenthwaite Lake CA15 9YE, England
Tel: 017687 76234, Fax: 017687 76002
18 Rooms, Double: £160–£210
Closed: Christmas, Credit cards: MC, VS

Situated behind high stone walls on a tree lined residential street, The Bath Priory dates back to 1835. A fine example of Gothic style architecture constructed of traditional honey-brown stone, it has been completely renovated and transformed into an award winning luxury hotel complete with Michelin starred dining, health club, spa and 4 acres of manicured grounds. The spaciously grand drawing room and library evoke visions of gracious country living, inviting soft furnishings, art bedecked walls, fresh cut flowers, gleaming brass and welcoming log fires. The guest rooms are sumptuously appointed, lavishly decorated with antiques and collectibles. Sparklingly modern bathrooms are outfitted with all the creature comforts expected by the sophisticated traveller. Menus are influenced by British and European cuisine, accented by the inventive use of organic produce from the kitchen gardens. A gymnasium and heated outdoor pool are available to work off those extra calories. For the less active there is The Garden Spa and Beauty Retreat with its sauna, steam room, treatments, manicures and massages. Guests can walk via Victoria Park and the Royal Crescent into the city center. *Directions:* Exit the M4 at junction 18, take the A46 into the center of Bath, then follow the A4 signposted Bristol. Pass Victoria Park on your right and at the end turn right into Park Lane then left into Weston Road. The hotel is on your left after 300 yards.

THE BATH PRIORY
Owners: Christina & Andrew Brownsword
Manager: Sue Williams
Weston Road
Bath BA1 2XT, England
Tel: 01225 331922, Fax: 01225 448276
31 Rooms, Double: £260–£445
Open: all year, Credit cards: all major

Renovated and restored to its original Georgian style, and with all the conveniences expected of a thoroughly modern townhouse hotel, Dukes enjoys a prominent position on Great Pulteney Street, one of Bath's more prestigious boulevards. As might be expected, the bedrooms and suites are named after dukes. Most are airy and spacious and have period plasterwork details and enormous sash windows looking out onto the bustle of the surrounding streets. Other rooms have views of the Bath skyline. The hotel's excellent Cavendish Restaurant and Bar, together with the adjoining peaceful patio garden, provide the perfect venue in which to enjoy a relaxing drink and meal. A level, five minutes' walk from the famous Pulteney Bridge, the hotel is superbly positioned to take advantage of this lovely city. *Directions:* Leave the M4 motorway at Junction 18 and head south on the A46. After approximately 9 miles, at the bottom of a long hill, follow signs to Bath. On the outskirts of town turn left at a traffic light, signposted A36 Warminster (Bathwick Road). At the next traffic light turn right into Sydney Place and approximately 150 yards farther on take a half right turn into Great Pulteney Street. Dukes is on the left. Double park on arrival, parking is usually available later in the day, and the hotel lends you a parking permit.

DUKES HOTEL
Manager: Tina Paradise
Great Pulteney Street
Bath BA2 4DN, England
Tel: 01225 787960, Fax: 01225 787961
17 Rooms, Double: £131–£232
Open: all year, Credit cards: all major

Catherine Andrew belongs to that school of dedicated and talented bed and breakfast owners who really take good care of guests with a warm and spontaneous hospitality. She welcomes you to her family home and takes you into her care, brewing you a cup of tea, getting the shortbread, and asking you where you've been and where you're going. Sitting on the sofa in her front room overlooking the garden, it's hard to believe that you're not in the countryside. A 15-minute walk finds you in the heart of the city and after a day's sightseeing, you can take a taxi or the bus back up the hill. Breakfast is served at separate little tables in the dining room with a fruit compote and specialties from Catherine's native Scotland on the menu as well as a traditional cooked breakfast. The three bedrooms offer twins, a double, and a queen bed. All are beautifully decorated, with the queen being my especial favorite both for its lovely blue and yellow decor and its wonderful view across the garden and rooftops to Bath. *Directions:* On aprroaching Bath follow signs for through traffic until A367 is signposted towards Radstock and Shepton Mallet. This is at an elongated roundabout by a railway viaduct. Bear left onto Wells Road up a hill to a small shopping area and onto a dual carriageway (The Bear pub is on your right). 300 yards past the shops, fork right into Bloomfield Road and take the 2nd right into Bloomfield Park, the house is on your right with plenty of off-road parking.

MEADOWLAND
Owners: Catherine & John Andrew
36 Bloomfield Park
Bath BA2 2BX, England
Tel: 01225 311079
3 Rooms, Double: £95–£120
Minimum Stay Required: 2 nights on weekends
Closed: Christmas, Credit cards: MC, VS

Located on a quiet cul-de-sac, a 10-minutes downhill walk to the Roman Baths and Pump House (save your legs, take the bus back), Paradise House offers magnificent views over the city from its half-acre of manicured, walled gardens at the rear of the property. Originally constructed in the 1720s, and the last house standing on the street after the second world war, it has been beautifully restored and modernized to provide eleven guestrooms in a range of shapes and sizes. Decorated in soft cream, yellow and beige tones offset by splashes of color, the rooms are furnished in an elegant country casual style, with pine antiques and wicker furniture. Features include a mix of brass beds, four-posters, antiques, and collectibles. All rooms have spotless, white-tiled bathrooms en suite, some with freestanding clawfoot bathtubs, some with Jacuzzis. A choice of vegetarian, continental, or "Full English" is served downstairs in the breakfast room. Next door, the cozy, guest sitting room with comfortable chairs and sofas has a fireplace and views over the garden for those cooler, damper days. *Directions:* From M4 at Exit 18 proceed south and onto the A4 into Bath. Turn left at the first major traffic lights onto the ring road, continue to the large traffic roundabout bisected by the main railway line. Turn onto A376, towards Radstock and Shepton Mallet. Proceed ¾ mile. At the shop front sign "Andrews Estate Agents", turn left and continue left down the hill.

PARADISE HOUSE HOTEL
Owners: Annie & David Lanz
86-88 Holloway
Bath BA2 4PX, England
Tel: 01225 317723, Fax: 01225 482005
11 Rooms, Double: £65–£185
Closed: Christmas, Credit cards: all major

The Queensberry, set in the heart of Georgian Bath, has been a hotel for over 100 years. Long ago it was 4 townhouses which accounts for the large central stairway with the criss-crossing stairs that rise 6 stories through the building—handily there's an elevator. This friendly boutique hotel hits just the right note between historic and modern: the building is a gem, there's a goodly number of appropriate antiques blended with modern furniture and stylish décor—look up in the brochure. Three lounges, and a shady patio, offer internet and butlered service—there's a collection of artisan after dinner drinks (malts, bourbons, rums and the like) that Laurence and his staff are happy to discuss with you. Quiet stylish guestrooms are priced according to size (Classic, Superior, Deluxe) with suites that were at one time enormous drawing rooms with tall and often decorative plaster ceilings. There is no shortage of restaurants in Bath but for a sophisticated place to enjoy modern British cuisine you can do no better than to slip below stairs to The Olive Tree—with a broad collection of over 220 wines. In the morning this serves as the breakfast room for Continental and full English breakfast. *Directions:* When you make your reservation, ask the hotel to send you the very specific directions on how to find The Queensberry, just a few minutes' walk from the Royal Crescent. On arrival double-park in front and the hotel valet will park your car.

THE QUEENSBERRY HOTEL
Owners: Helen & Laurence Beere
Manager: Lauren McCann
Russel Street
Bath BA1 2QF, England
Tel: 01225 447928, Fax: 01225 446065
29 Rooms, Double: £120–£450*
*Breakfast not included: £16
Open: all year, Credit cards: MC, VS

Rosamund and John Napier were delighted to find this lovely Georgian House on a quiet street in the conservation village of Bathford just 3 miles from Bath. It was just what they had been looking for—a large home, suitable for bed and breakfast. Over the years they have added bathrooms and showers, decorator touches, antiques and collectibles. It's more comfortably homey than decorator-perfect, with the Napiers' warmth of welcome adding the final ingredient. The spacious sitting room overlooks the grassy garden with its tennis court and guests are welcome to bring their own refreshments with ice and glasses being freely provided by the establishment. Upstairs, the larger bedrooms can be easily adapted to include an extra bed or two for children. Each room is well equipped with color TV, phone, tea-making facilities, hairdryer, and en suite shower or bathroom. If you would like complete privacy, opt to stay in one of the bedrooms in the walled garden cottage. Bathford is ideally situated for Bath (there are four buses an hour) and within easy reach of Bradford on Avon, Lacock, Longleat House, Stourhead Gardens, Bowood House, and Dyrham Park. *Directions:* From Bath take the A4 towards Chippenham for 3 miles, the A363 towards Bradford on Avon for 100 yards, then turn left up Bathford Hill. Church Street is the first right and Eagle House is on your right after 200 yards.

EAGLE HOUSE
Owners: Rosamund & John Napier
Church Street
near Bath
Bathford BA1 7RS, England
Tel: 01225 859946, Fax: 01225 859430
8 Rooms, Double: £72–£98
Closed: Christmas & New Year, Credit cards: MC, VS

Dating back in part as far as the 13th century, replete with a fascinating mix of mullioned windows, stone floors, heavy wooden beams, and large open fireplaces, The Bridge House is awash in character. Originally a clergy house, communal home to ten or twelve priests, it has been tastefully converted to a classic small country hotel and restaurant by owners Joanna & Mark Donovan. With flowers and books tucked away in various nooks and crannies, the public rooms are cozy and relaxed but on finer days guests may choose to retreat to the sunny conservatory or venture outside to the walled garden. Fourteen lovely bedrooms of different shapes and sizes are distributed between the main house and coach house across the courtyard to the rear. All have fresh flowers, fine linen from Italy, flat screen TVs and state of the art bath and shower rooms. Our favorites were the larger "superior" rooms in the main house. At the heart of the operation is the food—fresh ingredients from local farms and fishing ports are artfully transformed by the kitchen staff and served in the paneled dining room. Beaminster has some lovely Georgian houses and there are fine gardens at Forde Abbey and Clapton Court. Nearby are Sherborne (castle and abbey), Cricket St. Thomas Wildlife Park, and Cerne Abbas (abbey and giant cut in the chalk hills almost 2,000 years ago). *Directions:* Beaminster is on the A3066 between Crewkerne and Bridport.

THE BRIDGE HOUSE HOTEL
Owners: Joanna & Mark Donovan
3, Prout Bridge
Beaminster DT8 3AY, England
Tel: 01308 862200, Fax: 01308 863700
14 Rooms, Double: £116–£200
Open: all year, Credit cards: all major

Blockley is a delightful Cotswold village, a haven of peace and calm conveniently located just a few miles from the hustle and bustle of tourist-thronged Broadway, Bourton-on-the-Water, and Chipping Campden. Lower Brook House is created from two silk workers' cottages dating back to the early 1600's. The cottage origins are reflected in its exposed beams and wall timbers, the cozy parlor with large, stone-faced inglenook fireplace and the snug, flagstone-floored, dining room with its individual square tables and ladderback chairs. A narrow, winding staircase (don't bring huge cases) leads to the bedrooms, all named after various silk mills that have long since ceased to operate in the village. As might be expected, no two are the same, all having been carefully fit into the existing structure. Decorated in soft earth tones, all are artfully presented, comfortable beds, crisp linens, a carefully chosen mix of antiques and collectibles, flat-screen TV's and/or DVD players and modern luxuriously efficient bathrooms en suite. Free-standing baths, whirlpool spa tubs, walk-in showers. Take your pick, we liked them all. Use Lower Brook House as a base for your explorations from Oxford to Stratford-upon-Avon. *Directions:* From Moreton in Marsh take the A44 towards Broadway to Bourton-on-the-Hill, turn right for Blockley. Lower Brook House is on your right at the bottom of the hill.

LOWER BROOK HOUSE
Owners: Anna & Julian Ebbutt
Blockley GL56 9DS, England
Tel: 01386 700286, Fax: 01386 701400
6 Rooms, Double: £80–£185
Closed: Christmas & 2 weeks in Jan
Credit cards: all major

The Devonshire, previously a coaching inn, is now a traditional country house hotel resplendent with swimming pool and health spa. Rooms in the original coaching inn are especially lovely: Shepherd has lovely paintings of sheep; Crace has an elegant four-poster; and Chatsworth, with its fireplace, is especially spacious. Ground floor rooms are available in the Wharfedale wing. If you stay there, request a room that looks out across the garden and fields to the distant hills. The Duke and Duchess of Devonshire's family portraits add richness to the Long Lounge with its many groupings of comfortable chairs. Dinner in the Burlington restaurant, a Michelin star winner in a beautiful conservatory, is a formal affair. For a move from country house to modern, you might want to frequent the adjacent brasserie and bar, reached by a covered flagstone passageway. Just across the garden, the barns have undergone a skillful conversion to a spa with indoor swimming pool, gym, and beauty salons. Fast roads lead to York and Harrogate. Upper Wharfedale—one of the most scenic Yorkshire Dales—begins at your back door, the ruins of Bolton Abbey are across the fields, and a short drive brings you to Haworth and the Brontë sisters' parsonage. *Directions:* The hotel is on the B6160, 250 yards north of its roundabout junction off the A59, Skipton to Harrogate Road.

THE DEVONSHIRE ARMS
Owners: Duke & Duchess of Devonshire
Bolton Abbey BD23 6AJ, England
Tel: 01756 710441, Fax: 01756 710564
40 Rooms, Double: £225–£420
Open: all year, Credit cards: all major

Gill and David Taylor live in what was Boltongate's large, rambling rectory which dates from 1360 but was extensively "modernized" in Victorian times. Many of its rooms face south and have delightful views of peaceful countryside with distant views of the Lakeland fells and mountains. In summer the sun streams in and guests can enjoy the garden with its ponds and arbors, while during the cooler months log fires burn in the study and dining room. Dining in the cozy oak-beamed dining room is a delightful experience. In contrast to the old-world dining room, the bedrooms and sitting room are spacious, tall-ceilinged, large-windowed rooms. Bedrooms are large and comfortable. Two have en suite showers while the third has its bathroom (robes provided) down the hall. Boltongate is on the quiet, northernmost fringes of the Lake District, a perfect spot to break a journey to or from Scotland. Pretty towns and villages such as Caldbeck, Borrowdale, Ullswater, and Buttermere abound. William Wordsworth's birthplace is nearby in Cockermouth. *Directions:* From the Keswick bypass take the A591 for 7 miles. At the Castle Inn turn right at the sign for Ireby. Drive through Ireby to Boltongate (1½ miles). The Rectory is the first house on the right as you come up the hill.

BOLTONGATE OLD RECTORY
Owners: Gill & David Taylor
Boltongate CA7 1DA, England
Tel: 016973 71647
3 Rooms, Double: £100–£120
Closed: Christmas & New Year, Credit cards: MC, VS

Standing high in wooded grounds just outside Borrowdale with outstanding views across the surrounding countryside, The Leathes Head is a classic, small country house hotel. This gabled Edwardian house, constructed of local Lakeland stone, has been completely renovated and refurbished by owners Janice and Roy Smith, retaining many original architectural features, stained glass, old fireplaces, and plasterwork details to combine the charm of a bygone era with modern standards of comfort and convenience. The house has been tastefully decorated and furnished in keeping with its age. Bedrooms vary in size from spacious to snug with all having en suite bathrooms. Our favorites were the two superior double rooms with magnificent views to Catbells and Maiden Moor. Chef David uses local produce (as available), offers a wide-ranging, constantly changing menu and has established a fine reputation. The cuisine is supported by Roy's wine list, handpicked but very reasonably priced. Afternoon tea or pre-dinner drinks are served in the conservatory, furnished with comfortable wicker chairs and a thoughtful supply of games, magazines and books, and overlooks the grounds. On chillier, darker days, you might want to retreat to the snug bar. Breakfast ranges from "healthy" to "Full English" and caters to the hearty appetites of walkers who frequent the local hills. *Directions:* Leathes Hotel is on the left 3-1/2 miles south of Keswick on B5289 Borrowdale Road.

THE LEATHES HEAD HOTEL
Owners: Janice & Roy Smith
Borrowdale
Keswick CA12 5UY, England
Tel: 017687 77247, Fax: 017687 77363
12 Rooms, Double: £185–£215*
*Includes dinner, bed & breakfast
Open: mid-Feb to mid-Nov, Credit cards: MC, VS

Priory Steps, a row of 17th-century weavers' cottages high above the town of Bradford on Avon. The village tumbles down the hill to the banks of the River Avon, its narrow streets full of interesting shops and antique dealers. A few miles distant, the glories of Bath await exploration, easily accessible by car or local train. Hostess Diana is a gourmet cook and guests dine "en famille" in the traditionally furnished dining room. While Diana's cooking is reason enough to spend several days here, the adjacent library with its books and pamphlets highlighting the many places to visit in the area provides additional justification. The bedrooms are all very different, each accented with antique furniture. Each has a smart modern bathroom, television, and tea and coffee tray. On a recent visit we particularly admired Sue's room. There is a touch of whimsy in the bathroom of the dark-beamed Frog Room where an odd frog or two has inspired former guests to send their own contributions to an ever-growing collection of the creatures. If you are travelling with a family or would like to stay for several days consider staying in the adjacent apartment with its especially spacious open plan kitchen, dining, living room and snug twin beded bedroom. *Directions:* Take the A363 from Bath to Bradford on Avon. As the road drops steeply into the town, Newtown is the first road to the right. Priory Steps is 150 yards on the left.

PRIORY STEPS
Owners: Diana & Carey Chapman
Newtown
Bradford-on-Avon BA15 1NQ, England
Tel: 01225 862230, Fax: 01225 866248
4 Rooms, Double: £88–£104
1 Apartment: £90 daily–£490 weekly
Open: all year, Credit cards: MC, VS

Farlam Hall is a superb place to hide away for a relaxed holiday and be thoroughly spoiled, enjoying the pampering attentions of this family-run hotel. Mum, dad, son, daughter, and spouses make up the friendly team of one of only a handful of British hotels admitted to the prestigious Relais & Châteaux hotel group. Their presence is felt at all times; serving breakfast, welcoming guests and in the restaurant in an evening. They take a genuine interest in all their guests. The quality of everything, from the abundant antique furniture to the sumptuous food, is a delight. The same quality and good taste continue in the bedrooms, which vary greatly in shape and size. My favorite larger rooms are the Garden Room, a grand, high-ceilinged room with an enormous four-poster bed and the Guest Room, a spacious corner room whose large bathroom sports a Jacuzzi tub and separate shower. While Farlam Hall is a perfect place to break your journey if you are traveling between England and Scotland, it would be a shame to spend only one night in this charming hotel. Staff will drop you off and arrange to pick you up if you want to walk a section of nearby Hadrian's Wall. Carlisle, the Lake District and the Scottish border towns are also popular destinations. *Directions:* Leave the M6 motorway at junction 43 and take the A69 towards Newcastle for 12 miles to the A689 signposted Alston. The hotel is on your left after 2 miles (not in the village of Farlam).

FARLAM HALL
Owners: Quinion & Stevenson Families
Brampton CA8 2NG, England
Tel: 016977 46234, Fax: 016977 46683
12 Rooms, Double: £290–£340*
*includes breakfast & dinner
Closed: Dec 24 to 31, Credit cards: all major
Relais & Châteaux

Gently rolling hills with sheep grazing peacefully and shaded valleys with meandering streams surround the picturesque village of Broad Campden. The Malt House hugs the quiet main street and opens up to the most beautiful, secluded gardens at the rear. Years ago, barley was made into malt here for brewing beer. Now this most picturesque country house provides a perfect central location for exploring other Cotswold villages. Make yourself at home in the peaceful sitting room or relax by the massive inglenook fireplace in the lounge whose door opens to the gardens. Four lovely bedrooms are found in the house, each beautifully decorated and accompanied by top-of-the-line bathrooms, several of which have separate showers. I find Room 3, with its grand four-poster bed resplendent in blue toile de joie, especially appealing, though my favorite was Room 2, a king/twin decked out in soft shades of lime green and lilac. For complete privacy opt for a room in the adjacent stable block where an inviting ground floor suite and two additional bedrooms are to be found. Judi's garden is a real beauty. Garden lovers will also enjoy Kiftsgate, Hidcote Manor, and Batsford There are lots of lovely Cotswold villages to explore nearby. *Directions:* On entering Chipping Campden from B4081, take the first right: you know you are in Broad Campden when you see the Bakers Arms. The Malt House is opposite the wall topped by a tall topiary hedge.

THE MALT HOUSE
Owner: Judi Wilkes
Broad Campden
Chipping Campden GL55 6UU, England
Tel: 01386 840295, Fax: 01386 841334
7 Rooms, Double: £135–£160
Closed: Christmas, Credit cards: all major

Standing at the quieter end of High Street (no through traffic, just the occasional horse clip-clopping by) but a short walk to the bustle of Broadway village centre, The Olive Branch is a real find. Dating back to the 1590's the two-story building has been added to and expanded over the years. Functioning previously, among other things, as a shop and a bakery, it has been operated as a bed and breakfast since 1961 and under the watchful eye of the current owners since 1999. As expected in an old "listed" building, the guest accommodations rooms vary in size and format although quality is the watchword throughout. The rooms in the back of the house are larger but all are more than adequate, tastefully decorated, with comfy furnishings and functional bathrooms, all except the lone single room are en suite. Taller guest have plenty of opportunities to bump their heads on their way up the narrow staircase, all part of the adventure. Breakfast is served in the dining room with its original stone floor and exposed beams, and ranges from home-made muesli to fruit smoothies or David's classic "full English." Guests are welcome to use the cozy sitting room, comfortable sofas, as well as the walled garden to the rear (the source of Pam's flower arrangements). A stay at The Olive Branch is a handy for exploring Oxford, Stratford and Warwick. *Directions:* Drive up High Street to mini roundabout, go straight; Olive Branch is 30 yards on the left.

THE OLIVE BRANCH
Owners: Pam & David Talboys
78 High Street
Broadway WR12 7AT, England
Tel: 01386 853440
8 Rooms, Double: £85–£102
Open: all year, Credit cards: MC, VS

Named after the famous furniture manufacturing company whose ex-headquarters it now occupies, Russell's restaurant-with-rooms offers a refreshing alternative to the more staid, conventional hotels and bed and breakfasts that populate the Cotswolds. Located on Broadway High Street these superbly renovated and remodeled listed buildings offer bistro style cuisine and contemporary accommodations while at the same time conserving ancient beams, exposed stonework and inglenook fireplaces. The chef serves a fixed price (multiple choice) menu for lunch and early dinner (6 to 7pm). Thereafter guests eat a la carte. There is an ample and well-priced wine list. Meals can be served outside on the patio, or in the chic restaurant. Accommodations are to be found on the second floor (above the restaurant) and in the adjoining building, accessed via the patio. All are splendidly equipped, large comfortable beds, luxurious linens, sparklingly modern bathrooms and all the creature comforts demanded by the sophisticated traveler. Our favorite was Room 7 upstairs "next door" with its vaulted beam ceiling, and massive bathroom with huge "walk-in" shower. Broadway is an excellent base for Cotswold explorations and ideal for trips to Oxford, Stratford and Warwick. *Directions:* Broadway is off the A44 between Evesham and Stow-on-the-Wold. Russells is located on the High Street 100 yards down from the Lygon Arms. Park in front on arrival.

※ ■ ✍ 🚗 ☎ 🐕 @ W P ⁉ 🚭 🖼 ⚓ 🎋 👫 🏇

RUSSELL'S
Owners: Barry Hancox & Andrew Riley
20 High Street
Broadway WR12 7DT, England
Tel: 01386 853555, Fax: 01386 853964
7 Rooms, Double: £120–£295
Minimum Stay Required: 2 nights on weekends
Open: all year, Credit cards: MC, VS

The taste of Augill Castle is truly delicious. It is a most imposing home—a flamboyant Victorian castle built by a local eccentric who used to greet his guests regally from a dais in the hallway. No regality to Wendy and Simon's warm welcome! They have rescued this impressive place and returned it to its former glory, adding spacious bathrooms to the bedrooms, furnishing with antiques, and redecorating with their own hands the whole of this vast house. You will see what a task that has been when you look at the "before" picture in every room. Toast your toes by the fire in the magnificent music room and enjoy breakfast with your fellow guests round the 12-foot long dining table in the blue Gothic dining hall. The bedrooms are stunning and several are positively palatial—discuss your preferences when you book: magnificent four-poster bed, soaking tub for two, oak paneling, a walk-in turret, and Gothic leaded windows are just some of the choices. Sitting in the Eden Valley between the Yorkshire Dales and the Lake District, Augill Castle is an ideal several-day stopover on your way south or north. *Directions:* Exit the M6 at junction 38 and take the A685 through Kirkby Stephen towards Brough-in-Westmorland. Go through Brough Sowerby and turn right at the signpost for South Stainmore. The castle is on your left after 1 mile.

AUGILL CASTLE
Owners: Wendy & Simon Bennett
Brough-in-Westmorland
Kirkby Stephen CA17 4DE, England
Tel: 017683 41937
12 Rooms, Double: £160–£300
Closed: Christmas, Credit cards: MC, VS

Two miles from the hustle and bustle of Broadway is the pretty, small village of Buckland where, adjacent to the village church, sits Buckland Manor surrounded by acres of gorgeous gardens. Wisteria hugs the walls, blowzy roses fill the flowerbeds, and a rushing stream tumbles beside the woodland walk. The exterior sets the tone for an interior where everything is decorated to perfection. Add masses of flowers and enviable antiques and you have the perfect country house hotel. Relax and enjoy a drink before the huge fireplace in the richly paneled lounge, curl up with a book in the sunny morning room, and relish the sense of occasion in the refined dining room. Bedrooms are elegant and every attention has been paid to every luxurious detail. From the moment you are greeted at reception, you will be enveloped in the atmosphere of hushed gentility that pervades this most gracious Cotswold manor. Warm weather enables you to enjoy the tennis court, and croquet lawn. Surrounding Buckland are other Cotswold villages with such appealing names as Chipping Campden, Upper and Lower Slaughter, Stow-on-the-Wold, and Upper and Lower Swell. Stratford-upon-Avon, Worcester, Bath, and Oxford are all within an hour's driving distance. Garden lovers will enjoy Kiftsgate, Hidcote Manor, and Batsford. *Directions:* Buckland is 1½ miles from Broadway on the B4632.

BUCKLAND MANOR   **Cover painting**
Manager: Nigel Power
Buckland WR12 7LY, England
Tel: 01386 852626, Fax: 01386 853557
14 Rooms, Double: £285–£470
Minimum Stay Required: 2 nights on weekends
Open: all year, Credit cards: all major
Relais & Châteaux

Burford House, a charming half-timbered building on the corner of Burford's main street, is a small hotel of great character owned by Stewart Dunkley and Ian Hawkins. Just off the inviting entry with its old wood floors is the lovely restaurant aptly named Center Stage with its collection of theatre posters and pictures: on the other side is a most comfortable sitting room with sofas and chairs drawn around a log burning stove. The pretty morning room is especially attractive in the early hours. Doors open onto the lovely back courtyard and garden where guests often eat breakfast in the summer. Burford House has eight guestrooms, all named for local villages and all with en suite bathrooms (six of the rooms have separate walk-in showers in addition to a tub). Swinbrook is a spacious, pretty, garden-level room located in the wing off the courtyard, referred to as the "coach house" (although it is actually part of the main building). At the top of the stairs in the main house and overlooking the bustle of the main street is Sherbourne with its four-poster bed and an enormous bathroom complete with dramatic claw-foot tub. We especially enjoyed our stay in Windrush, a spacious king/twin looking over the courtyard. This small hotel is a real winner with award winning breakfasts. *Directions:* Burford is midway between Oxford and Cheltenham (A40). Burford House is on the main street.

BURFORD HOUSE
Owners: Stewart Dunkley & Ian Hawkins
99 High Street
Burford OX18 4QA, England
Tel: 01993 823151, Fax: 01993 823240
8 Rooms, Double: £145–£185
Minimum Stay Required: 2 nights on weekends
Open: all year, Credit cards: all major

The clomp of hooves as horses pulled carriages down the main street of Burford has long disappeared, but the inns that provided lodging and food to weary travelers remain. If you are in search of a delightful, quaint hostelry, but with modern food and service, you can do no better than to base yourself at The Lamb for the duration of your Cotswold stay. A tall, upholstered settee sits before the fireplace on the flagstone floor of the reception hall. There's an air of times long past pervading the place, particularly in winter when the air is heavy with the scent of woodsmoke and a flickering fire burns in the grate. Little staircases and corridors zigzag you up and down to the en suite bedrooms, all kitted out in modern country decor. Malt is a particularly spacious king-bedded room with a large bathroom. The restaurant offers a full à la carte menu or, if you prefer to eat less formally, a bar menu is available. It's lovely to eat out in the garden in the summer, but for atmosphere you cannot beat the homey little bar with its stone-flagged floor and little tables and chairs. Burford's main street is bordered by numerous hostelries, antique, gift, and teashops. There are mellow Cotswold villages to explore. Blenheim Palace and Oxford are less than an hour's drive away. *Directions:* Burford is midway between Oxford and Cheltenham (A40). The Lamb Inn is on Sheep Street, just off the village center.

THE LAMB INN
Manager: Andrew Swan
Sheep Street
Burford OX18 4LR, England
Tel: 01993 823155, Fax: 01993 822228
17 Rooms, Double: £150–£200
Open: all year, Credit cards: MC, VS

The Fell Hotel (as it was known) has long been serving visitors to this lovely part of the Yorkshire Dales and acquired the "Devonshire" in its title in 1998 when it was purchased by the Duke and Duchess of Devonshire to be a sister hotel to the Devonshire Arms, a country house hotel just down the road. Consequently, I expected a traditional interior for this sturdy Yorkshire hotel looking over the River Wharfe to the village of Burnsall, but the interior could not be further from traditional—it is dashingly modern. With the decor offering a broad palette of vivid colors, any rainy-day gloom is instantly dispelled. Relax in the boldly decorated bar and enjoy lunch or an evening meal in the restaurant or the conservatory. Selections are made from the menu or from daily specials posted on the board. Bedrooms are found on two floors (no elevator) and range from the crisp Linton room, all decked out in black and white, to oh-so-sunny Cracoe, all in bright yellow hues. Walking is de rigueur in this part of the world and scenic footpaths are on your doorstep. Just down the road are the ruins of Bolton Abbey, while just up the road is the village of Grassington. Harrogate is close at hand while York is an hour's drive away. Ask about the very-good-value-for-money B&B plus dinner rates. *Directions:* From the A59 (Skipton to Harrogate road) take the B6160 past Bolton Abbey and north to Burnsall. As you see the village below to your right, you find the hotel on your left.

THE DEVONSHIRE FELL
Owners: Duke & Duchess of Devonshire
Manager: Stephaine Leyreloup
Skipton
Burnsall ND23 6BT, England
Tel: 01756 718111, Fax: 01756 729009
12 Rooms, Double: £120–£208
Open: all year, Credit cards: all major

New House Farm sits beside the lane surrounded by green fields beneath rugged Lakeland peaks. Hazel grew up at a hotel and returned here with her young children to provide gracious guest accommodation in this 17th-century farmhouse and transform the barn into a tearoom and restaurant. Flagstone floors, beamed ceilings, and old fireplaces are the order of the day in the farmhouse. Hazel prepares a set, three or five-course dinner, but if you prefer a lighter, earlier and less formal meal, walk across to the barn where tables and chairs are arranged in the old cow stalls. Specials are posted on the board, and main courses include quiche, fish, and steak. Bedrooms and bathrooms are top of the line. Spacious zip-link beds are the order of the day. We especially enjoyed Lowfell whose dramatic bathroom has a roll-top tub sitting center stage. Two rooms lie a few steps from the house in the former stables—their ground-floor location making them ideal for those who have difficulty with stairs. After a day exploring the Lake District relax in the hot tub. Stride up Grasmoor or follow the country lane to Crummock Water and Buttermere from where the road winds and twists over the fells to Rosthwaite, Grange, and Keswick. *Directions:* From exit 40 on M6 take A66 past Keswick, and turn left onto the B5292 to Lorton. Follow signs for Buttermere on B5289 south and New House Farm is on your left after 2 miles.

NEW HOUSE FARM
Owner: Hazel Thompson
Near Cockermouth
Buttermere Valley CA13 9UU, England
Tel: 01900 85404, Fax: 01900 85478
5 Rooms, Double: £140–£160
Open: all year, Credit cards: MC, VS

Hotel Felix, which opened in November 2002, is situated just 1 mile northwest of Cambridge city center in 4-acres of tranquil landscaped garden. Its central core, a beautifully restored and renovated brownstone Victorian mansion, houses the restaurant and café-bar as well as four large, airy bedrooms, replete with old architectural features, fine plasterwork and moldings, tucked away on the first and second floors. All other guestrooms are located in two brand-new, custom-built wings that have been tastefully merged with the old building. All of the rooms embody an opulent simplicity complemented by state-of-the-art technology, internet and email access, satellite TV and pay-to-view movies. Pastel decorations are offset with vivid splashes of color. Large wooden headboards, contemporary furniture, white Egyptian-cotton sheets and pillowcases, and comfortable duvets complete the picture. Ample modern bathrooms feature earth-tone tiles and sparkling white fixtures. The restaurant and adjacent café-bar with their clubby atmosphere are the focal point of the Felix and on pleasant days service is available on the terrace overlooking the gardens. *Directions:* Exit the A14 onto the A1307 (Huntingdon Road) and Hotel Felix is located off Whitehouse Lane half a mile down on the left.

HOTEL FELIX
Manager: Shara Ross
Whitehouse Lane, Huntingdon Road
Cambridge CB3 0LX, England
Tel: 01223 277977, Fax: 01223 277973
55 Rooms, Double: £185–£300
Open: all year, Credit cards: all major

Magnolia House, a lovely Georgian home converted into the most welcoming of guesthouses, sits on a quiet street just a ten-minute walk from the heart of Canterbury. A small parlor is stacked with information not only on Canterbury but the surrounding area—you can easily keep busy for a week. Delightful guestrooms are found upstairs in the house ranging in size from a snug single to lovely double-bedded room, but the gem is the Garden Room with its private garden entrance, four-poster queen-sized bed, and the most spacious of bathrooms. In summer, breakfast is the only meal served; but on gloomy winter evenings very often guests do not want to venture out, so with prior arrangement supper can be provided. Canterbury is a lively historical city easily explored on foot. Its primary attraction is its cathedral, the Mother Church for all Anglicans. Begun in 1070, it became a pilgrimage site after the murder of Thomas à Becket. Join Chaucer's famous pilgrims in a 20th-century re-enactment of the "Canterbury Tales" at the Canterbury Tales Museum in town. *Directions:* Arriving in Canterbury from the A2, at the first roundabout turn left for the university. St. Dunstan's Terrace is the third street on the right and Magnolia House is the first house on the left.

MAGNOLIA HOUSE
Owner: Isobelle Leggett
36 St. Dunstan's Terrace
Canterbury CT2 8AX, England
Tel & Fax: 01227 765121
7 Rooms, Double: £95–£150
Closed: Christmas, Credit cards: all major

Carlisle makes an excellent place to break the journey when driving between England and Scotland. Your hosts, Pru and Mike, encourage guests to use Number Thirty One as a base for visiting the city and exploring the northern Lake District and Hadrian's Wall. Mike really enjoys cooking, and the three-course dinner he prepares for guests depends on what is fresh in the market that day. Upstairs, the three bedrooms are equipped to a very high standard with TV, trouser press, tea tray, and hairdryer; and furnished in a style complementing this large, Victorian terrace home. I admired the spaciousness of the Blue Room with its sparkling, Mediterranean bathroom and king-sized bed, and enjoyed the sunny decor of the smaller Green Room with its large, golden dragon stenciled on the black headboard. The equally attractive Yellow Room has a half-tester bed that can be king-sized or twin and faces the front of the house. A ten-minute stroll finds you in the heart of Carlisle with its majestic cathedral, grand castle, and Tullie House museum, which portrays Carlisle's place in the turbulent history of the Borders. *Directions:* Leave the M6 at junction 43 and follow Carlisle City Centre signs through five sets of traffic lights (the fifth is for pedestrians). Howard Place is the next turn on the right (before the one-way system).

NUMBER THIRTY ONE
Owners: Pru & Mike Irving
31 Howard Place
Carlisle CA1 1HR, England
Tel & Fax: 01228 597080
4 Rooms, Double: £90–£110
Open: all year, Credit cards: all major

Castle Combe is a picture-perfect example of a Cotswold village, gold-stone buildings, slate roofs, exposed timbers, and burbling stream. The last house was constructed in 1647. This idyllic setting with the complete absence of street lights and television aerials has won the "Prettiest Village in England" award many times and provided the backdrop for such famous movies as Dr. Doolittle. Nestled in the market place, you'll find the Castle Inn Hotel. Narrow hallways and staircases lead to guestrooms in a wide range of shapes and sizes with low doorways, crooked walls, beams and exposed stone walls. All are most attractively kitted out with antiques, nice bathrooms and flat screen televisions. Sophisticated cottage atmosphere without being cramped. Lie in bed in room 9 and admire the intricate support beams for the roof. Exposed beams are a real feature of spacious room 5. Room 4 is particularly glamorous with a large four-poster bed, two large windows overlooking the market cross, and an extra large bathroom. Breakfast is served in the conservatory or (weather permitting) outside on the patio. The old wood-beamed restaurant, walls hung with hunting scenes, is open for dinner and a reasonably priced international wine list is available. Retire to the fire in one of the lounges, or sample one of the impressive inventory of single malt whiskies. *Directions:* Castle Combe is 7 miles from junction 17 on the M4.

CASTLE INN HOTEL
Owners: Ann & Bill Cross
Castle Combe
Wiltshire SN14 7HN, England
Tel: 01249 783030, Fax: 01249 782315
11 Rooms, Double: £110–£175
Closed: Christmas, Credit cards: all major

A visit to Gidleigh Park is an experience not to be missed. The setting is stunning: a secluded woodland surrounding acres of beautiful garden with a tumbling stream in Dartmoor National Park. The house is a divinely decorated beauty full of lovely antiques and honey-toned paneling. Bedrooms are luxurious with sumptuous soft furnishings, antiques, original artwork, absolutely top-of-the-line bathrooms and a host of creature comforts. Know you deserve the best and request one of the spacious master rooms with panoramic views. Rooms at the top of the house are more contemporary in design. Some incorporate baths into the living space, some have a sauna and one a hot tub on the deck. While the exclusive style of the place merits a stay, THE reason to come here is the food. Executive Chef Michael Caine's flair for classic and modern food has earned him 2 Michelin stars and a clutch of culinary awards. Walks abound from gentle strolls around the garden to day-long hikes from the hotel into the wild beauty of Dartmoor. Guided walks can be arranged with Chris Chapman, well known for his knowledge of the moor and its natural history. Nearby Chagford is a delightful country town. *Directions:* From Chagford Square turn right (at Lloyds Bank) into Mill Street. After 150 yards fork right and go downhill to Factory Crossroad. Go straight across into Holy Street and follow the lane for 1½ miles to the end.

GIDLEIGH PARK
Owners: Christina & Andrew Brownsword
Manager: Sue Willaims
Chagford TQ13 8HH, England
Tel: 01647 432367, Fax: 01647 432574
24 Rooms, Double: £310–£1155
Minimum Stay Required: 2 nights on weekends
Open: all year, Credit cards: MC, VS

Cheltenham was a fashionable destination during the Regency period and today the classical squares and terraces built in delightful garden settings are the town's pride. Benjamin Bowen's boutique hotel and bistro occupies a fine Regency villa on the edge of Pittville Park. The hotel has recently received a total refurbishment giving it a chic modern look. Below the stairs is a small spa with a plunge pool, sauna, fitness room and treatment rooms. Bedrooms are top of the line—we were particularly intrigued with the bathrooms with their televisions and little refrigerators just large enough to hold ice-cream for two. Two extremely popular rooms have infinity baths where you are buoyed on bubbles, the water changes colors and a cascade comes down from the ceiling. Cheltenham offers excellent shopping and lots of specialist antique shops. Horseracing takes place at Cheltenham during the autumn and winter months. A ten-minute drive finds you in the midst of the Cotswolds. *Directions:* Arriving in Cheltenham, follow signs for town center onto the one-way system, then follow signposts for Evesham. The hotel is on the left, just as you reach Pittville Park (right) after passing a row of Regency townhouses.

HOTEL ON THE PARK
Owner: Benjamin Bowen
38 Evesham Road
Cheltenham
Glos GL52 2AH, England
Tel: 01242 518898, Fax: 01242 511526
12 Rooms, Double: £155–£795*
*Breakfast not included: £15
Open: all year, Credit cards: all major

Chipping Campden, rich in history and exquisite architecture, is home to the Cotswold House Hotel standing in Regency splendor next to the ancient market place. Its traditional exterior belies a splendid contemporary interior that emphasizes sublime comfort and luxury. Enjoy a drink in the bar before dining in the elegant Juliana's restaurant. For a more casual dining experience Hicks' Brasserie offers dishes with plenty of flair. Luxurious bedrooms range from those that blend lovely antique furniture with contemporary décor, cottage rooms in the garden that offer complete privacy (one comes with its own garden terrace) and ultra modern rooms—techno marvels with the most sublime bathrooms. The latter rooms are a destination in themselves: program your mood lighting, select the contents of your mini bar, preview your photos on the television, personalize your selection of pillows, watch TV from your tub. If you can tear yourself away head for Shakespeare's Stratford, Regency Cheltenham, Warwick Castle, and many historic houses and gardens. Add to this the hotel's special touches—tour guides, picnics, day-membership at local golf clubs—and you have the perfect recipe for a truly memorable stay. *Directions:* From Broadway take the A44 towards Moreton-in-Marsh and turn left for Chipping Campden. Turn right at the T-junction into the High Street, and Cotswold House is on your left in the main square.

COTSWOLD HOUSE HOTEL
Manager: Duncan Fraser
The Square
Chipping Campden GL55 6AN, England
Tel: 01386 840330, Fax: 01386 840310
28 Rooms, Double: £245–£650
Open: all year, Credit cards: all major

A Tudor manor house dating from 1550 set in a quiet, picturesque village above Bourton-on-the-Water, Clapton Manor is surrounded by its lovely gardens with only the birds to wake you in the morning and fabulous walking paths straight from the back gate. Inside the house, thick stone walls, exposed oak beams, and inglenook fireplaces set the scene. There are two tastefully decorated double rooms (one can be a twin or a king) with very comfortable beds, enormous goose-down comforters and top-of-the-line bathrooms. A cozy sitting room with comfy sofas, a wood fire, and books and magazines is the perfect setting for tea on less than perfect days. Otherwise, food is served in the garden where chickens waddle preparing to lay eggs for your breakfast. Karen, James and their four children have called Clapton Manor home for over 16 years. James runs his own garden tour company specializing in visits to private gardens in England and Europe. His and Karin's own garden is surrounded by hedges and old stone walls highlighting roses over arches and a wild-flower meadow. Karin and James will point you in the right direction for visiting nearby gardens. The manor is perfect as a base for visiting all the major sites: Blenheim Palace, Stratford, Warwick, Hidcote, Kiftsgate and Bath is only an hour and a half away. *Directions:* Coming from Cirencester towards Stow on the A429 turn right to Clapton and follow signs into the village. The manor is the large house by the church.

CLAPTON MANOR
Owners: Karin & James Bolton
Clapton-on-the-Hill
Bourton-on-the-Water GL54 2LG, England
Tel: 01451 810202
2 Rooms, Double: £100
Closed: Christmas & New Year, Credit cards: MC, VS

This pretty village of flint-walled, tile-roofed cottages is no longer "next the sea" but separated from it by a vast saltwater marsh formed as the sea retreated. The massive structure of Cley windmill is the villages most photographed building. The circular sitting room has large chintz chairs drawn round a stone fireplace whose mantel is a sturdy beam, a perfect place to enjoy a drink in the evening by the fire. Stacked above the sitting room are two large circular bedrooms with en suite bathrooms: the Wheat Chamber is where the grain was stored and the Stone Room is where the massive grinding stones crushed the flour. The very top of the tower is accessed by a steep ladder, views over the windmill sails to the distant sea are magnificent. I especially enjoyed my stay in the River Room with its private entrance and lovely view out over the reed beds. The old boathouse and stables in the yard are stylish little retreats. Dinner is available with advance reservations. It's a short walk to the village shops. Surrounded by reed beds and tranquility the windmill overlooks the salt marshes and Cley bird sanctuary with Blakeney harbor in the distance. Birdwatching, sailing, cycling, and walking are popular pastimes in the area. There are a great many stately homes to explore such as Sandringham House, the Royal Family's country residence, Fellbrigg Hall, Holkham, and Blickling Hall. *Directions:* From King's Lynn follow the A149 to Cley next the Sea.

CLEY WINDMILL GUEST HOUSE
Manager: Charlotte Martin
Cley next the Sea
Holt NR25 7RP, England
Tel & Fax: 01263 740209
9 Rooms, Double: £76–£155
Open: all year, Credit cards: MC, VS

Katherine Morgan has done the most magnificent job of converting an old barn, stable block, and oast house, originally used for drying hops, into an exquisite home. Traditional features include exposed timbers in the walls and ceilings and heavy rafters. Lovely pictures adorn the walls and enviable antiques furnish every nook and cranny. If you want to splurge, ask for the four-poster room and you will sleep in a king-size four-poster decked in lemon-and-green-sprigged fabric. Its ground-floor location within the roundel makes it ideal for anyone who has difficulty with stairs. A twin/king-bedded room has a third bed for a child, while the third bedroom is equipped with a queen bed. Like everything in the house, the bathrooms are absolutely spiffing and top of the line. Katherine enjoys meeting people and entertaining, so guests who order dinner (in advance) are in for a real treat. You are welcome to swim in the heated pool (summer only), relax on the deck by the pond, and enjoy the acres of gardens. Sissinghurst Gardens are a mile away, while Chartwell, Knole, Igtham Mote, Penshurt Place, and Batemans are within easy reach. *Directions:* Take the A21 south from Sevenoaks, turn left at the A262 before Lamberhurst and right onto the A229. Go into Cranbrook and take a sharp left after the school. Follow this road for about a mile, turn right just before the cemetery, and the entrance to Cloth Hall Oast is on your right.

CLOTH HALL OAST
Owner: Katherine Morgan
Coursehorn Lane
Cranbrook TN17 3NR, England
Tel & Fax: 01580 712220
3 Rooms, Double: £95–£135
Closed: Christmas, Credit cards: none

This quiet, rural spot is just minutes from Scotch Corner on the A1, making it an ideal place to break your journey between the south of England and Scotland. David's family has always farmed in Yorkshire, and when he inherited this small farm, he moved here with Heather and built Clow Beck House. The Armstrongs and their staff are relaxed, people who truly enjoy welcoming visitors. Guests have a large formal drawing room but more often gravitate into the roomy country kitchen and the spacious beamed dining room with its cheery fire. After a day of sightseeing it's nice to stay home for dinner. The menu has lots of choices and features local produce. One guestroom is in the main house with the remainder occupying a stable, a granary (where one is equipped for the handicapped), and a cottage. All the bedrooms are excellently fitted out with TV, phone, bathrobes, and large umbrellas. Decor ranges from the dramatic and colorful (particularly in the cottage) to the more quietly decorated rooms in the granary. Use Clow Beck as a base to explore the Yorkshire Dales and Moors, and the heritage coast with Whitby, Robin Hood's Bay and Runswick. Heather and David love planning routes for guests. *Directions:* From Scotch Corner go north on the A1 for a short distance to the Barton exit. Go through Barton and Newton Morell, turn right for Croft, and after 2½ miles turn left into the farm.

CLOW BECK HOUSE
Owners: Heather & David Armstrong
Monk End Farm
Croft on Tees
Darlington DL2 2SW, England
Tel: 01325 721075, Fax: 01325 720419
13 Rooms, Double: £135–£135
Open: all year, Credit cards: all major

The Punch Bowl lies nestled next to St Mary's Church in Cumbria's Damson Valley, famous for its display of white blossoms in April. Originally a small roadside inn dating back to the 17th century, it has been modernized and expanded by a succession of owners. Its latest incarnation is an interesting mix of old and new—exposed beams and high ceilings, comfortable beds, tasteful pine antiques, collectibles and flat screen televisions. Guest rooms are all named after past Vicars of St Mary's. All are comfortably furnished and have their own modernly appointed bathroom en suite, each with its own free-standing roll-top tub, separate shower and heated limestone floor. Our particular favorite was Noble which occupies the whole top floor, open to the eaves; massive bed and spacious bathroom with twin roll-top baths, luxury and seclusion combined. Afternoon teas are served in the sitting room, a comfortable spot to while away rainy day hours in front of the fire with a newspaper or board game. Traditional British fare with a contemporary twist, plus a carefully selected wine list, is served in the restaurant; more relaxed dining is available in rooms adjoining the slate-topped public bar. *Directions:* Exit the M6 at junction 36 towards Kendal (A591). At the roundabout take the Barrow exit and after 1 mile turn right towards Bowness and Windermere (A5074). After 2 miles turn right for Crosthwaite. The Punchbowl is on the right next to the church.

THE PUNCH BOWL
Owners: Paul Spencer & Richard Rose
Manager: Jenny Crompton
Crossthwaite
Lyth Valley LA8 8HR, England
Tel: 015395 68237, Fax: 015395 68875
9 Rooms, Double: £125–£310
Open: all year, Credit cards: all major

In the middle of the pretty redbrick village of Cuckfield you find Ockenden Manor, in part Tudor, with Victorian and contemporary additions. Viewing the manor from the garden, you appreciate that this combination of building styles is very pleasing. The spacious sitting room overlooks the garden and the adjacent dining room, with its dark-oak paneling and low, decorative-plasterwork ceiling, is most attractive. A maze of winding corridors and stairs leads to the atmospheric rooms in the older wing with their paneled walls, uneven floors, and plethora of four-poster beds (mostly queen-sized). I particularly enjoyed the Charles room with its large stone fireplace, Elizabeth for its third-floor isolation atop a narrow staircase, and Master, a spacious, paneled twin-bedded room with an adorable little parlor overlooking the garden. Avoid the possibility of getting lost in the maze of corridors and opt for easier-to-locate rooms in the Garden Wing with its new rooms made to look old. Less than a half-hour drive finds you in Brighton where seaside honky-tonk contrasts with the vivid spectacle of the onion domes of the Royal Pavilion, the Prince Regent's extravaganza of a home. Enjoy browsing in Brighton's Lanes where old fishermen's cottages are now antique and gift shops. *Directions:* From Gatwick airport take the M23/A23 to the B2115 signposted Cuckfield. In Cuckfield village, turn right into Ockenden Lane—the manor is at the end.

OCKENDEN MANOR
Manager: Adam Smith
Ockenden Lane
Cuckfield RH17 5LD, England
Tel: 01444 416111, Fax: 01444 415549
22 Rooms, Double: £183–£376
Open: all year, Credit cards: all major

Gravetye is a truly handsome Elizabethan manor house set in the most glorious of gardens. It is one of our favorite English country house hotels. You catch the spirit of the place as soon as you walk into the oak-paneled hall with its big fireplace and inviting armchairs. The lovely sitting room with its enormous stone fireplace has the same atmosphere of age-old welcome and comfort. Bedrooms are elegantly furnished with soft-toned fabrics, which contrast warmly with intricately carved wood paneling. Firescreens hide televisions and interesting books are close at hand. You will love the acres of gardens flourishing just as former owner William Robinson, who pioneered the natural look in English gardens, would have wished them to. His beloved kitchen garden has been restored and chef Mark Raffan puts its produce to good use. Other glorious English gardens within easy driving distance include Sissinghurst and Sheffield Park. Nearby is Standen, one of the finest Arts and Crafts houses, with furnishings by Morris and Benson. It's a very handy place to stay for both Glyndebourne and Gatwick airport. *Directions:* Exit the M23 at junction 10 onto the A264, signposted East Grinstead. After 2 miles, at the roundabout, take the B2028 (Haywards Heath and Brighton) straight through Turners Hill and watch for hotel signs on the left after another mile.

GRAVETYE MANOR
Owners: Andrew Russell & Mark Raffan
East Grinstead RH19 4LJ, England
Tel: 01342 810567, Fax: 01342 810080
18 Rooms, Double: £180–£350*
*Breakfast not included: £13–£18
*Service: 15%
Open: all year, Credit cards: all major
Relais & Châteaux

Sitting in acres of glorious gardens, Old Whyly is the most gracious of 17th-century manor houses and home to Sarah Burgoyne and her sons, a home they love to share with their guests. Sarah soon has guests feeling at home, encouraging them to relax in the beautiful drawing room, sit in the garden, swim in the pool, or take a peaceful walk through adjacent farms. Guests gravitate to the long pine table in the huge farmhouse kitchen where Sarah loves to talk to them—except when she is involved in one of the more complicated dinner dishes. Cooking is a passion for Sarah and it would be a shame to stay here and not enjoy dinner. Bedrooms are most attractive. Tulip offers the most spacious accommodation; French has blue toile wallpaper, drapes, and bedspread, and wisteria peeping in at the windows; Chinese has its large private bathroom across the hall. Old Whyly is perfect for opera fans as Glyndebourne is ten minutes away and hampers can be provided. Guests often visit Charleston Garden where the Bloomsbury set used to gather. Brighton is popular for its pavilion and interesting shops in the narrow lanes, while Nymans and Leonardslee are popular gardens. *Directions:* Take the A22 south from Uckfield past Halland for half a mile then take the first left off the large roundabout towards East Hoathly. After a quarter of a mile turn left into the drive by the post box. Where the drive divides into three, take the central gravel drive to Old Whyly.

OLD WHYLY
Owner: Sarah Burgoyne
East Hoathly BN8 6EL, England
Tel: 01825 840216
3 Rooms, Double: £90–£130
Open: all year, Credit cards: none

Ely has a fascinating history. The town got its name when St. Dunstan found monks living with women—he didn't approve of that sort of behavior and turned them into eels. The cathedral with its huge tower held up by eight 64-ft oak trunks is visible from miles away. A short walk from this lovely building you find Cathedral House, home to Jenny and Robin Farndale. Built in the mid-1800s, the house's unusual design has the side facing directly onto the street while its front faces a spacious walled garden. I particularly enjoyed the Oriel Suite with its brass bed, claw-foot tub, and separate sitting room. If you are traveling with a child, opt for the family suite, which has both a single-and a double-bedded room and a bathroom. Breakfast is enjoyed round the pine farmhouse dining-room table where you can plan your day's excursions. For dinner there are several restaurants and pubs within walking distance, the most famous and popular being the adjacent Old Fire Engine House. If you are interested in self-catering accommodation, ask about the Coach House tucked away behind Cathedral House. Ely is a perfect location for touring East Anglia —within an hour lie Cambridge, King's Lynn, Bury St. Edmunds, Wisbech, and Newmarket. *Directions:* Arriving in Ely, follow brown signs for the cathedral, pass the tourist office, and Cathedral House is the fourth house on your right. Park in front on the gravel.

CATHEDRAL HOUSE
Owners: Jenny & Robin Farndale
17 St. Mary's Street
Ely CB7 4ER, England
Tel: 01353 662124
3 Rooms, Double: £75–£100
1 Cottage: £500–£750 weekly
Open: all year, Credit cards: none

Legend has it that the French King John II was taken prisoner by the Black Prince and held captive here in 1356. Dating back to Jacobean times and substantially expanded thereafter, the house has been carefully restored by the Cunninghams, who have retained many of the original architectural features such as stone and inglenook fireplaces, stone mullioned windows with leaded lights, and heavy beams. Four bedrooms—Jacobean, Tudor, or Victorian—are available, all with either en-suite bathrooms and all comfortably furnished with a liberal mix of brass beds and antiques. A small family annex in the roof is linked to the Tudor room. Breakfast is served in the Jacobean dining room or on the terrace with Percy the peacock and views of the manicured lawn, lily pond, and the wild garden beyond with its rose walk. Guests are welcome to use the all-weather tennis court or swim in the pool. On gloomy days, retire to the Edwardian sitting room complete with snooker table or the quieter sitting room with its log fire. Four self-catering apartments are found in the barn. There are famous gardens galore nearby: just up the road is Scotney Castle, and Batemans, Great Dixter, Sissinghurst, Pashley Manor, and Merriments are all within a 30 minute drive. *Directions:* Go west off the A21 onto the A265 at Hurst Green. At the end of the village fork right (Burgh Hill) then turn right again into Sheep Street Lane. The house is 1 mile farther on the left.

KING JOHN'S LODGE
Owners: Jill & Richard Cunningham
Sheepstreet Lane
Etchingham TN19 7AZ, England
Tel: 01580 819232, Fax: 01580 819562
3 Rooms, Double: £90–£95
4 Apartments: £500–£1200 weekly
Minimum Stay Required: 2 nights
Closed: Christmas & New Year, Credit cards:

Surrounded by well-tended, arable farmland, Fulready Manor is a newly built Cotswold stone manor house and home to the Spencers, their King Charles spaniels, horses, sheep, and a breeding pair of swans on the two-acre lake. Ten years in the building, this was truly a family project. Daughter, Verity, provided the interior design. Mauveen and Michael's collection of original paintings, prints, antiques, and collectibles are featured throughout. All the stonework was individually hand-faced by local masons; the interior doors were rescued from old French railcars. Guests are welcomed with afternoon tea in the grand drawing room with its faux-painted paneling, comfortable sofas, and fireplace for cooler days. Upstairs, all three rooms come with en suite bathrooms. The Edwardian Room, resplendent in dark blue with wood paneling, has a miscellany of wartime caricatures and offers a four-poster. My favorite, the Tower Room, named for the octagonal sitting area adjacent to the bedroom with panoramic views, features a leather sleigh bed. The day begins with breakfast served in the Library (decorated with architectural prints) and finishes with chocolates, port and liqueurs in the drawing room. Ideally located as a base to explore nearby Stratford and the Cotswolds. *Directions:* From Stratford take A422 Banbury road to Pilerton Priors. Turn south on the B4551 to Halford and Fulready Manor is a half-mile down the hill on the left.

FULREADY MANOR
Owners: Mauveen & Michael Spencer
Ettington
Stratford-upon-Avon CV37 7PE, England
Tel: 01789 740152, Fax: 01789 740247
3 Rooms, Double: £126–£140
Open: all year, Credit cards: none

An ideal location for touring East Anglia, Fordham is within a half hour drive of Cambridge, Ely, Bury St., Edmunds, and Lavenham. It is just outside Newmarket, the horseracing capital of England, and no one is more passionate about all things equine than Malcolm Roper. He arranges and conducts day-long tours that take guests to early-morning gallop watching, around the trainers' yards, and visiting the studs (early booking essential). Back home Jan takes care of guests, always ready with a smile and a pot of tea. I especially liked the spacious twin-bedded room (beds can be zipped together) with its stripped-pine woodwork and furniture—its private bathroom is across the hall. Jan often rents it to families in conjunction with a small single-bedded room. A delightful double room has a tiny en suite shower room. For complete privacy, Jan has three simply furnished rooms (one en suite, two sharing a shower room)and a suite (bedroom and separate sitting room) in an adjacent converted barn. The first floor of the barn is a self-catering apartment for 4 to 6. There are excellent restaurants and pubs within walking distance. *Directions:* Fordham is on the A142 Newmarket to Ely Road. At the roundabout for the Fordham by-pass (A142) continue onto the B1102. Turn into Carter Street and Queensberry is on the left after half a mile.

QUEENSBERRY
Owners: Jan & Malcolm Roper
196 Carter Street
Fordham CB7 5JU, England
Tel & Fax: 01638 720916
6 Rooms, Double: £70–£95
1 Apartment: £165 daily
Open: all year, Credit cards: none

Fowey is one of Cornwall's most picturesque villages. Former fishermen's cottages and narrow streets step down the steep hillside to the river estuary where boats bob in the sheltered harbor. Sitting beside the water, The Marina Hotel was built in 1815 as a handsome townhouse on a residential street. It would be a shame to stay here and not have a bedroom with a view, the best being from rooms 4, 6 and 10 with French windows opening onto private balconies. At the top of the house, two lovely rooms capture the same outlook through little curved windows. Five rooms are found in Ashley house across the street. If you want to be beside the water, opt for the Focastle Suite, a wooden cabin on the lower patio with a nautical pine interior. While the bedroom and sitting room face the patio, French windows open to a private waterside terrace. Every table in the award-winning Restaurant Nathan Outlaw (named for the chef) looks out over the harbor and the menu always includes fish choices, such as turbot with leeks, mustard and brown shrimp. Guests often come to see the places where Fowey's most illustrious former resident, Daphne du Maurier, set her most famous novels. *Directions:* One mile after Lostwithiel (going south on A390) turn left onto B3269 to Fowey. Continue down into the narrow lanes of the village and turn right on the Esplanade. Park outside the hotel to unload, get parking directions, or use the hotel's valet parking.

THE MARINA HOTEL
Owner: Stephen Westwell
Manager: James Coggan
17 Esplanade
Fowey PL23 1HY, England
Tel: 01726 833315, Fax: 01726 832779
17 Rooms, Double: £160–£270
22 Apartments: £170–£300 daily
Open: Jan to mid-Dec, Credit cards: all major

The pretty village of Fowey, with its narrow lanes and little cottages cascading down the hillside to the harbor, is understandably a popular holiday spot. Besides its maritime history the town has literary associations with Daphne du Maurier, who lived and based her novels in the area. Right on the water in the center of town the Old Quay House was built in 1889 for the harbormaster. His boat dock is now the hotel's waterside terrace, offering a vista of hundreds of boats bobbing at anchor. The building has been a home for elderly seamen, but most recently Jane and Roy Carson have given the place a complete makeover, creating a beautiful boutique hotel. Bedrooms offer something to suit everyone from richly decorated rooms to those featuring softer beige tones. Several look out over the harbor, but without doubt rooms 6 and 12 offer the most spectacular views. Downstairs the Q restaurant is an excellent place to eat—the food is locally sourced and fish features prominently on the menu. There are spectacular walks along the coastal path. It's a perfect base for visiting the Eden Project, the Lost Gardens of Heligan and Llanhydrock House. *Directions:* Arriving in Fowey follow the one-way system down the narrow streets of the town. Go left past the church in the town center and the hotel is on your right next to Lloyds Bank. Stop in front, quickly unload bags and reception will give you a map and permit for parking 800 yards away.

■ ⚞ ⊟ ☎ @ W ¶ ▣ ⟁ ⚓ ⚑ ⚐ ⚘ ⚁ ⛴ ♞ ♘ ⛷ ❦

THE OLD QUAY HOUSE
Owners: Jane & Roy Carson
28 Fore Street
Fowey PL23 1AQ, England
Tel: 01726 833302, Fax: 01726 833668
12 Rooms, Double: £170–£300
Closed: Christmas, Credit cards: all major

The heart and soul of a successful country house hotel are its owners and at Stock Hill House Nita and Peter Hauser fill the bill perfectly, with the ebullient Nita presiding over the front of house and Peter being the chef. For over 20 years they have worked their magic on this delightful hotel. The result is a pleasing, eclectic decor and the mood is that of a luxurious private residence where you can stroll through the acres of garden to work up an appetite. At dinner vegetables from the garden and local Dorset produce are the order of the day, but remember to save room for one of Austrian-born Peter's decadent desserts. Bedrooms are delightful, and while I was particularly drawn to the opportunity to repose in the coach house in an ornate wrought-iron bed, which once belonged to a Spanish princess, I opted for the luxury of Room 4 in the main house. This lovely hotel is the perfect place for you to treat yourself to an extra-special getaway. If you are tempted to leave the grounds, you'll find the location ideal for visiting Sherbourne Abbey, Stourhead Gardens, Wells Cathedral, Glastonbury with its King Arthur connections, and the Saxon town of Shaftesbury. *Directions:* Leave the M3 at junction 8 and take the A303 towards Exeter for 54 miles, turning onto the B3081 for Gillingham and Shaftesbury. Stock Hill House is on your right after 3 miles.

STOCK HILL HOUSE
Owners: Nita & Peter Hauser
Gillingham SP8 5NR, England
Tel: 01747 823626, Fax: 01747 825628
9 Rooms, Double: £260–£320
Open: all year, Credit cards: MC, VS

A mile-long driveway meanders up from the picture-postcard village of Gittisham to this grand Elizabethan manor backed by ancient woodlands. The wow factor continues as you enter the Jacobean great hall with its massive open fireplace, oak paneling, imposing ancestral portraits and flagstone floor. There's a restored Georgian kitchen where private parties dine by candlelight. In a frescoed dining room you are treated to contemporary British cuisine with an emphasis on locally sourced produce. Bedrooms feature a variety of shapes and sizes, ranging from traditional principal bedrooms at the front of the house to smaller more contemporary rooms in the one-time servants' quarters. We were particularly impressed by the Linen Suite, the former Victorian laundry, and its contemporary decor in shades of cream and white with and large sash windows overlooking the walled garden. The piece de resistance, of the Linen Suite, is its 6-ft. diameter copper bathtub. It's just a short drive to the classic early Victorian resort of Sidmouth, a personal favorite, and Beer, a fishing village on a little bay. Nearby Honiton, a former lace-making center, is noted for its antique shops. *Directions:* Exit M5 at Junction 28, taking A373 to Honiton. At the T junction in town turn right, go straight at the roundabout and turn left at the BP/Budgen Garage towards Heathpark. From here follow brown hotel signs to Gittisham.

COMBE HOUSE
Owners: Ruth & Ken Hunt
Gittisham
Nr Exeter EX14 3AD, England
Tel: 01404 540400, Fax: 01404 46004
18 Rooms, Double: £175–£395
1 Cottage: £370–£395 daily
Open: all year, Credit cards: all major

With its acres of lovely gardens, grass tennis court, and heated swimming pool, Ennys is an idyllic, 17th-century manor house set deep in the Cornish countryside, 3 miles from St. Michael's Mount. You reach it along a private lane, and I timed my arrival perfectly—the kettle had just boiled, and I settled down for afternoon tea in the spacious country-pine kitchen. Polished flagstones line the hallway leading to the comfortable sitting room with its sofas drawn round the fire and mementos of Gill's extensive travels. Breakfast is the only meal served but Gill is happy to make reservations at excellent local inns and restaurants for dinner. Upstairs are three lovely bedrooms; one is a delectable four-poster, another has a king bed; and all have top-of-the-line bathrooms with "power showers". Families are welcome in the suites in the adjacent barn—bedrooms here are also delightfully appointed without bric-a-brac that can be so hazardous for children. Gill has three lovely self-catering cottages for longer stays. St. Michael's Mount is a "must visit." A delightful day trip involves taking a train to St. Ives to visit the Tate Gallery, which displays the work of 20th-century St. Ives artists. *Directions:* At Crowlas (4 miles before Penzance on the A30) take the A394 towards Helston and at the next roundabout turn left for Relubbus. Go through Goldsithney and St. Hilary, and when the Ennys' signpost is on the right, turn left and follow Trewhella Lane to the house.

ENNYS
Owner: Gill Charlton
St. Hilary
Goldsithney
Penzance TR20 9BZ, England
Tel: 01736 740262, Fax: 01736 740055
57 Rooms, Double: £90–£195
3 Cottages: £350–£1200 weekly
Minimum Stay Required: 2 night minimum
Open: mid-Mar to Nov 1, Credit cards: MC, VS

This cozy little hotel, tucked in a garden off the Ambleside to Grasmere road, has (like so many places hereabouts) associations with the poet William Wordsworth. He lived just down the road at Rydal Mount and bought White Moss House for his son whos descendents kept it until the 1930s. Now, it is owned by Susan and Peter Dixon who lavish their guests with a level of personal attention usually found at much fancier establishments. Peter's culinary talents shine in the delicious breakfasts he prepares that are served in the cottage-style dining room. The spacious Wordsworth lounge has a log fire on cooler days. When warmer the flower filled garden terrace or the benches dotted around the grounds are great places to relax. Bedrooms are on the smaller size, each accompanied by a snug, bath and shower room. Room 1, an attractive twin-bedded room with a ribbon-and-bow-motif running through the bedspread fabric, has a tiny shower room and small patio. Brockstone Cottage, a two-bedroom self-catering cottage, is nearby. For dinner guests are directed to nearby restaurants. You can fish on nearby Rydal Water and have free use of a local leisure club. Lakeland scenery is glorious whether you come in spring when the famous daffodils bloom, in summer with the crowds, or in autumn. You can stroll to Rydal Mount and Dove Cottage—Wordsworth's famous homes. *Directions:* White Moss House is on the A591 between Ambleside and Grasmere.

■ ♨ ⬜ ☎ @ W P 🖼 🏌 🚶 ⛵

WHITE MOSS HOUSE
Owners: Susan & Peter Dixon
Rydal Water
Grasmere LA22 9SE, England
Tel: 015394 35295, Fax: 015394 35516
5 Rooms, Double: £84–£114
1 Cottage: £590–£850 weekly*
* Breakfast not included with Cottage
Open: Mar to Dec, Credit cards: MC, VS

There are many good reasons to visit Leicestershire and this exceptional home at the edge of a peaceful village with many picturesque thatched cottages is one of them. Here old furniture is polished till it gleams, the windows sparkle, and everything is in apple-pie order. The evening sun streams into the drawing room where books on stately homes and castles invite browsing. Breakfast is served in a small dining room with a long trestle table. If there are several people for dinner, Raili (who grew up in Finland) sets the elegant table in the large dining room and serves a variety of meals using organic vegetables from her garden. The principal bedroom has en suite facilities, while the other guestrooms have either private bathrooms or shower rooms. Bedrooms have televisions and someone is always on hand to make a pot of tea. Nearby are a great many stately homes (Burghley House and Rockingham Castle, for instance), lots of antique shops, cathedrals at Ely and Peterborough, historic towns (Stamford and Uppingham), and ancient villages. *Directions:* From Uppingham take the A47 and turn left at East Norton for Hallaton. Drive through the village and The Old Rectory is next to the church.

THE OLD RECTORY
Owners: Raili & Tom Fraser
Hallaton
Market Harborough LE16 8TY, England
Tel & Fax: 01858 555350
5 Rooms, Double: £95
Open: all year, Credit cards: none

Near the center of England lies Oakham, the proud capital of England's smallest county, Rutland. Close by is Rutland Water where you drive onto a spit of land stretching out into the middle of the lake. At its end is the quiet village of Hambleton and a jewel of a hotel, Hambleton Hall. The staff are caring, anxious above all else to please. The motto over the front door echoes the relaxed, happy atmosphere: "Fay Ce Que Voudras" or "Do As You Please". I cannot imagine anyone leaving Hambleton Hall discontented. The garden tumbles towards the vast expanse of water with rolling hills as a backdrop and behind a wall is a sheltered, heated pool. The interior is decorated with great flair and made lovely with enormous flower arrangements. The drawing room with its large inviting windows provides glorious water views. In fine weather enjoy lunch and tea on the terrace. Delicious smells will tempt you to the award-winning restaurant. The bedrooms are adorable, the decorations varying from soft English pastels to the vibrant rich colors of India. If you want total privacy, opt for the luxurious two-bedroom croquet pavilion. Sightseeing covers shopping in Oakham and Stamford, visits to the country houses of Burghley and Belton, and trips to Cambridge and Lincoln. *Directions:* From the A1 take the A606 (Oakham road) through Empingham and Whitwell and turn left for Hambleton.

HAMBLETON HALL
Owners: Stefa & Tim Hart
Hambleton LE15 8TH, England
Tel: 01572 756991, Fax: 01572 724721
18 Rooms, Double: £205–£600*
*Service: 12.5
Minimum Stay Required: 2 nights on weekends
Open: all year, Credit cards: all major
Relais & Châteaux

Harrogate's Hotel du Vin has its origins in eight Georgian style townhouses built facing "The Stray", a 200-acre, green parkland in the center of the city. Conjoined and a hotel since the 1930s, it has been completely renovated to take its rightful place as a member of the Hotel du Vin's stylish group. From the moment you step through the front door, you realize that you have arrived somewhere very special. The comfy, old leather armchairs in the entrance hall contrast with the starkly modern elegance of the oak and stainless steel staircase curving up to the guest rooms; the open-plan bar with its hand-wrought, pewter-like stainless steel top and Cruvinet machine dispensing a variety of wines by the glass drawn directly from the cellar and the billiard table just off the wine cellars. The bustling, bistro-style restaurant features more than 600 bins of wine, each one carefully chosen to accentuate the hallmark cuisine. The rooms are contemporary in décor, and even the smallest double is more than ample; all are luxuriously appointed to fulfill the needs of the most exacting traveler. The two "attic" suites approach decadence with eight-foot beds, dual side-by-side soaking tubs, and massive walk through showers. You are just steps from the heart of Harrogate. *Directions:* From A1, take A59 into Harrogate. Follow signs for "town centre" to Prince of Wales roundabout. Take the third exit (West Park). The hotel is on the right after the church.

HOTEL DU VIN
Manager: Nick Lawson
Prospect Place
Harrogate HG1 1LB, England
Tel: 01423 856800, Fax: 01423 856801
48 Rooms, Double: £105–£395*
*Breakfast not included: £9.50–£13.50
Open: all year, Credit cards: all major

Hathersage is a typically picturesque Derbyshire village situated in the lovely Hope Valley. It is a place that has impressed many visitors over the years, the most famous being Charlotte Brontë who was said to be so taken with it that she based parts of her novel "Jane Eyre" on it. The George sits imposingly at one end of the main street that runs through the village. Parts of the hotel date back to the 14th century when it was an alehouse, but it wasn't until the 1770s that The George became an inn. The heart of the hotel is the large airy lounge divided into sitting nooks by lots of plush sofas with a library nook in an alcove and a bar occupying the front turret. The contemporary feel is carried into the restaurant by a series of low-ceilinged rooms with beams and exposed stone walls. Upstairs, the bedrooms have the same light and airy feel. While room 3 with its double four-poster bed and unusual round stained-glass window depicting St. George has lots of appeal, you may want to select a room with a larger bed. Hathersage is well placed for visiting the Peak District. *Directions:* Exit the M1 at junction 29 towards Baslow then take the A623 to the B6001 through Grindleford to Hathersage. At the junction with the main road The George faces you.

THE GEORGE
Manager: Philip Joseph
Hathersage S32 1BB, England
Tel: 01433 650436, Fax: 01433 650099
22 Rooms, Double: £130–£185
Open: all year, Credit cards: all major

Bordering the market square in the center of the village, this traditional old Yorkshire coaching inn, part of which dates back to Tudor times, has served travelers well for a couple of hundred years. More recently it has expanded into two old adjoining properties—a classic Georgian house and a black-and-white Tudor rectory. A wing of rooms has been added next to the lovely back garden with its tables and chairs for sunny days on the patio outside the bar. Bedrooms overlooking the marketplace have lots of old world charm. As might be expected, the modern rooms in the stone wing extending to the rear are identical in size, each with French doors that open to either a balcony or tiny patio. Toast your toes by the fire in the cozy little parlor, partake of a traditional afternoon tea in the tearoom and enjoy the conviviality of the bar before going in to dinner. Helmsley has interesting shops, an ancient market cross (market day Friday) and a Norman castle. The most popular places to visit are Rievaulx Abbey, York, Castle Howard, Robin Hood's Bay, Whitby, and the folk museum at Hutton-le-Hole. *Directions:* Helmsley is on the A170 midway between Thirsk and Pickering. The Black Swan faces the market square. Pull up in front to unload. The hotel has a large car park to the rear.

THE BLACK SWAN
Owner: Simon Rhatigan
Manager: Chris Falcus
Helmsley
York Y06 5BJ, England
Tel: 01439 770466, Fax: 01439 770174
45 Rooms, Double: £110–£200
Open: all year, Credit cards: all major

Just off Helmsley's main square lies the Feversham Arms & Verbenna Spa, an interesting mix of old and new that is a luxurious destination in its own right. A country comfortable public lounge has the obligatory fireplace for those cooler, damper, north Yorkshire interludes; smartly modern dining room features local produce and "real food" menus and a cozy bar. The luxurious spa offers a complete range of treatments and the outdoor heated pool adds to the chic surroundings. As might be expected of a property that has been expanded over the last hundred years, rooms come in a variety of shapes and sizes, out of the 33 bedrooms 22 are suites all of which have beautiful, large bathrooms with double ended deep soaking tubs and walk in showers. The suites surround the central courtyard with its flagstone patio areas and swimming pool. The majority are very spacious, furnished on a contemporary theme and provided with all the luxuries expected by the savvy traveler. Locally manufactured "mouseman" furniture is juxtaposed with modern art. Leave your car in the spacious underground parking garage and allow yourself to be pampered. *Directions:* From Thirsk take the A170 for 14 miles to Helmsley. Arriving at the top of the market square, turn left at the mini roundabout and go right past the church. Feversham Arms is on the right.

THE FEVERSHAM ARMS HOTEL & VERBENA SPA
Owner: Simon Rhatigan
Helmsley
York YO62 5AG, England
Tel: 01439 770766, Fax: 01439 770346
33 Rooms, Double: £150–£445
Minimum Stay Required: 2 nights on weekends
Open: all year, Credit cards: all major

The first thing you notice when you come through Woodhayes's front door is the portraits, huge paintings that sometimes stretch from floor to ceiling. Once you have made yourself at home in this friendly house, you may be inclined, as I was, to do a "who's who" of Noel's forbears, ascertaining how the congenial pictures in your room are related to all the others. This is no place for minimalists to stay—for in addition to hundreds of paintings the house is packed with fine antiques. Guests dine by candlelight around the polished dining-room table in what was at one time the home's kitchen—hence the flagstone floors and huge Inglenook fireplace, which now contains a wood-burning stove. The twin-bedded room at the front of the house has commanding views across the valley while the four-poster room overlooks the rose garden at the side of the house. Both have en suite bathrooms. A single bedroom has its private bathroom down the hall. Dumpdon Celtic hill fort rises behind the house and beyond lies the rolling green of the Blackdown Hills. Nearby Honiton is the historic center for lace making and a small museum chronicles the industry's history. A 20-minute drive brings you to the Victorian resort of Sidmouth and Beer, a fishing village in a little bay. *Directions:* Woodhayes is prominently visible on high ground 1½ miles northeast of Honiton. Take the Dunkeswell road and take the first turn right. Woodhayes's drive is on the left.

WOODHAYES
Owners: Christy & Noel Page-Turner
Honiton EX14 4TP, England
Tel & Fax: 01404 42011
3 Rooms, Double: £90
Open: all year, Credit cards: MC, VS

Formerly a cottage and barn dating back to the late 1800s, Underleigh House is tucked away at the end of a quiet Derbyshire lane in the heart of walking country. Now the home of Vivienne and Philip Taylor, it has been transformed to provide six nicely furnished, comfortable bedrooms, all with en suite shower or bath. My favorite was the Thornhill Suite with a small bedroom and sitting room and a grand high-ceilinged bathroom. The spacious residents' lounge downstairs is fully equipped with comfortable chairs, games, books, and a cozy wood stove for those occasional rainy days. On sunny days and summer evenings, relax outside on the terrace where countryside views and sounds abound. Breakfasts are a special treat, a generous buffet includes Philip's home- made muesli, fruit compotes and yogurt; Derbyshire oatcakes with eggs and tomatoes or the full English with sausage and black pudding from the local butcher; and to finish toast and home-made preserves. All this is enjoyed at a large table in the dining room with its flagstone floor and exposed beams. There are numerous excellent restaurants and pubs in Hope, Hathersage, and Castleton. From the ruins of the castle at Castleton to the opulence of Chatsworth House, this is an interesting area to explore. *Directions:* Leave Sheffield west on the A625 and connect with the A6187 to the village of Hope. Turn right opposite the church onto Edale Road and fork left to Underleigh House after 1 mile.

UNDERLEIGH HOUSE
Owners: Vivienne & Philip Taylor
Off Edale Road
Hope S33 6RF, England
Tel: 01433 621372, Fax: 01433 621324
5 Rooms, Double: £85–£105
Open: Feb to Dec, Credit cards: MC, VS

Langshott Manor is a beautiful Elizabethan house with 3 acres of gorgeous gardens and ponds, which, with just 22 bedrooms in the main house and adjacent mews wings, still retains the intimate feeling of a home. The interior more than exceeds the promise of the historic exterior: at every turn you admire low-ceilinged, beamed rooms, polished-oak paneling, and stained-glass windows with motifs of flowers in bloom and birds in flight. The Mulberry Restaurant is an especially spacious room overlooking a small lake and lovely gardens. Bedrooms are an absolute delight. I especially enjoyed Leeds with its four-poster bedroom and whimsical four-poster bath and Lewes, a most spacious room whose windows frame the rose garden. Two smaller bedrooms (Hever and Wakehurst) are found on the ground floor. Equally lovely rooms are found across the gardens in the former stables, now a luxurious mews offering spacious, bright rooms with king-sized beds and comfortable seating areas. The manor is just 2½ miles from Gatwick airport (not on the flight path) and offers complimentary transfer to the airport on departure. Churchill's home, Chartwell, and Brighton are amongst the most popular visitor attractions. *Directions:* From Gatwick take the A23 north (Redhill) for 2½ miles to the large roundabout with a garage in the middle and bordered by the Chequers pub. Take the Ladbroke Road exit from the roundabout and follow the lane to the hotel on the right.

LANGSHOTT MANOR
Owners: Deborah & Peter Hinchcliffe
Manager: Mathew Callard
Horley RH6 9LN, England
Tel: 01293 786680, Fax: 01293 783905
22 Rooms, Double: £130–£290
Open: all year, Credit cards: all major

Originally a classic hall house dating back to the early fifteenth century, Wilton House is to be found on the High Street in the bustling market town of Hungerford, known for its many antique shops. The flagstone-floored entry hall with its exposed timbers sets the tone for this lovely old house, now home to Deborah and Jonathan Welfare and their friendly black Labradors. Two tastefully decorated, comfortable, double guest rooms are to be found upstairs past the antique rocking horse, both with bathrooms en suite, one with a shower. Both overlook the quintessentially English garden with its brickwork pathways, lawns and flowerbeds to the rear of the house. Breakfast is served next to the fireplace in the wood-paneled dining room downstairs. Conveniently located midway between Heathrow and the Cotswolds, and five minutes walk from the local train station with regular service into London. *Directions:* Exit the M4 at Junction 14 and take the A338 south to Hungerford. After three miles, turn right onto the A4, then left at The Bear Hotel. Over the canal and into the High Street, Wilton house is on your right, 200 yards beyond the town hall with its clock tower.

WILTON HOUSE
Owners: Deborah & Jonathan Welfare
33 High Street
Hungerford RG17 0NF, England
Tel: 01488 684228, Fax: 01488 685037
2 Rooms, Double: £78–£84
Closed: Christmas, Credit cards: none

Set amidst the gently rolling, verdant Cheshire countryside, the plain white façade belies the history that lies within. In the spacious lounge hall, log fire blazing in the brick-faced open fireplace, one's attention is immediately drawn to the magnificent hand-carved Elizabethan staircase. Made of "armada oak" (timber salvaged from Spanish vessels defeated by the Royal Navy), it reaches up two floors to the bedrooms above. The original building dates back to the 13th century and has been tastefully expanded ever since. The comfortable drawing room, completed in 1780, has views across the expansive gardens. The dining room, furnished entirely with family antiques, is in the oldest part of the house and includes a "diamond-paned" leper window and ancient fireplace complete with stone lintel. Retaining many of the old architectural features, bedrooms have been refurbished and redecorated to include modern creature comforts and en suite facilities. They all share spectacular views of the surrounding countryside. Just 7 miles away, Chester can be reached by foot along the bridal path of the Shropshire Union Canal. *Directions:* Take A41 from Chester towards Whitchurch. Turn 4th left after the roundabout signpost, Waverton and Huxley. Continue straight over crossroads and follow the canal. 1.4 miles after the humpback bridge, turn right into the hall drive.

HIGHER HUXLEY HALL
Owners: Pauline & Jeremy Marks
Huxley CH3 9BZ, England
Tel: 01829 781484
5 Rooms, Double: £90
Minimum Stay Required: 2 nights on holidays
Open: all year, Credit cards: all major

The Faulkners (thought to be a derivative of "falconers") started out as a Wealden Hall House in the 15th century. The second-floor bedrooms were incorporated some 200 years later and feature numerous exposed beams. The two single rooms share a private bathroom while the double has its own facilities and also expansive views over the grounds and garden. Home to the Rigby family the house showcases Celia's antiques and a fascinating array of collectibles: locks, hats, cane baskets, galvanized buckets, bread boards, and carved wooden decoys, to mention but a few. Set in 5 acres of meadowlands complete with paddock, ponds, and gardens, guests are free to wander and relax in the tranquil surroundings. Take a seat in a sunny corner of the walled garden or curl up in front of the stove in the drawing room. Breakfast in the dining room is the only meal served. The seaside town of Brighton with its extravaganza of a Royal Pavilion and narrow, twisting lanes full of antique shops is a great attraction and the famous opera house at Glyndebourne is a ten-minute drive away. *Directions:* Heading north on the A26, approximately 4 miles north of Lewes take the turnoff signposted Isfield just after the Old Ship Inn. Follow the road into the village, make a left turn over the old railway crossing, and The Faulkners is approximately 1 mile farther, on the right-hand side at the second bend.

THE FAULKNERS
Owner: Celia Rigby
Isfield TN22 5XG, England
Tel: 01825 750344
3 Rooms, Double: £80–£85
Closed: Christmas & New Year, Credit cards: none

No need to request a room with a view at Nonsuch House. Every room offers a spectacular panorama of the sheltered harbor of Dartmouth with its castle, houses stepped down the wooded hillside to the river, and yachts tugging at their moorings. After a day of sightseeing, enjoy tea by the fire, in the plant-filled conservatory or on the terrace on warm days. Enjoy the same spectacular views of the activity in the harbor as you enjoy a three course evening meal—Kit posts the menu on the board and offers a choice in each of the three courses (not Tue, Wed or Sat). You are welcome to bring a bottle of wine to accompany your meal. Bedrooms, which come with a choice of queen, king, or twin beds, are absolutely delightful and each is accompanied by an immaculate modern bathroom. Fun daytrips include: taking a ferry up to Totnes, taking a steam train to Paignton, visiting the nearby Coleton Fishacre gardens (of D'Oyley Carte fame), and exploring Greenway (of Agatha Christie fame). You can make a day trip to the Eden Project or stick close to home walking the coastal path or taking the ferry to Dartmouth for dinner on the nights that Kit does not cook. *Directions:* Two miles before Brixham on the A3022 take the A379. After 2 miles fork left onto the B3205 for Kingswear, go onto the one-way system through the woods, and take the first left up Higher Contour Road. Go down Ridley Hill and Nonsuch House is on the seaward side at the hairpin bend.

NONSUCH HOUSE
Owners: Kit & Penny Noble
Church Hill
Kingswear
Dartmouth TQ6 0BX, England
Tel: 01803 752829, Fax: 01803 752357
4 Rooms, Double: £105–£145
Minimum Stay Required: 2 nights on weekends
Open: all year, Credit cards: MC, VS

The magnificent scenery of the Lake District, the Yorkshire Dales and Hadrian's Wall are all within easy driving distance of Hipping Hall. Contemporary decor sits very nicely within this three-hundred-year-old, wisteria-clad house. Enjoy the traditional sitting room, relax in the bar with its red leather armchairs, and dine in the great hall with its soaring beamed ceiling and minstrels gallery. Feast on chef Jason Birkbeck's modern interpretation of traditional British fare with its origins in Yorkshire, Lancashire, and Cumbria—much of the fresh produce comes from a nearby farm. A conservatory connects the main house to the great hall and in warm weather tables and chairs are set up outside. Upstairs the bedrooms are decked out in pale shades of cream and white. Bathrooms come with power showers; some have deep soaking tubs, all have lots of fluffy white towels and Kew Gardens toiletries. Room 2 has exposed beams, a limestone bathroom and views of the garden. Room 6 is the largest with a separate little sitting area, and its garden-view bathroom has a big whirlpool bath. Three bedrooms are found in the adjacent cottage where we particularly like room 7 with its sitting room downstairs and a spiral staircase leading to the bedroom above. Country walks abound. *Directions:* Leave the M6 at junction 36 and follow the A65 through Kirkby Lonsdale towards Skipton. Hipping Hall is on the left, 3 miles after Kirkby Lonsdale.

HIPPING HALL
Owner: Andrew Wildsmith
Kirkby Lonsdale
Cowan Bridge LA6 2JJ, England
Tel: 01524 271187
9 Rooms, Double: £160–£265
Closed: Jan, Credit cards: all major

At the Sign of the Angel is a black-and-white timbered inn at the heart of the lovely National Trust Village of Lacock. This 15th-century wool merchant's house is easy to spot as it contrasts strikingly with the neighboring stone buildings. Heavy old beams, low ceilings, and crooked walls are the order of the day at this old inn. Three delightful little dining rooms have their candlelit tables set before blazing fires for dinner. Choose from the set dinner menu or an a la carte featuring British specialties such as steak and kidney pie, Welsh rack of Lamb and Scottish salmon, with sticky toffee pudding and strawberries, meringues and clotted cream desserts (vegetarian fare available). Guests have a spacious paneled sitting room—upstairs. What we thought was a secret passage turned out to be the access to room 4 with its high beamed ceiling. Room 3 overlooking the front street, the most spacious, has 5' doorways to both the bedroom and the bathroom. We loved the coziness of our four-poster bedroom overlooking the garden (room 2). If you are If you are looking for more space for larger luggage opt for rooms in the cottage across the garden where room 11 is the prize, it has a private entrance and lots of room. Lacock is just 12 miles from Bath. *Directions:* If you are arriving from London, exit the M4 at junction 17 and take the A350 Melksham road south to Lacock.

AT THE SIGN OF THE ANGEL
Owners: Lorna & George Hardy
Church Street
Lacock SN15 2LB, England
Tel: 01249 730230, Fax: 01249 730527
11 Rooms, Double: £120–£145
Closed: last week of Dec, Credit cards: all major

The village of Lastingham is unhurried and peaceful, an oasis of green surrounded by the rugged, untamed beauty of the North York Moors National Park. Lastingham Grange preserves a 1950s style—everything is in apple-pie order, with such things as flowery wallpapers, and patterned carpets giving an old-fashioned air. I love the long lounge crowded with intimate groupings of sofas and chairs where in the morning the smell of furniture polish mixes with fresh-brewed coffee as you enjoy your morning coffee and homemade biscuits. The charm of the house extends outside where a broad terrace leads to the rose garden and acres of less formal gardens, which give way to fields and the distant moor. Guests of all ages and their dogs are welcome—there are listening devices for babies and a large adventure playground tucked beyond the formal garden where older children can play. The village church dates back to 1078 when a group of monks built a crypt to house the sacred remains of St. Cedd, which now remains a church beneath a church. Thirty miles distant lies medieval York and, closer at hand, narrow roads lead you to the coast with its fishing villages and long sandy beaches. *Directions:* Take the A170 from Thirsk towards Pickering. Just after Kirbymoorside turn left to Hutton-le-Hole where you turn right and cross the moor to Lastingham. The hotel is on your left in the village.

LASTINGHAM GRANGE
Owners: Jane, Bertie & Tom Wood
Lastingham
North Yorkshire
Lastingham Y062 6TH, England
Tel: 01751 417345, Fax: 01751 417358
12 Rooms, Double: £125–£210
1 Cottage: £385 weekly
Closed: Dec to Feb, Credit cards: MC, VS

Lavenham with its lovely timbered buildings, ancient Guildhall, and spectacular church is the most attractive village in Suffolk. The Great House on the corner of the market square, a 15th-century building with an imposing 18th-century façade, houses a lovely French restaurant-with-rooms run by Martine and Regis Crepy. Dinner is served in the oak-beamed dining room where up to the moment modern décor is married with exposed beams and an open brick fireplace. From Tuesday to Friday a particularly good value for money fixed-price menu is offered. On Saturday you dine from the à-la-carte menu. The restaurant is closed on Sunday and Monday. In summer you can dine al fresco in the flower-filled courtyard. Four of the large bedrooms have a lounge or a sitting area; all are stylishly decorated with oversize headboards, striking pieces of furniture and modern art from local artists. The en suite bathrooms are state of the art. Enjoy the village in the peace and quiet of the evening after the throng of daytime summer visitors has departed. Next door, Little Hall is furnished in early-19th-century style and is open as a museum. Farther afield are other historic villages such as Kersey and Long Melford, and Constable's Flatford Mill. *Directions:* Lavenham is on the A1141 between Bury St. Edmunds and Hadleigh.

LAVENHAM GREAT HOUSE & RESTAURANT
Owners: Martine & Regis Crepy
Market Place
Lavenham CO10 9QZ, England
Tel: 01787 247431, Fax: 01787 248007
5 Rooms, Double: £90–£190*
*Breakfast not included: £8.50–£12.50
Closed: Jan, Credit cards: MC, VS

I could spend hours sitting in Lavenham Priory's old Great Hall just soaking up the atmosphere of this impressive Elizabethan merchant's home which began life in the 13th century as a Benedictine priory. It's an absolutely superb room with its stone-flagged floor, huge sofas drawn round the massive inglenook fireplace, and beams patterning the simple white walls rising to the rafters. Bedrooms enjoy the same airy spaciousness and are furnished to utter perfection. Whether you choose the Great Chamber with its ornately draped bed; the Painted Chamber with its four-poster bed and Elizabethan wall paintings; or the snugger quarters of the twin-bedded Garden Chamber, you will be completely charmed by your room. Breakfast is the only meal served but there is no shortage of places to walk to for dinner. Because of the popularity of this exceptional home it is advisable to make reservations well in advance. Lavenham, in Tudor times one of England's wealthiest towns, is now a picturesque village with leaning timbered houses lining its streets and continuing into its market square where the Guildhall presents displays of local history and the medieval wool industry. *Directions:* Arriving in Lavenham, turn down the side of The Swan into Water Street, then go right after 50 yards into the private drive and Priory's car park.

LAVENHAM PRIORY
Owners: Gilli & Tim Pitt
Water Street
Lavenham CO10 9RW, England
Tel: 01787 247404, Fax: 01787 248472
6 Rooms, Double: £100–£165
Closed: Christmas & New Year, Credit cards: MC, VS

Hall End is an exquisitely decorated, quintessentially Georgian country house set in several acres of gardens and equestrian estate. Angela and Hugh really know how to make guests feel welcome, relaxed and at home. Guests have full run of the house—conservatory, drawing room, TV room, library, and formal dining room. Up the main staircase two beautifully decorated country house bedrooms have enviable bathrooms. he front bedroom is the larger and features a luxurious modern bathroom with double washbasins and separate shower and tub. The bathroom for the equally lovely but slightly smaller four-poster room is equipped with a shower. The third bedroom has its own private entrance and is reached via a spiral staircase off the conservatory. It has views on three sides, a double bed, sofa bed and bathroom with shower. Breakfast is served on a large circular table in the breakfast room off the designer kitchen, which is worth a visit in its own right. On warm days guests eat breakfast in the conservatory or on the patio next to the outdoor pool. Angela will give you with ideas on where to go and what to see that will keep you busy for a week. *Directions:* From Ledbury take the A449 Ross-on-Wye road to Much Marcle. Turn right between garage and stores/post office. After 300 yards, turn right at sign for Rushall and Kynaston. Follow this lane for 2.5 miles and Hall End is on your left.

HALL END
Owners: Angela & Hugh Jefferson
Ledbury
Kynaston HR8 2PD, England
Tel: 01531 670225, Fax: 01531 670747
3 Rooms, Double: £95–£120
Closed: Christmas & New Year, Credit cards: none

As you walk directly into the oak-paneled hall, you catch the spirit of this lovely house with its enormous stone fireplace, ornate stone-mullioned windows, and plump sofas enticing you to sit and relax. The dark-oak paneling, carvings, ornate plasterwork ceilings, family portraits and Jacobean furniture are the grand embellishments added by Lewtrenchard Manor's most famous owner, the Reverend Sabine Baring Gould, composer of many well-known hymns. Speculation has it that George Bernard Shaw based Pygmalion on the Reverend and his wife Grace. An illiterate Yorkshire mill girl when they first met, Gould sent her away to be educated before they married. His portrait hangs in the front hall, Grace's is in the back dining room. Upstairs the lovely bedrooms are all different, with the most popular being those off the broad upstairs hallway. The Bridal Tower occupies a separate turret in the garden. Within an easy drive are Castle Drogo, a fanciful Lutyens house, the Lost Gardens of Helligan, the Eden Project, Lydford Gorge, Dartington Glass, wild Dartmoor, and the north and south coasts of Devon. *Directions:* From Exeter (the M5) take the A30 for Okehampton and Bodmin and after 25 miles take the A386 slip road off the highway. Immediately turn right and then left for Bridestowe and Lewdown. After 6 miles just after The Blue Lion, on the right, turn left and Lewtrenchard Manor is on your left in ¾ mile.

LEWTRENCHARD MANOR
Owner: Von Essen Hotels
Manager: Jason Hornbuckle
Lewdown EX20 4PN, England
Tel: 01566 783222, Fax: 01566 783332
14 Rooms, Double: £155–£445
Open: all year, Credit cards: all major

The Arundell Arms is a traditional fishing inn that provides its guests the opportunity to fish for salmon, trout, and sea trout in miles of river and a 3-acre lake. Owner Anne Voss-Bark, an expert fisherwoman, ably assisted by fly-fishing instructors and guides David Pilkington and Tim Smith, offers a variety of residential fishing courses. Fisherfolk gather in the morning in the hotel garden's 250-year-old cock pit (a long-since retired cock-fighting arena), now the rod-and-tackle room. In the evening the catch of the day is displayed on a silver platter on the hall table. The traditional fishing inn has been extended over the years to encompass the village assembly rooms—now the elegant, tall-ceilinged dining room where you enjoy the most delectable of dinners—and the courthouse and jail—now the adjacent village pub. Cozy bedrooms, all but five of which face the garden, are found in a converted stable block and the main house. Non-fisherfolk can enjoy walking, riding, golf, and, of course, traditional cream teas. Pheasant and snipe shooting are offered in the winter. Sightseers head for Dartmoor and the north Cornish coast with the ruins of Tintagel Castle and the ancient fishing villages of Boscastle and Port Isaac. *Directions:* Exit the M5 at Exeter and take the A30 (signposted Bodmin) for about 40 miles to the Lifton Village exit. Once off the dual carriageway turn right for Lifton and the hotel is on your left in less than a mile.

ARUNDELL ARMS
Owner: Anne Voss–Bark
General Manager: James Storey
Lifton PL16 0AA, England
Tel: 01566 784666, Fax: 01566 784494
21 Rooms, Double: £170–£195
Closed: Christmas, Credit cards: all major

Tucked in an unspoilt valley high above the hustle and bustle of the well-known Lake District tourist routes, this traditional pub lies surrounded by the ruggedly beautiful Lakeland scenery. Built of local slate in 1872 as a resting place for travelers, the hostelry is still a base for tourists, many of whom come here for the walking. They gather by the bar, the sound of their hiking boots echoing against the slate floor, poring over maps and discussing the day's activities. By contrast, the carpeted and curtained dining room and lounge with its comfy chairs seem very sedate. The Stephenson family pride themselves on the quality of their food and offer home-cooked fare served in the dining room or the bar—I was pleased to see a selection of vegetarian dishes, as well as beef-and-ale pie and Cumberland sausages on the menu. Bedrooms maintain the character of a 19th-century inn with those at the front enjoying superlative countryside views—I particularly liked room 3. For travelers who enjoy tastefully decorated, country-style, bedrooms with modern bathrooms, the Three Shires fits the bill. Just a few miles away are some of the Lake District's most popular villages: Hawkshead (home of Beatrix Potter), Ambleside, Coniston, and Grasmere. *Directions:* From Ambleside, take A593 (Coniston Road), cross Skelwith Bridge, and take the first right, signposted The Langdales and Wrynose Pass. Take the first left to Little Langdale, the Three Shires Inn is on the right.

THREE SHIRES INN
Owners: Elaine, Jane & Ian Stephenson
Little Langdale
Ambleside LA22 9NZ, England
Tel: 015394 37215, Fax: 015394 37127
10 Rooms, Double: £80–£110
1 Cottage: £400–£575 weekly
Closed: Jan, Credit cards: MC, VS

From the front, Wood Hall appears to be a substantial, classic Georgian home, but step round the back and you discover beams and plasterwork, for the Georgian frontage is a façade placed on a 1480 Tudor home. A Victorian owner made his contribution to the house in the 1840s when he added tall windows that flood the entire house with light. This blend of architectural periods gives Susan and Patrick Nisbett's home great charm. While Patrick has the interesting occupation of designing church vestments, Susan takes care of her guests, the family, and the pets. The building is large enough to give guests their own "end" of the house where a vast dining room with a polished table sitting center stage in the tall bay window doubles is the guests' breakfast room. A broad staircase leads up to the bedrooms. The very pretty queen-bedded room has a shower, while the lovely twin-bedded room has a bath. Both are large enough to accommodate seating areas where you can relax or watch TV. With advanced notice Susan may provide dinner though you'll find that there is no shortage of excellent eating places nearby, among them The Swan at Monks Eleigh or The Red Rose at Lindsey. Just up the road lies Lavenham with its many leaning timbered houses. *Directions:* Take the B115 from Sudbury towards Lavenham for 3½ miles. Turn right to Little Waldingfield and the house is on the left 200 yards beyond The Swan pub.

WOOD HALL
Owners: Susan & Patrick Nisbett
Little Waldingfield CO10 0SY, England
Tel: 01787 247362
2 Rooms, Double: £85–£90
Closed: Christmas through New Year
Credit cards: MC, VS

Originally a monastery with cellars dating back to the 14th century, this house was confiscated from a past owner by Henry VIII. More recently a working farmhouse, it has now been purchased and renovated by owners Sybil and Robert Gisby, no newcomers to the bed and breakfast business. Upstairs are two spacious bedrooms, each with its own thoroughly modern and luxurious bathroom en suite, as well as expansive views across the surrounding countryside. My particular favorite features an enormous crimson soaking tub. Downstairs, guests can relax in the sitting room with its comfortable sofas, inglenook fireplace equipped with wood-burning stove, and a plentiful supply of reading matter. A window seat provides views of the front garden. Breakfast is served farmhouse-style in the kitchen or in the conservatory, which is shaded by an impressive Black Hamburg grapevine or, weather permitting, outside on the patio next to the decorative fishpond. Lower and Upper Swell date back to Roman times, as evidenced by the coins found when Lower Swell's church was being restored. Exploring Cotswold villages is a popular pastime, with Bourton-on-the-Water, Stow-on-the-Wold, Chipping Campden, and Broadway being popular destinations. *Directions:* From the A429 at Stow-on-the-Wold take the B4068 signposted to Lower Swell. Turn left into a private driveway just before the Golden Globe Inn.

RECTORY FARMHOUSE
Owners: Sybil & Robert Gisby
Lower Swell
Cheltenham GL54 1LH, England
Tel: 01451 832351
2 Rooms, Double: £93–£96
Closed: Christmas & New Year, Credit cards: none

Ludlow is an absolutely charming town of cobblestone streets rising from the River Teme to its Norman castle. The most delightful street in town is Lower Broad Street, whose architecture runs the gamut from Tudor through Georgian to Victorian. Half way up the street you find Bromley Court, three absolutely adorable little Tudor cottages forming a secluded haven round a small, walled garden. Each cottage has a beamed sitting room, adorable bedroom, top-of-the-line bathroom, and breakfast bar with stocked refrigerator for your "local to Ludlow" produce Continental breakfast. The owner Philip is a mine of information on what to see and where to go locally—he can keep you busy for a week. They have a comprehensive list ogf information of the fine restaurants and bistro's in and around Ludlow, many of which need booking in advance. Explore the immense Norman castle and wander the lanes with their many book and antique shops. *Directions:* From the south, fork left off the A49 onto the B4361, signposted Ludlow south and Richards Castle. Cross the river and go straight into Lower Broad Street. Park on the right near the red mailbox. Parking is on the street.

BROMLEY COURT B&B
Owner: Maggie Wright
Lower Broad Street
Ludlow SY8 1PQ, England
Tel: 01584 876996
3 Cottages: £75–£125
Open: all year, Credit cards: all major

Assuredly one of the most beguiling "restaurant with rooms" that we have in our guides, Mr Underhill's combines an idyllic setting overlooking the River Teme, hunkered down beneath the imposing walls of Ludlow castle, and cuisine that has established its reputation amongst the highest in the country. With fine cuisine, a constantly changing and innovative menu, a carefully chosen wine list, and attentive service in relaxed, comfortable surroundings, clearly dining is the focal point. The dining room offers views across the river and the opportunity to spot herons, kingfishers, assorted wildfowl, and otters in the protected freedom of their own domain. The guestrooms are all comfortably furnished and decorated to very high standards with handmade beds (two in maple, two in oak and two in cherry), crisp linens, and soft, fluffy down comforters. All have gleaming, modern bathrooms. Our favorite room was, without a doubt, the suite that is found across the garden in the misleadingly named "shed"—stylishly modern, its expansive interior handcrafted from blond oak, a magnificent ensuite bathroom, and remotely operated drapes that allow you to savor the river view without leaving the enormously comfortable bed. Doze off and awaken to the sound of water in the old mill race. A foodie haven in a very special location. *Directions:* Located in Ludlow below the castle on the banks of the River Teme.

MR UNDERHILLS
Owners: Judy & Chris Bradley
Dinham
Ludlow SY8 1EH, England
Tel: 01584 874431
84 Rooms, Double: £145–£270
Open: all year, Credit cards: all major

Set just off the market place across from the historic church, the Spread Eagle dates back to 1430 and has been welcoming guests ever since. Now completely renovated and restored, the hotel retains a wealth of period architecture. Several of the premier "feature" bedrooms located in the older parts of the building are named after prior patrons such as H. G. Wells, Hilaire Belloc, and even Queen Elizabeth I. Our favorites were Egremont, a most spacious room, with its very tall four-poster bed, and the elegantly panelled White Room, both with large, well-appointed bathrooms. Other smaller but no less comfortable rooms are in a modern wing sympathetically designed to meld with its older surroundings. Meals are served in the dining room with its Flemish stained glass windows, massive open fireplace, and Christmas puddings hanging from the beams. Enjoy a quiet pre-dinner drink by the fire in the classically English bar or indulge yourself with a special treatment in the impressive on-site health spa, exercise in the gym, or relax in the magnificent indoor pool. This very attractive hotel makes a good base for visiting Chichester, Fishbourne Roman palace, Petworth House, and the Weald and Downland open-air museum. *Directions:* From the M25 take the A3 south towards Portsmouth, exit at Milford, and take the A286 to Midhurst. The Spread Eagle sits by the market square in the old part of town.

SPREAD EAGLE HOTEL
Manager: Edward James
South Street
Midhurst GU29 9NH, England
Tel: 01730 816911, Fax: 01730 815668
39 Rooms, Double: £180–£405
Open: all year, Credit cards: all major

This peaceful little corner of Norfolk boasts miles of flat sandy and shingle beaches backed by salt marshes lined with quaint villages of gray-flint houses trimmed with red brick. One of these villages is Morston with its pub, 13th-century church, and Morston Hall. Fortunately for visitors, Galton (the masterful chef) and Tracy Blackiston opened Morston Hall as a small country house hotel. Being seduced by Galton's exquisite dinners is a huge part of your stay here—fortunately, there are plenty of opportunities for exercise, so you can afford to repeat the divine experience. Bedrooms and suites are extremely large, beautifully decorated, and accompanied by sparkling new bathrooms. Birdwatchers will find nearby marshes a paradise. Guests often take a boat from Morston's little quay to visit the seal sanctuary at Blakeney Point. Nearby Holkham Hall, an imposing Palladian mansion, contains grand paintings and items of bygone days. Blickling Hall is elegantly furnished. *Directions:* Morston Hall is situated on the A149 King's Lynn to Cromer road between Wells-next-the-Sea and Cley-next-the-Sea.

MORSTON HALL
Owners: Tracy & Galton Blackiston
Morston NR25 7AA, England
Tel: 01263 741041, Fax: 01263 740419
13 Rooms, Double: £270–£320*
*Includes dinner, bed & breakfast
Closed: Jan, Credit cards: all major

Mousehole (pronounced Mowzel) is a picture-postcard Cornish fishing village full of little cottages. Narrow streets surround its sheltered, boat-filled harbor making it a quaint spot popular with artists. Just beyond the harbor you find the Old Coastguard Hotel occupying, as the name suggests, the one-time headquarters of the coastguard. Built in 1903 the property is now a comfortable modern hotel. Coastal views abound across a broad expanse of a sub-tropical garden. With twelve of the fourteen bedrooms featuring sea views, we recommend you request one with a terrace or balcony—all the better for enjoying those balmy summer evenings. Rooms are generally not large and, as expected in an old building, several that we saw had unusual configurations. The restaurant and sun lounge also share magnificent views across the bay. Food is locally sourced and there are always several fish choices on the menu. Enjoy the swimming hole on the rocky shore or walk the coastal footpath to explore both faces of this most southerly peninsula. The north coast is pounded by wild Atlantic rollers and the south is more protected. Travel to the artists' colony of St Ives to visit The Tate museum and St Michaels Mount, an isle in Mount's Bay linked to the mainland by a causeway. *Directions:* Follow the A30 to Penzance and then signposts to Mousehole. The hotel is on your left as you enter the village. Park in the hotel's car park or the large public car park next door.

THE OLD COASTGUARD
Manager: Neil Slade
Mousehole
Penzance TR19 6PR, England
Tel: 01736 731222, Fax: 01736 731720
15 Rooms, Double: £120–£210
Open: all year, Credit cards: MC, VS

In her younger years, Beatrix Potter used to visit Ees Wyke House with her family. Now it is a pleasant hotel run by Margaret and Richard Lee, who have painted and decorated the house from top to bottom in a comfortable style. Richard cooks to order and his dinner menu always offers choices of starter, main course, and dessert. Dinner is served in the large dining room with glorious views across the countryside. The bedrooms have tall windows framing gorgeous countryside views and many overlook nearby Esthwaite Water. Tucked under the eaves, two airy, spacious, attic bedrooms have super views. One has a bathroom en suite, while the other has a private bath just next door. The other bedrooms also have a mix of en suite and adjacent bathroom arrangements. When the hotel is full, guests may be offered the smallest bedroom, on the ground floor, which is usually reserved for visitors who have difficulty with stairs and has a garden view. A short stroll up the village brings you to Hill Top Farm, where Beatrix Potter wrote several of her books. Walks abound in the area and the more oft-trod Lakeland routes are easily accessible by taking the nearby ferry across Lake Windermere. *Directions:* From Ambleside, take the A593 towards Coniston. After about a mile, turn left on the B5286 to Hawkshead. Skirt Hawkshead village and follow signs for the ferry. Ees Wyke House is on the right just before Sawrey.

EES WYKE COUNTRY HOUSE HOTEL
Owners: Margaret & Richard Lee
Near Sawrey
Hawkshead LA22 0JZ, England
Tel: 015394 36393
8 Rooms, Double: £120–£132
Open: all year, Credit cards: MC, VS

The quiet country lane in front of Fosse Farmhouse is the historical Fosse Way, built by the Romans to connect their most important forts from Devon to Lincolnshire. Caron Cooper has furnished her rooms very simply with French country antiques. Charming knickknacks and china adorn the sitting and breakfast rooms. Upstairs are three extremely comfortable guest bedrooms and a magnificent old blue and white porcelain Loo. My favorite is the Pine Room, a double, with its mellow pine furniture and especially spacious, bathroom. Pink, also a large room, can either be twin or king-bedded. Blue is a smaller double room. With advance notice, Caron enjoys preparing an imaginative, two or three-course dinner, and is happy to cater to vegetarian palates. Try her home-made apple cider. In the summer Caron opens the garden for delicious afternoon teas. At Christmas, Caron offers a three-day festive holiday. For longer stays inquire about self-catering accommodation: a studio loft and a one bedroom cottage with a glass-roofed dining room, cozy living area, and fireplace. A half hour drive will find you in Bath, Bristol, Tetbury or Cirencester. The picture-perfect village of Castle Combe is within walking distance. *Directions:* Exit M4 at junction 17 towards Chippenham, turn right on the A420 (Bristol) for 3 miles to the B4039, which takes you around Castle Combe to The Gib, where you turn left opposite The Salutation Inn. The house is on the right after 1 mile.

FOSSE FARMHOUSE
Owner: Caron Cooper
Nettleton Shrub
Nettleton
Chippenham SN14 7NJ, England
Tel: 01249 782286, Fax: 01249 783066
4 Rooms, Double: £95–£160
2 Cottages: £650–£1250 weekly
Minimum Stay Required: 3 nights for self catering
Open: all year, Credit cards: MC, VS

Chewton Glen was voted "best hotel in the British Isles" by Conde Nast Traveler US Readers in Dec 2006. It's an image that is carefully nurtured and Chwton Glens efforts have been rewarded by considerable success—we had difficulty getting a room midweek in the summer. The secret of their success is not just the luxuriousness of the entire place—though it is indeed decadently luxurious, with lovely suites and bedrooms decked out with all the mod cons—but their understanding that luxury extends to offering absolutely outstanding, genuine service. To experience this level of service is one of the true pleasures in life. In between Nirvana-like meals you relax completely—perhaps with a little croquet on the lawn, a splash in the pool, or tea on the terrace. You can exert yourself in the spa and health club complex with its magnificent indoor pool, gym, indoor and outdoor tennis, and indulge yourself in various beauty treatments; disport yourself on the nine-hole golf course; or walk through the grounds and along the glen to the beach. If you feel the urge to go sightseeing, the New Forest, where wild deer and ponies roam is nearby. Stonehenge, Salisbury, and Winchester cathedrals are within an hour's drive. *Directions:* From the A35 follow signposts for Highcliffe (not New Milton), go through Walkford, then turn left down Chewton Farm Road—the hotel is on your right.

CHEWTON GLEN
Manager: Andrew Stembridge
New Milton BH25 6QS, England
Tel: 01425 275341, Fax: 01425 272310
58 Rooms, Double: £299–£1280*
*Breakfast not included: £20–£25
Open: all year, Credit cards: all major
Relais & Châteaux

The Vineyard at Stockcross takes its name and inspiration from the Peter Michael Winery in California's world-renowned Sonoma Valley. Nestled in the Berkshire countryside between Newbury and Hungerford, and conveniently located midway between Heathrow and the Cotswolds. The "Fire and Water" reflecting pool sets the scene for over 1,000 pieces of original art displayed in this exquisite property with its origins in an 18th-century hunting lodge. Guestrooms, (named after vineyards in California, France, and Italy) with a sprinkling of four-posters, share a common opulence, all with beautiful marble bathrooms en suite. The Atrium Suites are decorated in a more contemporary style. Choose between those on the first floor, with their private balconies, or those the ground floor with bay windows opening to the patio. Indulge yourself with a visit to the spa with its circular indoor pool, steam rooms, gym, and treatment rooms. The aspiring two Michelin star restaurant is exquisite. Chocoholics this is the place—the kitchen has a room dedicated to magnificent chocolate confections. As might be expected, California wines feature prominently in the 25,000-bottle cellar; 500 California vineyards blend with 1,500 from around the world to accent and support the fine cuisine. *Directions:* The hotel is close to junction 13 on the M4 motorway. Take the A34 south towards Winchester, and then the A4 (3rd exit) towards Stockcross (B4000).

THE VINEYARD AT STOCKCROSS
Owner: Sir Peter Michael
Manager: Nicholas Peth
Newbury RG20 8JU, England
Tel: 01635 528770, Fax: 01635 528398
39 Rooms, Double: £382–£582
Open: all year, Credit cards: all major

Set in the picturesque moorland village of North Bovey, frequent winner of the best-kept Dartmoor village award, Gate House has a lovely location just behind the tree-lined village green. The location and warm welcome offered by Sheila and John Williams add up to the perfect recipe for a countryside holiday. The sitting room has an ancient bread oven tucked inside a massive granite fireplace beneath a low, beamed ceiling, and the adjacent dining room has a large oak table in front of an atmospheric old stove. A narrow stairway leads up from the dining room to two of the guest bedrooms, each with a neat bathroom tucked under the eaves. The third bedroom is found at the top of another little staircase off the sitting room and affords views through a huge copper beech to the unheated swimming pool and idyllic green countryside. Sheila prepares a lovely country breakfast and a supper tray including vegetarian dishes as requested. Apart from walking on the moor and touring the moorland villages, guests enjoy visiting the many nearby National Trust properties. The Devon coast is easily accessible and many guests take a day trip into Cornwall, often as far as Clovelly. *Directions:* From Exeter take the A38 to the A382, Bovey Tracy, turnoff. Turn left in Mortenhampstead onto the Princetown road, then immediately left again to North Bovey. Go down the lane into the village and Gate House is on the left beyond the Ring of Bells.

GATE HOUSE
Owners: Sheila & John Williams
North Bovey TQ13 8RB, England
Tel & Fax: 01647 440479
3 Rooms, Double: £76–£80
Open: all year, Credit cards: none

As you drive by on the busy A442, it would be easy to dismiss this as "just another pub" but step inside the door and you realize how big a mistake you could have made! The name originates from the Middle Ages when the shires of Merry England were divided into "Hundreds." The 14th-century, half-timbered, thatched building in the parking lot was originally used as a courthouse (the stocks are on the green across the road). The main building, of Georgian origin, has been completely renovated by its current owners, the Phillips family. Entering through the public rooms is an experience in itself as you encounter a maze of bars and dining rooms decorated with baskets of local produce, tables with centerpieces of fresh herbs, and menus sophisticated enough to entrance the culinary writers of such British institutions as the Sunday Telegraph and the Observer. Heading upstairs to the bedrooms, you are struck by the brightly colored carpets, the pea green paintwork and the flowery wallpaper. The rooms themselves are a sight to behold, sumptuously decorated with period-style four-poster and half-tester beds, patchwork drapes, lavender-scented sheets, and potpourri. Superior rooms at the top of the house are provided with garden swings under the eaves. If you are looking for a place to break your journey on the way north or a base from which to explore Wales, this is well worth the diversion. *Directions:* Hundred House is next to the A442 just north of Bridgenorth.

HUNDRED HOUSE HOTEL
Owners: Sylvia, Henry, Stuart & David Phillips
Bridgenorth Road
Norton
Telford TF11 9EE, England
Tel: 01952 730353, Fax: 01952 730355
10 Rooms, Double: £99–£125
Open: all year, Credit cards: all major

This 1889 Victorian merchant's house has been transformed into a delightful bed and breakfast, just a bus ride away from the historic heart of Oxford. Burlington House is impeccably maintained and its rooms are immaculately decorated. Contemporary design, featuring plain walls with touches of color and designer fabrics, reigns throughout. The overall effect is most inviting, uncluttered and functional. The ten guestrooms in the house are supplemented by two across the Japanese-influenced, walled courtyard. The beds are very comfortable and the bathrooms are absolutely modern with power showers, glass, and tile—each one is artfully crafted in the space available. Breakfast is served in the cozy dining room, dominated by its turn-of-the-century German Arts and Crafts dresser, its walls decorated with blue ironstone pottery and large framed prints of exotic fruits. The accent is on freshness, with fresh orange juice, freshly ground and brewed coffee, vine-ripened tomatoes, homemade granola, and breads and cookies direct from the kitchen. Please ask management for suggestions on what to visit in Oxford. Be sure to visit the Cotswolds, Blenheim Palace, Bath and Stratford-Upon-Avon. *Directions:* Leave the M40 at Junction 8 for Oxford and follow the dual carriageway to the A40, northern bypass. At the next roundabout take the first exit (to Summertown) into Banbury Road. Burlington House is on the left after about half a mile.

BURLINGTON HOUSE
Manager: Nes
374 Banbury Road
Oxford OX2 7PP, England
Tel: 01865 513513, Fax: 01865 311785
12 Rooms, Double: £85–£110
Closed: Christmas & New Year, Credit cards: all major

The Old Bank Hotel is housed within an attractive, four-story building dating from 1780, which was formerly—you guessed it—a bank. Fronting on the bustling high street, guestrooms are found on the upper levels and down the two back wings along the south-facing courtyard. Very luxurious, the two top-floor bedrooms enable "sleeping amongst the spires" with views over the surrounding college rooftops. The guestroom interiors, are beautiful, all having the same theme of understated elegance and sumptuous well-appointed marble bathrooms. As befits a modern town hotel, the rooms are fully equipped to accommodate the needs of today's traveler with air conditioning, broadband internet connection, mini-bar, sound system, LCD flat-screen televisions and DVD players. Guests enjoy the peace and quiet of the library bar. Quod, the stylish bar and brasserie located on the ground floor, serves meals from breakfast onwards. Open to non-residents, as well as resident guests, the restaurant has a contemporary design with stone floors, wooden tables, and an oval zinc-topped bar. In summer, weather permitting, guests can enjoy dining and barbeque on the rear terrace, a secluded haven from the bustle of the city. The hotel enjoys a prestigious location in the very heart of Oxford, neighboring some of the oldest colleges and perfectly situated for exploring the city on foot. *Directions:* Located on High Street. Private parking is to the rear of the hotel.

❄ ⚡🛏 💳 ☎ 🛗 @ P ‖ ♿ 🎭 🐎

THE OLD BANK HOTEL
Owner: Jeremy Mogford
92–94 High Street
Oxford OX1 4BJ, England
Tel: 01865 799599, Fax: 01865 799598
42 Rooms, Double: £185–£325*
*Breakfast not included: £10–£13
Open: all year, Credit cards: all major

Between Keble and Somerville colleges you find the Old Parsonage Hotel, a wisteria-draped, golden-stone building dating back to 1660. Years past, the Old Parsonage grew like Topsy with a higgledy-piggledy collection of rooms and corridors added to the rear. Now it is a very smart boutique hotel perfect for walking to everything Oxford. The main bar with its Russian red walls covered with original cartoons and interesting portraits is open from breakfast until late. You can enjoy lunch, afternoon tea, a cocktail and dinner. In summer dining moves to the walled terrace where there's live jazz on a Friday evening and a lobster barbeque at weekends. Bedrooms are delightful. We particularly like rooms 8, 9 and 10 (standard rooms) which open up to a garden terrace. Several larger rooms overlook the leafy, rear garden. The largest rooms, our favorites, are the four rooms in the original house. Reached through a pretty sitting room and up a narrow flight of stairs, they have slanting doors, uneven floors, and little windows peeking out through the wisteria. Take a picnic and borrow one of the hotels bicycles or punts to explore the real Oxford. Enjoy a personal walking tour of the town every afternoon at 2pm or relax and enjoy an in-house beauty treatment at any time. *Directions:* The Old Parsonage is just beyond St. Giles Church on the A4260, Banbury Road.

OLD PARSONAGE HOTEL
Owner: Jeremy Mogford
Manager: Marie Jackson
1 Banbury Road
Oxford OX2 6NN, England
Tel: 01865 310210, Fax: 01865 311262
34 Rooms, Double: £170–£260*
*Breakfast not included: £12–£14
Open: all year, Credit cards: all major

On a narrow cobbled street overlooking the harbor, The Abbey Hotel dates back to the 17th century and is a delightful bed and breakfast full of period features. Make yourself at home in the high-ceilinged sitting room whose tall windows also serve as doors to the walled garden. Breakfast is the only meal served in the oak-paneled dining room. The second floor contains the three choice bedrooms. Number 1 is an especially attractive large room with comfy chairs and a huge, pine-paneled bathroom with large antique bath. Room 3 has a delightful sitting nook and a bathroom hidden behind a bookcase door. Room 4 has twin beds, inviting window seats providing views of the harbor and its dry dock, and a shower and WC tucked into a large closet. A two-bedroom apartment offers the most spacious accommodation. It's an excellent location in the heart of town. Just up the street are two great pubs, The Admiral Benbow and The Turk's Head. Nearby are St. Michael's Mount, Mousehole, and Land's End (very commercialized). *Directions:* On entering Penzance stay on the seafront road. Just before the bridge (across the harbor) turn right and immediately left up the slipway—The Abbey Hotel is at the top of the hill.

THE ABBEY HOTEL
Owners: Jean & Michael Cox
Penzance TR18 4AR, England
Tel: 01736 366906, Fax: 01736 351163
6 Rooms, Double: £130–£200
1 Apartment: £150–£210 daily
Open: all year, Credit cards: all major

Christine and Charles Taylor feel very lucky to live in some of most beautiful countryside in Cornwall, looking down across fields to the sea and St. Michael's Mount. Their farmhouse is a converted barn and outbuildings. Inside, beamed ceilings, whitewashed granite walls, and flagstone floors all contribute to the traditional farmhouse look. The Pink Room in the main house has its four-poster bed decked out in crisp white linen and its adjoining bathroom has bath for two in the center of the room. Just across the courtyard are two more lovely rooms—Apricot, all dainty and delicious with a tiny private patio, and the Blue Room, the most spacious with its large bathroom and French windows opening onto a private terrace with views across the fields to Perranuthnoe and the sea. Breakfast is served at the 9-foot-long oak refectory table in Charles and Christine's open-plan family room/kitchen upstairs. For dinner it is just a short walk across the fields to Perranuthnoe and the Victoria Inn. The garden is a masterpiece in the making and sometimes open to the public. There's lots to see in the area. You must not miss St. Michael's Mount or St. Ives, home to a branch of the Tate Gallery. *Directions:* From the A30 after the Crowlas roundabout take the A394 towards Helston. A quarter mile after the next roundabout, take the first right towards Perranuthnoe and the first left, which leads to Ednovean Farm.

EDNOVEAN FARM
Owners: Christine & Charles Taylor
Perranuthnoe
Penzance TR20 9LZ, England
Tel: 01736 711883
3 Rooms, Double: £90–£110
Minimum Stay Required: 2 nights on weekends
Closed: Christmas, Credit cards: MC, VS

No railroad noise for the lord of the manor in this neighborhood—he lobbied for the Petworth train station to be built beyond earshot, almost 2 miles from town. The last train ran in 1966 and the gingerbread-style Victorian station has been cleverly converted to a home. The former waiting room is now a spacious sitting room, with sofas gathered round the fire and individual pine tables set for breakfast on cool days. Warmer days find guests breakfasting outside on the platform beside the sweep of lawn that was once the train tracks. Two bedrooms occupy one side of the building—downstairs, a room with a brass-and-iron queen-sized bed and spacious modern full bathroom and upstairs, an equally romantic room set beneath a soaring beamed ceiling with high skylights instead of windows. Eight more are found in four Edwardian Pullman cars (as used on the Orient Express) which have been restored to reflect an era of bygone elegance. No dinner is served so guests often pop next door to The Badger Inn. Petworth is an ideal base for exploring stately homes (Petworth, Goodwood, Uppark), viewing gorgeous gardens (Westdean, Nymans), and visiting the Weald and Downland Museum. *Directions:* From Guildford take the A3, Portsmouth road, to Milford, the A283 to Petworth, and leave Petworth on the A285, Chichester road. After 1½ miles The Badger pub is on your left. Take the slip road in front of the pub—this leads to The Old Railway Station.

THE OLD RAILWAY STATION
Owner: Gudmund Olafsson
Petworth GU28 0JF, England
Tel: 01798 342346, Fax: 01798 343066
10 Rooms, Double: £90–£199
Minimum Stay Required: 2 nights on weekends
Open: all year, Credit cards: all major

This lovely Edwardian house sits high above the pretty village of Porlock and was designed as a home where every room has views of the distant sea across the roofs and chimneys of the village. Anne and Tim have worked hard to keep the feel of a private home while adding all the amenites of a small hotel. Downstairs, guests have a snug hallway parlor with chairs drawn round a log fire and an airy sitting room with flowered sofas and pink velvet chairs arranged into conversational groupings. The dining room has been extended and picture windows added so that, no matter where you sit, you have sea views across the fields or village views across the rooftops. Upstairs, the bedrooms enjoy identical interesting views. Though some are a bit larger than others, all rooms are priced alike and offer the same high standards, and each retains its own individual character. Stroll around the village with its attractive houses and shops and drive the short distance to the harbor of Porlock Weir. Just inland is Lorna Doone Country—the church at Oare was the scene of her wedding. *Directions:* From Dunster, as you enter Porlock down the hill on the one-way system, turn left into the hotel just as the road becomes two-way.

THE OAKS HOTEL
Owners: Anne & Tim Riley
Porlock TA24 8ES, England
Tel: 01643 862265, Fax: 01643 863131
8 Rooms, Double: £150
Open: mid-Mar to Oct, Credit cards: all major

Sitting beside the harbor, the whitewashed Lugger Hotel was for many years the village hostelry and reputedly the haunt of smugglers. Indeed, for such a crime, the landlord, Black Dunstan, was hanged in the 19th century. Nowadays Portloe, while having its share of holiday homes, remains a real working fishing village with crab and lobster pots just where we wanted to park the car. Fishing boats rested in the tiny harbor, sheltered by imposing cliffs and all but invisible from the sea. Outfitted in a tasteful contemporary style, the Lugger includes the reception area, a bar, a cozy beamed sitting room, the harbor-overlook restaurant and several bedrooms, the majority of which are to be found in three additional village buildings. The premier rooms have harbor views and/or a terrace. A few steps from your front door you may stride along the Cornish coastal path with its ocean panoramas. A short drive puts you in St Mawes or on the unspoiled white sandy beaches at Pendower and Carne. The Eden Project is a 40- minute drive away while the Lost Gardens of Heligan are closer. St Ives with its artists and galleries is a worthwhile daytrip. *Directions:* From St Austell travel west on the A390 toward Falmouth. Turn left on the B3287 to Tregony and left onto A3078 towards St Mawes. After 2 miles, take the left fork for Portloe; left at T-junction and you'll find the hotel by the harbor slipway in the heart of the village.

THE LUGGER HOTEL
Manager: Richard Hartley
Portloe
Truro TR2 5RD, England
Tel: 01872 501322, Fax: 01872 501691
21 Rooms, Double: £150–£300
1 Cottage: £350 daily
Open: all year, Credit cards: all major

The Yorke Arms nestles beside the village green in Ramsgill, a handful of houses and farms and a tiny church. This delightful Nidderdale hostelry (one of Yorkshire's quietest and most attractive dales) is now a foodie haven (Michelin Star) where Frances Atkins and her brigade perform culinary magic. There is plenty of old world charm: flagstone floors, two beautiful dining rooms and blazing log fires. The bedrooms within The Yorke Arms are comfortable and individually decorated in tasteful hues. Knowing you deserve the best request one of the largest rooms: Gouthwaite twin or king-bedded or Longside with its grand four-poster bed. Loft, set under the eaves with its large tub for two in the bedroom, stands out as a particularly memorable bedroom. A charming cottage in the village has now been added to the accommodation and is perfect if you enjoy tranquil surroundings and privacy and is only a 200 yard stroll away. You can take beautiful walks from the restaurant, which vary in length from strolls by Gouthwaite reservoir to daylong hikes over the moorlands. The ruins of nearby Fountains Abbey are an awesome sight and medieval York and the 18th century spa town of Harrogate are popular day trips. *Directions:* From Ripon take the B6285 to Pateley Bridge where you cross the river and turn right for Ramsgill. The Yorke Arms is beside the village green.

THE YORKE ARMS
Owners: Frances & Bill Atkins
Manager: John Tullett
Ramsgill HG3 5RL, England
Tel: 01423 755243, Fax: 01423 755330
12 Rooms, Double: £180–£240
1 Cottage: £300 daily
Open: all year, Credit cards: all major

The Burgoyne family were people of substance hereabouts for they secured the premier building site in this picturesque Swaledale village and built an impressive home that dwarfs the surrounding buildings, a most welcoming hotel run for many years by Derek Hickson. Derek makes guests feel thoroughly at home and he makes certain that they live up to the motto, "Tis substantial happiness to eat." A fixed-price, four-course meal is offered every evening with plenty of choices for each course. The handsome lounge is warmed by a log fire in winter and full of inviting books on the area. There's abundant scope for walking and driving in this rugged area using Reeth as your base, though you'll be hard-pressed to find a lovelier dales view than the one from your bedroom window of stone-walled fields rising to vast moorlands (one bedroom faces the back of the house). Redmire, being more spacious, is the premier room, while Marrick is a most luxurious four-poster suite. Robes and slippers are provided for the occupants of Keld, Grinton, and Thwaite who have to slip across the hall to their bathrooms. Richmond with its medieval castle and the Bowes Museum, near Barnard Castle, with its fine collection of French furniture and porcelain, are added attractions. *Directions:* From Richmond take the A6108 towards Leyburn for 5 miles to the B6270 for the 5-mile drive to Reeth. The Burgoyne Hotel is on the village green.

THE BURGOYNE HOTEL
Owner: Derek Hickson
Reeth DL11 6SN, England
Tel & Fax: 01748 884292
9 Rooms, Double: £132–£195
Closed: Jan 2 to Feb 12, Credit cards: MC, VS

Millgate House's unassuming street frontage disguises one of Richmond's finest Georgian homes. Faux-painted marble columns draw you through the wide hall into the drawing room packed with serendipitous heirlooms, treasures and antiques collected by Tim Culkin and Austin Lynch. Tall windows overlook the lush, secluded, garden that terraces down to the river far below. The same splendid view is enjoyed by the delightful dining room with its enviable antiques and lovely paintings. A bountiful offering of fruits heads up the breakfast menu. The two premier bedrooms, a twin and a queen, face the river. Both are very large and beautifully furnished, and have spacious bathrooms and wonderful views. The third bedroom, at the front of the house, has a king-size bed and a bathroom across the hall. A five-bedroom coach house beside the river is available for three to seven day lets. You are just steps from Richmond's cobbled market square (the Frenchgate Hotel is an excellent place to eat) and just down the road from the 11th-century Norman castle. Tours of the Yorkshire Dales and Moors and York itself give you an excuse to spend several nights to soak up the atmosphere of this remarkable house. *Directions:* Directions: From the A1, take the A6136 to Richmond. Head for the central Market Place. Millgate House is at the bottom of the hill opposite Barclays Bank.

MILLGATE HOUSE
Owners: Tim Culkin & Austin Lynch
Richmond DL10 4JN, England
Tel: 01748 823571, Fax: 01748 850701
3 Rooms, Double: £95–£125
Coach house: £720–£1620 weekly
Open: all year, Credit cards: none

The St. Enodoc Hotel occupies an exquisite location on one of England's most scenic coastlines overlooking the broad Camel estuary. Combine this with a refreshing, stylishly chic, Mediterranean interior and you have a real winner. Enjoy the peace and quiet of the comfortable sitting room or take advantage of the well-stocked library featuring books on Cornwall and some by Cornish authors. Soak in the panoramic water view from the smart, split-level bar and restaurant specializing in modern European cuisine, or stroll down the lane and take the little ferry across to the ancient fishing port of Padstow with its array of shops and restaurants. Bedrooms are very nicely decorated with those at the front having lovely views. There is a choice of king- or twin-bedded rooms, several with a large window seat that can be converted to a small child's bed, though families often opt for one of the more spacious family suites. With its heated outdoor pool (May through September), billiard room, gym, children's playroom and adjacent golf course, the St. Enodoc is an ideal holiday hotel. The nearby little fishing village of Port Isaac with its craft and antique shops is charming, but also drive to Carbis Bay and take the little train to St. Ives for a visit to the Tate Gallery, or meander up the coast to Tintagel of King Arthur fame. *Directions:* At the Wadebridge roundabout follow signs for Wadebridge, then at the next roundabout turn right for the 4-mile drive to Rock.

ST. ENODOC HOTEL
Manager: Kate Simms
Rock PL27 6LA, England
Tel: 01208 863394, Fax: 01208 863970
20 Rooms, Double: £130–£400
Closed: mid-Dec to mid-Feb, Credit cards: all major

Romaldkirk epitomizes a traditional north-of-England village with honey-colored stone cottages set spaciously round the large village green where the old pump and even older stocks (for punishing wrongdoers) still stand. The surprisingly sophisticated Rose and Crown pub bordering the village green has a pretty sitting room (where guests can escape the hubbub of the bar) and a paneled dining room serving four-course dinners. However, like all great pubs, The Rose and Crown also has an excellent traditional bar where beams are decorated with horse brasses and locals gather for a pint in the evenings. Delectable bar meals are served here or in the adjacent Brasserie. Up the narrow stairs you find five attractive bedrooms (room 10 is a lovely large double-bedded room overlooking the village green) and two suites, under the eaves, which are especially suitable for families as the sofas in the sitting rooms make into beds for children. Five additional, modern bedrooms are in the courtyard beside the carpark. Walking is a popular pastime hereabouts and a few minutes' drive brings you into quiet Pennine countryside. Barnard Castle is a lively local market town where the Bowes Museum merits an all-day visit. A 40-minute drive finds you at Beamish Museum, a turn-of-the-century mining town hosted by costumed staff. *Directions:* Romaldkirk is 6 miles NW of Barnard Castle on the B6277 in the direction of Middleton in Teesdale.

THE ROSE & CROWN
Owners: Alison & Christopher Davy
Barnard Castle
Romaldkirk DL12 9EB, England
Tel: 01833 650213, Fax: 01833 650828
14 Rooms, Double: £135–£190
Closed: Christmas, Credit cards: MC, VS

Rosedale Abbey nestles in a sheltered green valley below the gently rolling moorland. High above the village lies Thorgill, a few houses strung out along a narrow road just beneath the moor. Here you find Sevenford House, a large residence built at the turn of the century for the vicar of the village church, and now home to Linda, Ian and their family. The three large bedrooms have excellent views, are delightfully furnished and decorated and each has a snug en suite shower room. Enjoy a welcoming cup of tea and a chat in the lovely drawing room and browse through the books that highlight the many things to do in this lovely part of Yorkshire. Ride a steam train on the North Yorkshire Moors Railway, visit the vast array of stately homes, explore the lovely villages nestled beneath the moor, and visit the coastside towns of Whitby, Runswick Bay, and Robin Hood's Bay. Should you want to stay for a week you can do no better than the three-bedroom cottage in the adjacent stables. There's no shortage of good pubs and cafes close at hand. Just above the house you can follow the path of an old railway line that takes you on a spectacular four-hour walk. *Directions:* From Pickering take the A170 towards Helmsley for 3 miles, then turn right for the 7-mile drive to Rosedale. Just as you enter the village, turn sharp left and go up the hill to the White Horse Hotel where you turn right (signposted Thorgill). Sevenford House is the first house on your right.

■ ⚙ @ W P 🚭 🖼 ⚓ 🚶 🥾 ⚓

SEVENFORD HOUSE
Owners: Linda Sugars & Ian Thompson
Thorgill
near Pickering
Rosedale Abbey YO18 8SE, England
Tel: 01751 417283
3 Rooms, Double: £75–£80
1 Cottage: £395–£700 weekly
Closed: Christmas, Credit cards: none

With a backdrop of mountain peaks and a lush green lawn sweeping down towards Rosthwaite village, this award-winning establishment has a superb location in Borrowdale, one of the loveliest and quietest Lake District valleys. All the rooms are comfortable, light, airy, and uncluttered. The bedrooms, named after nearby mountains, vary from spacious to snug, though even the snuggest has a corner to accommodate comfortable chairs and a TV—we particularly admired Dalehead. After a day out walking or sightseeing, relax over a drink in the sitting room before one of Anton's award-winning dinners. This is walking country so the house has a drying and ironing room for clothing. Just behind the house, overlooking the garden, is a delightful little self-catering cottage for two people. An excellent day out is had by driving high over the adjacent pass to Buttermere and Crummock Water. Visit Wordsworth House in Cockermouth, drive along Bassenthwaite Lake to Keswick, and after sightseeing, continue along Derwent Water back to Rosthwaite. *Directions:* Hazel Bank is 7 miles south of Keswick on the B5289. Turn left over the little humpbacked bridge just before entering the village of Rosthwaite.

HAZEL BANK
Owners: Rob Van der Palen & Anton Renac
Rosthwaite CA12 5XB, England
Tel: 017687 77248
8 Rooms, Double: £140–£170*
1 Cottage: £375–£475 weekly
*Includes dinner, bed & breakfast
Open: all year, Credit cards: MC, VS

On the edge of the village of Rowsley, standing in its own grounds, distanced from the road by a winding, tree-lined, private driveway, the East Lodge dates back to the late 1700's. As the name implies, it started out as a hunting lodge on the Haddon estate. Today is has retained many of the old architectural features and combined them with a sleek modernity and creature comforts resulting in an upscale, chic, country house hotel. From the reception area with its black iron and tile fireplace to the four-poster beds, free-standing tubs and flat-screen TV's in the bathrooms, there is an unmistakable air of attention to detail throughout. The "hands-on" management style of the Hardman family ensures there is always an owner on site. Rooms vary in size: our favorites were larger, at the front of the house and looked over the gardens and pond. Light meals and snacks are served in the conservatory bar, breakfast and dinner in the more formal dining room. It's a perfect central location for exploring the most interesting villages in the Peak District National Park. *Directions:* From the south exit the M1 at junction 28, taking the A38 towards Derby for 3 miles, the A615 to Matlock and the A6 towards Bakewell for 5 miles to Rowsley. East Lodge is on your right before you reach the river.

☕ 🏃 💳 @ P ⅋ 🚭 🖼 🏃 👫 🐎

EAST LODGE
Owners: Joan & David, Carly & Iian Hardman
Rowsley DE4 2ET, England
Tel: 01629 734474, Fax: 01629 733949
12 Rooms, Double: £160–£350
Open: all year, Credit cards: all major

Dating back to the mid-1600's The Peacock was originally built as a Manor House by John Stevenson. Once the Dower House for Haddon Hall and still part of the Haddon Estate, its name derives from the Peacock in the Rutland Family coat of arms. The hotel has more recently been sympathetically renovated and restored as a classic country house hotel. Stone mullioned, leaded-light windows rub shoulders with antique furniture from nearby Haddon Hall and Belvoir (pronounced "beaver") Castle. Exposed wood beams, open fireplace and comfortable furnishings complete the picture. The dining room and snug bar feature "mouseman" wooden tables and chairs, locally produced in Kilburn, by not only the original Mousey Thompson but also his son. See if you can find the small critter carved into your chair and ask about the difference in styles. The hotel grounds lead down to the River Wye home to sizeable rainbow trout. Fishing can be arranged for hotel guests. It's a 2½ mile walk to Chatsworth House (10% discount) through lovely countryside while Haddon Hall (50% discount) lies just 1½ miles up the road. It's a perfect central location for exploring the most interesting villages in the Peak District National Park. *Directions:* From the south leave the M1 at junction 28 taking the A38 towards Derby for 3 miles, the A615 to Matlock and the A6 towards Bakewell for 5 miles to Rowsley. The Peacock is on your right immediately after you cross the river.

THE PEACOCK
Owner: Lord Edward Manners
Managers: Jenni & Ian Mackenzie
Bakewell Road
Rowsley DE4 2EB, England
Tel: 01629 733518, Fax: 01628 732671
16 Rooms, Double: £145–£210
Open: all year, Credit cards: all major

We found Lizzie Newton weeding a flowerbed in her prize-winning garden, which looks out over peaceful fields. The same combination of care and flair that Lizzie displays in her garden she applies to her delightful thatched cottage where she welcomes guests. The comfortable twin-bedded guest bedroom is bright and cheery and accompanied by an en suite shower room. In the evening guests are welcome to join Lizzie in her comfortable sitting room. Breakfast is the only meal served here and while you can walk across the fields to the Charlton Cat, there are lots of delightful pubs within easy driving distance. Just up the road is the picturesque village of Pewsey. Less than a half-hour drive finds you wandering amongst the ancient stones of Avebury and Stonehenge, wondering why Bronze Age man spent what has been estimated at millions of manhours constructing such temples. Another local phenomenon is crop circles, mysterious, elaborate patterns that appear overnight in crop fields. Much more down-to-earth are Georgian Bath, Salisbury with its exquisite cathedral, and the handsome town of Marlborough with its Georgian buildings and little alleys of old timbered cottages. *Directions:* From Marlborough take the A345 towards Amesbury to Pewsey (8 miles) and 2 miles after Pewsey, turn for Devizes at a small roundabout with the Woodbridge Arms on your right. On reaching Rushall go past the school and Little Thatch is on your left.

LITTLE THATCH
Owner: Elizabeth Newton
Rushall
Pewsey SN9 6EN, England
Tel & Fax: 01980 635282
2 Rooms, Double: £58–£65
Open: mid-Jan to mid-Dec, Credit cards: none

Stone House, the manor house for Rushlake Green, has belonged to the Dunn family for over 500 years. Built in 1495 with an addition in 1778, this glorious house, set on a 1,000-acre estate, is filled with wonderful antique furniture and old English china, which is complemented by chintzes and family memorabilia. Bedrooms vary in size from small and cozy to large and spacious. Most feature old exposed beams. All are furnished with care and provided with practically everything you might need from TV to hot-water bottles, sewing kits, books, and tempting biscuits. Two rooms are especially gorgeous, with four-poster beds and equally lovely bathrooms. Sumptuous dinners and breakfasts are served in the oak-paneled dining room, and continental breakfast is available in your bedroom. There is a croquet lawn and a billiard table. The 18th-century walled garden, old-fashioned rose garden, and lime walk are yours to enjoy. Other glorious gardens include Sissinghurst, Great Dixter, Scotney Castle, and Sheffield Park. Going to Glyndebourne then take along a sumptuous Stone House picnic. Ask about the popular cooking and vegetable gardening courses. *Directions:* From Heathfield take the B2096 towards Battle and then the fourth turn on the right to Rushlake Green. Turn left in the village (with the green on your right) and Stone House is on the far left-hand corner of the crossroads.

STONE HOUSE
Owners: Jane & Peter Dunn
Rushlake Green TN21 9QJ, England
Tel: 01435 830553, Fax: 01435 830726
8 Rooms, Double: £135–£260
Closed: Dec 23 to Jan 6, Credit cards: MC, VS

Rye, a busy port in medieval times, has become marooned 2 miles inland since the sea receded. Once the haunt of smugglers who climbed the narrow cobbled streets laden with booty from France, Rye is now a picturesque town that invites tourists to walk its cobbled lanes. On Rye's most historic street, Jeake's House dates back to 1690 when it was built by Samuel Jeake as a wool storehouse (wool was smuggled to France while brandy, lace, and salt were brought into England). From the street you enter a small reception area, which leads to a Victorian parlor and bar. This opens up to a large galleried hall, now the dining room, where a roaring log fire blazes in winter. At some point in its history the house was owned by the Baptist Church who built this room as a chapel. From the spacious attic bedroom to the romantic four-poster rooms. No two rooms are alike. All are most attractively decorated and furnished with antiques in keeping with the historical mood of the house. All offer modern amenities such as tea-making trays, television, and telephone and all have en suite bathrooms. Within easy driving distance are Winchelsea, Battle Abbey (built on the site of the Battle of Hastings in 1066), Bodiam Castle, and Sissinghurst Gardens. *Directions:* Rye is between Folkestone and Hastings on the A259. Mermaid Street is off the town's main street—park in front to unload and you will be directed to nearby private parking.

JEAKE'S HOUSE
Owner: Jenny Hadfield
Mermaid Street
Rye TN31 7ET, England
Tel: 01797 222828
14 Rooms, Double: £90–£128
Open: all year, Credit cards: MC, VS

Surrounded by open farmland on the edge of the Vale of Evesham, Salford Farm House dates back to the 19th century and showcases many of the original architectural features, beams, flagstones, and fireplaces. Traditionally decorated with antiques and family heirlooms, silverware gleams on the dining-room sideboard. A contented herd of ceramic cow creamers sits on the windowsill of the comfortable sitting room. A fascinating collection of French costume prints bedecks the hall stairs leading to the two lovely king (or twin) bedrooms, both with top of the line bathrooms one pink, one cream, the latter with its own separate dressing room. On arrival guests are invited to afternoon tea in the sitting room before a roaring fire or, on warmer, sun-dappled days, in the flower-filled garden. Jane prepares sumptuous breakfasts and dinners on her Aga in the country kitchen. Fresh local produce—fruits, vegetables, meat, and game from the Marquess of Hertford's Ragley Estate—features largely on the menu. Salford Farm House is just 8 miles from Stratford-upon-Avon and 15 miles from Warwick Castle. Ragley Hall, Kenilworth, the Cotswolds, and an abundance of National Trust properties are nearby. *Directions:* From Stratford-upon-Avon or Evesham take the A46, following signs to Salford Priors. Turn right opposite the church in the center of the village (signposted Dunnington). Salford Farm House is approximately 1 mile along on the right.

SALFORD FARM HOUSE
Owners: Jane & Richard Beach
near Stratford-upon-Avon
Salford Priors WR11 8XN, England
Tel: 01386 870000
2 Rooms, Double: £85
Closed: Christmas, Credit cards: none

Tim knows how to look after guests: For many years he was a hotelier at one of London's splendid little townhouse hotel, Number Sixteen. After selling his share of the hotel, he came back to his native Devon to run Parford Well. Set within a walled garden, the comfortable house is totally dedicated to guest accommodation while Tim lives in the tiny adjoining cottage. Sink into the oh-so-comfortable sofas in the sitting room and toast your toes before the fire. The decor is of such a high standard that, apart from the smaller proportions of the house, you would think you are in a grand country house hotel. Breakfast is the only meal served round the farmhouse table in the dining room. If you want complete seclusion, ask to eat in the tiny private dining room with grand draperies that once belonged to the Queen Mother and has just enough room for a table for two. Upstairs are three delightful small bedrooms, two en suite and one with its private bathroom across the hall. He is an expert on where to walk, what to see, and which tea shops and restaurants to frequent. Castle Drogo is just up the lane. He can suggest enough activities to keep you busy for a fortnight. *Directions:* From Moretonhampstead take the A382 towards Okehampton for 3 miles. Turn right at the Sandy Park crossroads towards Castle Drogo and Parford Well is 100 yards along on your left.

■ ⚏ @ W P ⊘ ⊥ ⊀ ⋔ ⫯

PARFORD WELL
Owner: Tim Daniel
Sandy Park
Chagford TQ13 8JW, England
Tel: 01647 433353
3 Rooms, Double: £75–£95
Open: Feb to Dec 23, Credit cards: none

While the house dates back to the 17th century, the estate is mentioned in the Doomsday book of 1086 when monks from nearby Glastonbury ran a prosperous farm here. The house has receive a new lease on life as a luxury country house hotel. With its rich theatrical decor there are a touches of whimsy and opulence throughout. Nowhere more so than in the spa, a Moroccan style retreat replete with indoor/outdoor hydrotherapy pool, gym, sauna and treatment rooms that include couples rooms. Stylishly comfortable drawing rooms lead to the award-winning conservatory restaurant which specializes in organic meats and produce, much of it coming from the hotel's estate. This includes spelt, an ancient cereal grain, used instead of wheat in the hotels muesli, breads and pastries. Bedrooms are a delight, varying from spacious rooms to decadent suites. Request one with a verandah, tiny garden or terrace. The historic City of Wells with its beautiful cathedral and twice weekly markets is just a few miles away, as is Glastonbury with its myths of the Holy Grail and King Arthur. Bath with its abbey, Roman baths and museums is a popular day trip. *Directions:* From the M4, exit Junction 17, signposted Chippenham A350. Pass Chippenham toward Trowbridge until you meet the A361 to Frome. Follow the A361 past Frome towards Shepton Mallet. Charlton House is on the left, one mile before Shepton Mallet.

CHARLTON HOUSE
Owner: Von Essen Hotels
Shepton Mallet BA4 4PR, England
Tel: 01749 342008, Fax: 01749 346362
25 Rooms, Double: £155–£415
Open: all year, Credit cards: all major

A cozy hilltop refuge from winter storms, an outstanding spring, summer, or autumn base for exploring Derbyshire by car or on foot, Dannah Farm is a delightful place for all seasons. The solid Georgian farmhouse is turned over entirely to guests, with delightful cottagey bedrooms and two cozy, tastefully furnished sitting rooms. I particularly liked the suites, two of which have their private entries from the old stableyard. One has a snug sitting room with an open-tread spiral staircase leading to the low-beamed bedroom while the other is a lofty raftered room with a four-poster bed. Bathrooms have double spa baths and large showers, one has a private sauna and another a hot tub. Another part of the old stables is a convivial country-style restaurant where guests enjoy breakfast and by prior arrangement dinner. There is no shortage of good pubs round and about where you can enjoy dinner. Adults and children love the animals—the kune kune pigs are a great attraction and Cracker and Jack, the two English setters, will take you for a walk. The Peak District National Park is on your doorstep full of walks, bike trails, and appealing little villages. The stately homes of Haddon Hall and Chatsworth House are well worth a visit. *Directions:* From Belper take the A517 (Ashbourne road) for 2 miles and after the Hanging Gate Inn take the next right (at the top of the hill) to Shottle (1½ miles). Go straight at the crossroads and after 200 yards turn right into Dannah Farm.

DANNAH FARM
Owners: Joan & Martin Slack
Bowmans Lane
Shottle
Belper DE56 2DR, England
Tel: 01773 550273, Fax: 01773 550590
8 Rooms, Double: £110–£285
Closed: Christmas, Credit cards: MC, VS

Set in two acres of its own grounds, with magnificent views over the local countryside, Holmby House is an impressive old wisteria clad Victorian dating back to 1884. Previously home to the Bishop of Oxfordshire it has been lovingly renovated by current owners Sally and John Wass. From its vantage point on the edge of the Cotswolds Holmby is handily located for day trips to the various attractions of Stratford-upon-Avon, Stowe on the Wold, Warwick and Oxford. Guest rooms, two in the house and two in converted stables are named after operatic heroines. All are spacious, decorated with soft tones, splashes of color, antiques and collectables. Comfortable beds, luxurious linens and all modern amenities complete the picture. A self-catering cottage to the same high standards can accommodate up to eight people. Tennis, croquet and swimming (in the outdoor heated pool) are available on site for the more actively inclined. The classically smart drawing room is available for those less than perfect days. Breakfast (and dinner by request) is served in the dining room. In the summer dinner can also be served on the terrace or by the swimming pool. Sally is an aficionado of Claire MacDonald's cuisine and indulges her guests in good food featuring local produce. *Directions:* From Banbury take the B4035 towards Shipston. After Swalecliffe, at the top of the hill, turn left to Sibford Ferris. Holmby House is the first house in the village on the right.

HOLMBY HOUSE
Owners: Sally & John Wass
Sibford Ferris OX15 5RG, England
Tel & Fax: 01295 780104
6 Rooms, Double: £80–£100
1 Cottage: £450–£1200 weekly
Open: all year, Credit cards: all major

Because of its close proximity to The Potteries and Leek, Rose Cottage is an ideal countryside base for shopping for fine china and antique pine. It really is the most quintessentially countryside spot—a darling cottage set on a quiet country lane just up the road from Snelston, a very pretty village. The term "cottage" conjures up visions of a modest-sized house but though Rose Cottage has its origins in a small residence, it has been expanded over the years into a substantial house of great character. Toast your toes by the fire in the snug little parlor or spread out in the spacious sitting room with its large windows framing panoramic countryside views. The same lovely view is enjoyed by the bedrooms, the largest of which also offers bucolic views from its bathroom. One bedroom has its private bathroom across the hall. Breakfast is the only meal served. Nearby Ashbourne has some excellent restaurants but we preferred the "real ale", excellent food, and old-world pub atmosphere of the Coach and Horses in the neighboring village of Fenny Bentley. Just down the road is Ashbourne with its splendid church and antique salesrooms and to the north lie the beautiful Derbyshire Dales. *Directions:* From Ashbourne take the A515 towards Lichfield. After 3 miles turn right on the B5033 in the direction of Norbury. Take the second lane to the right towards Snelston and Rose Cottage is the second house on the right.

ROSE COTTAGE
Owners: Cynthia & Peter Moore
Snelston
Ashbourne DE6 2DL, England
Tel: 01335 324230, Fax: 01335 324651
3 Rooms, Double: £74–£78
Closed: Christmas, Credit cards: none

The Lynch Country House was built for an attorney and his bride in 1812 and was owned by their family for over a hundred years. Roy Copeland purchased the house with the intention of running a country house hotel, but later decided that bed and breakfast was more his cup of tea. Roy shares the house with his guests so several rooms are labeled private though guests have a small sitting room and a large conservatory where breakfast is served. Roy encourages guests to enjoy the lovely gardens with their topiary hedges and the lake with its resident family of black swans. Bedrooms vary in size from snug low-ceilinged rooms under the eaves (Alderley is an especially attractive attic room) to Goldington, a large high-ceilinged room with a grand Georgian four-poster bed. Four additional rooms are found in the coach house. Roy finds that guests usually stroll into the village to eat at one of the pubs or the restaurant. Somerton village has some interesting shops and pretty streets lined with old stone houses. Glastonbury, the cradle of English Christianity, and Wells with its magnificent cathedral are just up the road. Bath is just under an hour away. *Directions:* From the Podimore roundabout on the A303 follow signposts for Langport and Somerton. Join the A372 and turn right after a mile for Somerton. Take the third left by the dairy. Lynch Country House is at the top of the hill by the mini roundabout.

THE LYNCH COUNTRY HOUSE
Owner: Roy Copeland
4 Behind Berry
Somerton TA11 7PD, England
Tel: 01458 272316, Fax: 01458 272590
9 Rooms, Double: £70–£100
Open: all year, Credit cards: all major

At its heart St. Ives is a lovely old fishing town with narrow cobbled streets and quaint cottages. While the fishing industry is gone, the town's artistic legacy thrives. The splendid Tate as well as many lesser known private galleries feature dramatic seascapes with white beaches. These seascapes are reminiscent of the views from the four ocean-facing rooms at Primrose Valley on Porthminster Beach. Be it a room with a view or no view, you'll appreciate the clean uncluttered lines of the modern design and the thought that has gone into every aspect of the stylish decor. Sue and Andrew Biss are believers in the use of local produce for breakfast and work hard to keep the hotel "green." For dinner the famous Porthminster Beach Cafe is, as its name suggests, on the beach just the other side of the railway line. A five-minute walk finds you in the heart of St Ives with its array of restaurants. There is a lot to see and do in this part of Cornwall—driving along the picturesque north coast, visiting St Michael's Mount, exploring Mousehole (a picture-postcard fishing village), or shopping in Penzance. *Directions:* Arriving in St Ives on the A3074 signal right as you see the hospital sign on your left and turn sharp right down a narrow, steep lane (small signpost Primrose Valley). Go under the railway bridge and turn left (both a road and a footpath); take the next left and Primrose Valley is the second house facing you.

PRIMROSE VALLEY
Owners: Sue & Andrew Biss
Porthminster Beach
St Ives TR26 2ED, England
Tel & Fax: 01736 794939
9 Rooms, Double: £100–£235
Closed: Christmas & Jan, Credit cards: MC, VS

Hosts Jane and Steve Epperson previously owned a country house hotel so they know what guests want. Consequently their modern Georgian-style home offers more guest facilities than many hotels: indoor heated lap pool, hot tub, sauna, and gym facilities. Sparkling bedrooms and suites have contemporary/chic decor accented with antiques and packed with everything to make you happy and very comfortable. They have king-sized beds, satellite television, plush carpets and curtains, stone-tiled bathrooms with huge baths, separate power showers and names like Stunning, Pleasurable, Charming and Sensational. I particularly admired Desirable in the cottage which is handicap friendly and offers a huge tub for two in the bathroom. Candlelit suppers are sometimes available. There are excellent pubs and restaurants within a few minutes' walk or drive. Anchorage House's location on a quiet cul-de-sac just off the A390 makes it ideal for those who want to avoid navigating narrow Cornish lanes to reach their accommodation and also means that it is handily placed for driving forays to places as near as the Eden Project (5 minutes) or the Lost Gardens of Heligan (15 minutes), and as far away as Land's End, St. Ives, and St. Michael's Mount (1 hour). *Directions:* Just off the A390, 1 mile west of St. Blazey, 2 miles east of St. Austell. Opposite the St. Austell Garden Center turn into a small lane signposted Tregrehan and then immediately left to Anchorage House.

ANCHORAGE HOUSE
Owners: Jane & Steve Epperson
Nettles Corner, Tregrehan Mills
St. Austell PL25 3RH, England
Tel: 01726 814071, Fax: 01726 813462
5 Rooms, Double: £115–£160
Open: Mar to Nov, Credit cards: all major

This lovely Georgian home set in five acres of grounds in a peaceful countryside has the Eden Project just 2 miles up the road. Bedrooms come in two sizes, small and large. Rashleigh is an enormous room, its double bed having an artfully draped bedhead matching the curtains and bedspread; Treffry has a six-foot bed that can be two single beds; and Prideaux has a dainty white four-poster. Each bedroom has an en suite bathroom with spa bath, tea- and coffee-makings, television, telephone, and a huge umbrella for guests to use during their stay. Guests have their own entrance into a lofty hallway where double doors open up to a vast sitting room all decked out in warm cream shades. Beyond lies a sunny conservatory with wicker chairs and little tables set for breakfast, the only meal served. Local dining spots range from formal restaurants to a pub on the beach in a smugglers' cove. Outside are vast lawns, a summertime swimming pool, a hot tub, and a paved terrace with spectacular views across rolling countryside. Local attractions include the picturesque town of Fowey, the fishing village of Mevagissey, and National Trust properties such as Lanhydrock. *Directions:* Pass over the Tamar Bridge into Cornwall and take the A390 (St. Austell turnoff), following it through Lostwithiel and into St. Blazey. Cross the railway lines and opposite the Jet garage turn right into Prideaux Road, following it to Nanscawen on your right.

NANSCAWEN MANOR HOUSE
Owner: Keith Martin
Prideaux Road, Luxulyan Valley
St. Blazey PL24 2SR, England
Tel: 01726 814488, Fax: no fax
3 Rooms, Double: £98–£122
Open: all year, Credit cards: MC, VS

Enjoy utter tranquility and the magnificent coastal panorama from Boskerris Hotel in Carbis Bay, located a scenic three-minute train ride away from the heart of bustling St Ives. Sit on the deck and be spellbound by the ocean view that stretches from St Ives harbor to Godrevy lighthouse—sunsets are spectacular. The Bassetts bought the hotel in 2004 and embarked on a complete refurbish to give it a contemporary, airy feel that works just perfectly. Bedrooms vary in size: most have magnificent views, all are spacious with bathrooms that come with all the bells and whistles. The stylish lounge is a terrific place to relax and enjoy the books and magazines reflecting the owners' interests in interiors (Marianne and Annette), surfing (Jono) and opera (George). The white sands of Carbis beach are a short stroll away while St Ives is a half hour walk along the coastal path. A huge map of Cornwall fills an entire wall and highlights the Bassetts' favorite places from where to buy the best Cornish pasties to gardens, walks, and favorite restaurants—you may well want to dine in house one night. *Directions:* From the A30 take the A3074 towards St. Ives into Carbis Bay where you turn right on Boskerris Road. The hotel is on your left halfway down the hill.

BOSKERRIS HOTEL
Owners: Marianne & Jono, Annie & George Bassett
Boskerris Road
St. Ives
Carbis Bay TR26 2NQ, England
Tel: 01736 795295
15 Rooms, Double: £100–£210
Closed: mid–Nov to mid–Feb, Credit cards: MC, VS

The delightfully pretty little fishing village of St. Mawes, with its narrow, steep streets and boat-filled harbor strung along the River Fal, sports quite a Mediterranean look. The town's sheltered position makes it a warm hideaway even in winter and there is no more splendid place to hide away than in the elegant Hotel Tresanton. Terracing up steep steps, this spectacularly located, scrumptious hotel is dashingly modern, with a nautical, Mediterranean flair. Its easy-on-the-eye decor—mainly in white and soft, neutral tones with royal-blue accents—is a perfect balance between classic and modern. Bedrooms all have magnificent sea views and two are spacious family suites for up to five people. Naturally, the restaurant features fish on the menu. Enjoy the hotel's extensive library or choose a film to watch in the hotel's cinema. Follow the coastal path past the castle to the 14th-century church at St. Just in Roseland. You can hire many different boats including the hotel's 48-foot classic yacht. Sightseers have lots of scope, from St. Michael's Mount to the Tate Gallery at St. Ives, while garden lovers are spoilt for choice: Trelissick, Glendurgan, Trebah, the Lost Gardens of Heligan, and The Eden Project. *Directions:* From St. Austell take the B3287 for 16 miles to St. Mawes where you follow the road along the front of the harbor, coming to the Tresanton on your right. Park in front, go up to reception, and the staff will unload your bags and park your car.

HOTEL TRESANTON
Manager: Federica Bertolini
St. Mawes TR2 5DR, England
Tel: 01326 270055, Fax: 01326 270053
26 Rooms, Double: £190–£360
3 Suites: £315–£495
Open: all year, Credit cards: all major

The gallows sign outside The George stood as a warning to highwaymen not to rob coaches departing from the Stamford inn. The waiting room for London coaches is now an oak-paneled private dining room, while the adjacent York waiting room serves as a friendly bar. History positively oozes from this place and the staff is always happy to enliven your stay with tales of resident ghosts and secret passages. Do not be put off by the hotel's austere façade directly on the main road because most bedrooms face a peaceful inner courtyard and you are not aware of the road once you are inside the hotel. Horses once clip-clopped across the cobbled courtyard where overflowing tubs of flowers paint a pretty picture and tables and chairs are set beneath umbrellas for traditional afternoon tea. Most bedrooms face this pretty courtyard and I particularly enjoyed the historic ambiance of room 29 (a deluxe double) with its dark-oak paneling (apparently Princess Anne has slept here) and room 49 decked out in maroon and blue and overlooking a quiet garden. Traditional roast dinners are the hallmark of the dining room—be sure to save room for an old-fashioned pud—while lighter, more casual fare is served in the indoor Garden Lounge. Stamford has lots of antique shops. *Directions:* From Peterborough take the A1 north for 14 miles to the first roundabout where you take the B1081 to Stamford. The George is on the left by the traffic lights.

THE GEORGE OF STAMFORD
Manager: Chris Pitman
71 St. Martins
Stamford PE9 2LB, England
Tel: 01780 750750, Fax: 01780 750701
48 Rooms, Double: £130–£245
Minimum Stay Required: 2 nights
Open: all year, Credit cards: all major

Plumber Manor has been a country home of the Prideaux Brune family since the early 17th century. Portraits hanging in the upstairs gallery hint at the grandeur of the family's past. (There is also a portrait of Charles I, which he personally presented to his mistress, a member of the family.) Billed as a restaurant with bedrooms, Plumber Manor is under the personal supervision of the family. Richard and Alison Prideaux Brune look after guests; Brian Prideaux Brune, the chef, conscientiously provides a high standard of cuisine and wine. Six comfortable, spacious bedrooms are in the main house and, just across the garden, ten rooms surround a courtyard. Our favorites are 14, 15, 16, and 17—spacious, two-level rooms with luxurious modern bathrooms. Ten miles away lies Milton Abbas, a picture-perfect village of thatched cottages built in 1770 by the Earl of Dorchester who had the old village razed because it interfered with his view. Another pretty village is Cerne Abbas with thatched and Tudor cottages, 7 miles north of Dorchester (Hardy's Casterbridge). Within reach are Salisbury, Longleat, and the many attractions in and around Bath. *Directions:* In Sturminster Newton turn left from the A352 onto the road leading to the village of Hazelbury Bryan. Plumber Manor is 1¼ miles beyond on the left.

PLUMBER MANOR
Owner: Prideaux Brune family
Hazelbury Bryan
Sturminster Newtown DT10 2AF, England
Tel: 01258 472507, Fax: 01258 473370
16 Rooms, Double: £120–£180
Closed: Feb, Credit cards: all major

Just a twenty-minute drive from Salisbury and Stonehenge, Howard's House sits in two acres of lovely gardens in the picture-book village of Teffont Evias. Honey-colored stone cottages are strung along a quiet country lane beside the tumbling tiny River Teff. Just down the road from the grand manor house and hidden behind a tall wall, Howard's House, built in 1623, was for many years the estate's dower house. In 1837 the house was extended. Inspired by the architecture of Switzerland, the owner gave the house an Alpine air. The sitting room offers a large stone fireplace and French windows opening to the garden with places to sit and enjoy a drink on a warm summer evening before going in to dinner. The attractive bedrooms are decorated in quiet, restful colors. All but one (a twin) are furnished with king-sized beds. I especially liked rooms 1 and 2 with their views down the long expanse of garden. Room 3 has a romantic four-poster. Salisbury Cathedral is close by and a great draw for visitors, as are Stonehenge, Stourhead Gardens and Longleat House. An hour's drive will bring you to the hustle and bustle of Georgian Bath or the calm serenity of the Dorset coast. *Directions:* From Salisbury take the A36 to Wilton and the A30 (Shaftesbury). After 3 miles turn right (B3089) towards Mere and Teffont, then after 4½ miles, at Teffont turn left, following the sign to the hotel, 400 yards down the lane.

■ ✗ 📧 @ W P ⑪ ⊘ ⫯ ⫯⫯ ⪫

HOWARD'S HOUSE HOTEL
Owner: Grahame Senior
Manager: Noele Thompson
Teffont Evias
Salisbury SP3 5RJ, England
Tel: 01722 716392, Fax: 01722 7168202
9 Rooms, Double: £165–£185
Closed: Christmas, Credit cards: all major

Thomas Luny, the marine artist, had this home built in 1792 in the center of Teignmouth. It's just a short walk through narrow streets from the sheltered harbor, which has a long history as a fishing and ship-building center. Now this handsome house is home to Alison and John Allan Guests enjoy a spacious sitting room and a nice dining room where breakfast is served. All the rooms have an en suite bathroom, television, mineral water, and a lovely old sea chest. Each is decorated in a contrasting style: Chinese offers painted Oriental furniture; Clairmont (twin or king) has an Edwardian feel; Luny (twin or king) is nautical; and Bitton is contemporary with its impressive four-poster bed. There is no shortage of eating places in the old town or across the bridge in Shaldon. Follow the narrow streets of old Teignmouth to the working harbor and along to the Victorian section of town with its long sandy beach, cheerful pier, and esplanade popular with the bucket-and-spade brigade. Just across the estuary lies Shaldon where every Wednesday, from May to September, residents dress in 18th-century costume. *Directions:* From Exeter take the A380 towards Torquay for 3 miles to the B3192 to Teignmouth. Turn left at the traffic lights at the bottom of the hill, then turn immediately right at the next set of traffic lights, signposted Quays, and immediately left into Teign Street. Thomas Luny House is on your right.

THOMAS LUNY HOUSE
Owners: Alison & John Allan
Teign Street
Teignmouth TQ14 8EG, England
Tel: 01626 772976
4 Rooms, Double: £75–£98
Open: all year, Credit cards: MC, VS

Dale Head Hall, set in beautiful gardens, dates from the 16th century and was, for over 100 years, the Lord Mayor of Manchester's country retreat. It occupies a stunning, isolated position on the shores of Thirlmere, one of Cumbria's most central, tranquil lakes, and provides a central base for exploring the entire Lake District. Marie, Philip and daughter Jane offer a warm welcome. On a February 2008 visit we found the family in the midst of redecorating: removing wallpaper from the bedrooms and replacing it with painted walls, replacing flowery fabrics with those in solid colors. They were in a quandary as to whether to paint the hall purple and considering carpets to replace the acres of bold blue Axminster that was commissioned by Manchester City council. Lakeside bedrooms offer fabulous views and tend to be on the more spacious side while those in the Elizabethan part of the house, at the rear, have period features. One room has a small cradle room snug above the Inglenook fireplace. The beamed Elizabethan dining room becomes a cozy lounge in the summer when the restaurant is moved to one of the lake-view lounges. For a week's stay, Dale Head Hall has apartments in the adjacent stables. *Directions:* Exit the M6 at junction 40 and take the A66 towards Keswick then the B5322 signposted Windermere to join the A591, which you take in the direction of Windermere for ½ mile to the hotel entrance.

DALE HEAD HALL
Owners: Marie & Philip Hill
Thirlmere
Keswick CA12 4TN, England
Tel: 017687 72478, Fax: 0871 900 7234
12 Rooms, Double: £140–£330*
8 Apartments: £260–£650 weekly
*Includes dinner, bed & breakfast
Open: Feb to Dec, Credit cards: all major

Standing in over an acre of carefully tended gardens and surrounded by parkland, Spital Hill provides a tranquil retreat just a ten-minute drive from the busy A1. The house is of Georgian origin, with Victorian additions. Hosts Ann and Robin Clough have named the three large and comfortably furnished bedrooms after family relatives and friends. Emmie has a queen-size double bed, Muriel has two full-size twins, and Anthony is equipped with not only a large double bed but also its own piano, which guests are actively encouraged to play. The house is furnished throughout with family heirlooms and antiques. Robin entertains guests with pre-dinner drinks in the sitting room while Ann applies the meal's finishing touches in the kitchen, often using fresh produce from the garden. Just up the road, shops overlook Thirsk's cobbled market square. Here you can visit the Herriot Centre, the former veterinary surgery of James Herriot, quiet local vet-turned-author. Nearby villages include Kilburn and Coxwold, the former associated with the "mouse man" and his oak furniture and the latter famous for Shandy Hall, the home of Laurence Sterne. York, Castle Howard, and the Yorkshire Moors all make excellent day trips. *Directions:* Spital Hill is 1 mile south of the A19 (A170)/168 junction on the A19, Thirsk to York road. The entrance to Spital Hill is marked by two short white posts at the roadside.

SPITAL HILL
Owners: Ann & Robin Clough
Thirsk Y07 3AE, England
Tel: 01845 522273, Fax: 01845 524970
3 Rooms, Double: £90–£105
1 Cottage: £300 daily, £1200 weekly
Open: all year, Credit cards: MC, VS

Tucked away at the edge of the small town of Thornbury is Thornbury Castle and from the moment you see it you will be enchanted. Construction began in 1510 at the order of the 3rd Duke of Buckingham, but ceased when he was beheaded in 1521 at the Tower of London. The castle was then appropriated by Henry VIII who stayed her in 1535 with Anne Boleyn. The current owners continue the upkeep of this partially restored castle, leaving other areas as a romantic ruin. All 27 bedchambers (one with the largest hotel bed in the UK) are fabulously atmospheric, some with four-poster or coronet beds, stone walls, tapestries, roaring fires and ornate carved ceilingst—this is no longer a castle of drafty stone passages. Dinner in the baronial dining rooms is a leisurely affair and can be accompanied by a glass or two of the wine made from the estates vineyard. Nearby Slimbridge Wildfowl and Wetlands Centre was founded by Sir Peter Scott (son of the explorer) in 1946. Just south of Slimbridge you find Berkeley and Berkeley Castle where Edward II was murdered in the dungeon in 1327. Also in the grounds is the Jenner museum, a tribute to Edward Jenner, discoverer of the smallpox vaccination. *Directions:* At the junction of the M4 and M5 motorways take the A38 north to Thornbury. At the bottom of the hill in the High Street fork left down Castle Street and the entrance to the castle is on the left of the parish church. Follow brown historic signs.

THORNBURY CASTLE
Owner: Von Essen Hotels
Manager: Brian Jarvis
Thornbury BS35 1HH, England
Tel: 01454 281182, Fax: 01454 416188
32 Rooms, Double: £200–£800
Open: all year, Credit cards: all major

You'll have no difficulty finding the Gurnard's Head. Its bright lemon yellow exterior and name painted boldly on the roof stand out from the surrounding heathland. To step into the country pub is to experience rustic simplicity; flagstone floors, open fires in the bar, color washed walls hung with interesting artwork and paperback books (yours to borrow) filling every shelf. It's a low-key friendly place that prides itself on excellent pub fare—simply delicious food that can be enjoyed in the bar, the restaurant, or outside in the beer garden in summer. The wine list is well priced, the beer is local. Upstairs the no frills bedrooms have twin or double beds with soft white linens, fluffy pillows, Welsh blankets, Roberts radios, checked Roman shades and tea makings. Each is provided with a simple shower or bathroom. The rugged headland (after which the hostelry is named) is just down the lane, past the cluster of farms and cottages that comprise Treen. Go walking along the coastal path to appreciate the stunning coastal views. St Ives, with its galleries and artists, and Penzance are just 7 miles distant. The Eden project and Lost Gardens of Heligan are popular daytrips. *Directions:* Exit the A30 and take the A3074 to St Ives; then the B3306 towards St Just. Gurnard's Head is on the right after 7 miles.

■ ⚄ ▭ 🐕 @ W ⑪ ⚓ ⚲

THE GURNARD'S HEAD
Owners: Charles & Edmund Inkin
Manager: Andy Wood
Treen
Zennor, St. Ives TR26 3DE, England
Tel: 01736 796928
7 Rooms, Double: £85–£150
Open: Christmas, Credit cards: MC, VS

Victorians flocked to Tunbridge Wells—in fact, the young Princess Victoria always stayed here when she came to town. The Hotel du Vin's interior has changed considerably since those days, now presenting a light, airy, and uncluttered look. Like its sister hotel in Winchester, the hotel's theme is wine—the wine list is extensive and very well priced as is the accompanying bistro menu with its tempting selections of top-quality food. Bedrooms are stylishly simple in their decor yet equipped with all the modern conveniences. They are generally high-ceilinged rooms, very smartly decorated in a tailored style with superb beds made up with Egyptian cotton linens. Each bedroom is accompanied by a sleek modern bathroom with oversized tub, power shower, and fluffy towels. Splurge and request a larger room with a view of the park. A short walk finds you in the heart of the town with its elegant Regency parades and houses designed by Decimus Burton. The Regency meeting place, The Pantiles, a terraced walk with shops behind a colonnade, is especially memorable. You can also use Tunbridge Wells as your base for visiting the gardens at Scotney Castle and Sissinghurst and exploring Hever and Bodian castles, and the lovely town of Cranbrook with its white-board houses. *Directions:* From the railway station in Tunbridge Wells go up the hill and at the first set of traffic lights turn right onto Crescent Road. The hotel is on your right in 150 yards.

HOTEL DU VIN
Manager: Mike Auld
Crescent Road
Tunbridge Wells TN1 2LY, England
Tel: 01892 526455, Fax: 01892 512044
34 Rooms, Double: £125–£340*
*Breakfast not included: £9.95–£13.50
Open: all year, Credit cards: all major

Upper Slaughter, just up the hill from its sister village, Lower Slaughter, is a quiet, tranquil collection of idyllic cottages surrounded by bucolic Cotswold countryside. In the center of the village lies the grand former home of the Witts family, "lords of the manor" hereabouts for over 200 years. A massive portrait of the Reverend Witts, sitting regally on his stallion, graces the drawing room and other family portraits decorate the walls in the public areas which set the tone for the hotel, a crisp modern decor accented with antiques. Facing the lake (built as a skating pond for one of the Witt children), the main house offers the opportunity to stay in grand high-ceilinged bedrooms with decadent bathrooms. Cleverly blended into this large home is a curving wing of rooms built to appear like other farm buildings. Overlooking the narrow lane, it offers well proportioned bedrooms and top-of-the-line bathrooms. A path leads through the fields to the old mill at Lower Slaughter. It is a perfect location for forays through the Cotswolds; nearby Lower and Upper Swell are very picturesque. Broadway and Bourton-on-the-Water are best visited early in the morning to avoid the crowds. The Cotswold Farm Park with its rare farm animals is nearby. *Directions:* From the A429 on the outskirts of Bourton-on-the-Water, a small signpost indicates "The Slaughters." Follow the lane through Lower to Upper Slaughter.

LORDS OF THE MANOR HOTEL
Manager: Ingo Wiangke
Upper Slaughter
Cheltenham GL54 2JD, England
Tel: 01451 820243, Fax: 01451 820696
29 Rooms, Double: £191–£362
Open: all year, Credit cards: all major

Standing on the corner of St. John's Hill, a charming little square on the edge of the very attractive little town of Wareham, Gold Court House was built in 1762 on the foundations of a 13th-century cottage where the local goldsmith lived. Now it is the spacious, lovely home of Anthea and Michael Hipwell and, fortunately for guests, they continue to offer the same hospitable welcome (along with a tail-wagging greeting from Merlin, the Labrador) as they did for over 15 years at The Old Vicarage in Affpuddle. All the spacious, well-decorated bedrooms overlook the lovely walled garden. Two are found up the main staircase, while the third has a private entry off the garden. Breakfast is the only meal served most of the year but Anthea offers advice on pubs and restaurants to walk to for dinner. Likewise, Anthea helps guests plan their exploration of Hardy country or visits to the haunts of Lawrence of Arabia. The Dorset coast (Lulworth Cove, Dirdle Door, and Ringstead Bay) is close at hand. Nearby are the historic towns of Dorchester, Sherbourne, and Poole, with lots to see and good shopping. *Directions:* Wareham is on the A351 between Poole and Swanage. Cross the River Piddle and go down North Street into South Street. As you see the River Frome in front of you, turn left into St. John's Hill. Gold Court House is on the corner.

GOLD COURT HOUSE
Owners: Anthea & Michael Hipwell
St. John's Hill
Wareham BH20 4LZ, England
Tel & Fax: 01929 553320
3 Rooms, Double: £75
Closed: Christmas to New Year, Credit cards: none

Standing on the River Frome on the edge of the lovely town of Wareham, this 16th-century building was once the priory of Lady St. Mary, a Benedictine monastery, and is now a particularly lovely hotel. The entrance, through a little walled courtyard, sets the tone for this most delightful hotel. Decorated in soft colors, the dining room is most inviting. Lovely furniture and a grand piano highlight the beamed living room whose French windows lead under the wisteria-laden trellis to a broad expanse of lawn, which slopes down to the lazily flowing river—a perfect place to enjoy lunch on a warm summer day. A narrow maze of corridors and stairs winds amongst the rooms, which are on the small side but very smartly outfitted. If you are looking for the most deluxe of quarters, request one of the suites in the riverside boathouse. The gardens are a delight, full of roses in the summer, with a series of small, sheltered walled gardens. Wareham is an interesting mix of architectural styles encircled by earth banks built by the Saxons. Lawrence of Arabia's home is open to the public at nearby Clouds Hill. There are many wonderful places to visit, such as Lulworth Cove, Corfe Castle, Poole Harbor, Wool, Bindon Abbey, and Durlston Head. *Directions:* Wareham is on the A351 between Poole and Swanage.

THE PRIORY
Manager: Jeremy Merchant
Church Green
Wareham BH20 4ND, England
Tel: 01929 551666, Fax: 01929 554519
13 Rooms, Double: £225–£325
5 Suites: £315–£395
Open: all year, Credit cards: all major

This is a particularly lovely part of England with miles of unspoilt coastline, little villages and mighty castles such as Bamburgh which commands a rocky outcrop above the dunes. The stone cottages of the village nestle below in its shadow. To see all that the area has to offer there is no better place to stay than Waren House Hotel, a delightful Georgian country house overlooking a sheltered coastal bay. The chandelier-lit entrance hall is home to a grand piano and many dolls from Anita's extensive collection. The ornately decorated drawing room is furnished with deep sofas, the library with traditional leather. By contrast, the large dining room, decorated in soft peach, is much more restful on the eye, with family portraits and pictures adorning the walls. Bedrooms are decorated in a range of different styles. I particularly enjoyed Duke and Duchess with their toile wallpaper and drapes and Baywatch, named for its distant view of the bay. It's a great spot to spend time on your way to or from Scotland. A short drive brings you to Holy Island, historically known as Lindisfarne. Caution: the causeway connecting the island to the mainland is flooded at high tide. *Directions:* Forty-five miles north of Newcastle on the A1, turn right to Waren Mill and the hotel is on your right at the far end of the village.

🛏 🎿 💳 ☎ 🐕 P ⑪ ⚓ 🧍 👬 🏇 ⚓

WAREN HOUSE HOTEL
Owners: Anita & Peter Laverack
Belford
Waren Mill NE70 7EE, England
Tel: 01668 214581, Fax: 01668 214484
10 Rooms, Double: £137–£175
3 Suites: £168–£223
Open: all year, Credit cards: all major

Wartling Place is a fine white Victorian house with Georgian origins in the heart of the Sussex countryside. It stands well back from the road in acres of grounds in the pretty village of Wartling, close to the 13th-century church. The home of the Gittoes family, it's a captivating place—relaxing and happy—and large enough for guests to have lots of privacy and space. Two of the large bedrooms have antique queen-sized four-poster beds and two have brass beds that can be either twins or kings. All are delightfully kitted out and accompanied by en suite bathrooms. Breakfast is served in the spacious guest sitting/dining room. Dinner is available by prior arrangement and there are lots of pubs and restaurants nearby (the Lamb Inn serves excellent food). If you would like to stay for a week, there's a delightful two-bedroom cottage in the garden. Just up the road is Herstmonceux Castle, a romantic, fortified 15th-century house complete with moat and crusaders' tombs in the old church opposite the castle entrance. Other popular places to visit include Charleston, Monks House (Virginia Wolfe's home), Bodiam Castle, quaint Rye with its cobbled streets, and the gardens at Pashley Manor and Great Dixter. *Directions:* Five miles outside Eastbourne leave the A22 and take the A271 towards Bexhill and Hastings through Herstmonceux and turn right after Windmill Hill for Wartling. Wartling Place is just after the Lamb Inn on the right.

WARTLING PLACE
Owners: Rowena & Barry Gittoes
Wartling
Herstmonceux BN27 1RY, England
Tel: 01323 832590
4 Rooms, Double: £125–£165
1 Cottage £500–£750 weekly
Open: all year, Credit cards: all major

Beryl, a Gothic Revival mansion on thirteen acres of grounds just a mile from Wells Cathedral, is a grand house full of lovely antiques and home to Holly Nowell and her family. The measure of her success is the large number of returning guests who bring their family, friends, and even dogs (provided that they are compatible with the resident toy poodles and cats). The green room (where you can help yourself to drinks from the honesty bar and watch the telly), and the drawing room are yours to enjoy. If you have difficulty with stairs there's a stair lift. All the bedrooms have special features with most of the principal bedrooms being larger and grander. Choose Winston if you have a passion for grand, old-fashioned, climb-into bathtubs, Butterfly (a twin or king) or Master (a grand four-poster with a view from the loo) if you enjoy space and want to wake up with Wells Cathedral framed in the enormous bay windows. Attic rooms are cozy by comparison though all are very nicely furnished and decorated. For dinner there's a choice of several restaurants or the local pub a short drive away. Be sure to visit daughter Mary-Ellen and Edward's jewelry boutique in the coach house. Wells is England's smallest city, with a most glorious cathedral. *Directions:* Leave or approach Wells on the B3139 in the direction of The Horringtons. Turn into Hawkers Lane (bus shelter on the corner). Drive to the top of the lane and continue into Beryl's driveway.

BERYL
Owner: Holly Nowell
Hawkers Lane
Wells BA5 3JP, England
Tel: 01749 678738, Fax: 01749 670508
9 Rooms, Double: £75–£140
Closed: Christmas, Credit cards: MC, VS

The Citadel sits like a mighty fortress on a knoll overlooking verdant countryside. As soon as you cross the threshold, you realize this is not a "castle" of drafty halls and stone chambers, but a lovely home built to a fanciful design. A spacious sitting room occupies one of the turrets and leads to the large billiard room. You are welcome to bring your own wine to accompany supper in the dining room. Up the broad staircase, two of the en suite bedrooms occupy turrets. A lovely twin-bedded room has an en suite shower room. As an added bonus there are 3 acres of glorious gardens to admire. The adjacent golf club is a popular venue, but the real magic of the area lies in a visit to Hawkstone Park where you follow an intricate network of pathways through woodlands and across a narrow log bridge to high cliffs, a ruined castle, mystical grotto, and giant obelisk. The Ironbridge Gorge Museums, Shrewsbury, and Chester are within an hour's drive. *Directions:* From Shrewsbury, take the A49 (north) for 12 miles, turn right for Hodnet and Weston-under-Redcastle, and The Citadel is on your right, a quarter of a mile after leaving Weston-under-Redcastle (before Hawkstone Park).

THE CITADEL
Owners: Sylvia & Beverley Griffiths
Weston-under-Redcastle
Shrewsbury SY4 5JY, England
Tel: 01630 685204
3 Rooms, Double: £100–£120
Closed: Christmas & Easter, Credit cards: MC, VS

Tucked behind a rambling, timbered façade with mullioned windows and steeply pitched roof, Wesley House is a delightful "restaurant with rooms" offering fabulous fare to appreciative travelers and faithful locals. From the entry with its comfortable seating, you can look through to the staggered levels of the attractive restaurant whose enticing menu makes for difficult choices. Ask to be seated in the atrium with its countryside views. Not looking for a big meal then consider wine and tapas in the adjacent bar. Climb the narrow little stairs of this inn, whose oldest part dates to 1435, to five snug guestrooms, each named for a local meadow. The smallest, charmingly named Mumble Meadow, has a double bed and is attractively decorated in fabrics of cream and reds. Preachers, the oldest room and housed in what was once the fireplace, has twin beds and a sloping floor. At the back, Sandy Hollow has a twin or double bed; while Almsbury, enjoys a private terrace and views across to Sudeley Castle. Setchley is also identified as the emergency fire escape, so residents of this room would be the first ones out! On Saturday nights dinner, bed and breakfast rates apply from £180 to £200 per room. *Directions:* Winchcombe is on the B4632 between Cheltenham and Broadway. Wesley House is easy to find on the main street at the corner of Castle Street.

WESLEY HOUSE
Owner: Matthew Brown
High Street
Winchcombe GL54 5LJ, England
Tel: 01242 602366, Fax: 01242 609046
5 Rooms, Double: £80–£95
Open: all year, Credit cards: all major

Sudeley Lodge, built in 1760 as a hunting lodge on the Sudeley Castle estate, sits high on a hill overlooking rolling countryside beyond its acres of gorgeous gardens. Jim grew up here and shares the family home with his parents, with Jim, Susie, and their family having the Westward wing. Jim and Susie welcome guests with tea and cake, encouraging them to make themselves at home, relax by the fire, sit on the terrace, wander through the gardens, and go walking on the estate—there's the ruins of a Roman villa in the adjoining woods. Upstairs, the spacious bedrooms have lovely views across the garden to the countryside. Susie offers lots of choices for her breakfasts including kedgeree and fishcakes as well as the traditional English breakfast. There is no shortage of excellent places to eat both in nearby Winchcombe and the surrounding villages. Just down the road is Sudeley Castle with its parklike setting, magnificent medieval exterior, and recently restored gardens. This is an ideal spot for exploring Cotswold towns and villages, gardens, and houses, with Broadway, Chipping Campden, Lower Slaughter, Cirencester, and Stow-on-the-Wold all being within easy reach. *Directions:* Winchcombe is on the B4632 between Cheltenham and Broadway. Turn into Castle Street (in the center of the village) and proceed up the hill. Pass the farm buildings on the right and turn right, signed for Sudeley Lodge. Pass two cottages on the way to the house.

WESTWARD AT SUDELEY LODGE
Owners: Susie & Jim Wilson
Winchcombe GL54 5JB, England
Tel: 01242 604372, Fax: 01242 609198
3 Rooms, Double: £80–£100
Closed: Dec 1 to Mar 1, Credit cards: MC, VS

Centrally located in the historic city of Winchester sits the most attractive Hotel du Vin and Bistro in an elegant townhouse designed by Christopher Wren (of St. Paul's fame). The hotel's theme is wine, with each bedroom named for its sponsoring winery that provided the photos and memorabilia decorating the walls. The rooms' overall decor is very similar —smart striped curtains, a duvet-topped queen- or king-sized bed (there is one king four-poster), television, and bathroom with oversized tub and Victorian shower with power head. I particularly enjoyed the most expensive and very large Courvoisier room with its ornate plasterwork ceiling, large window framing the garden, and two-part bathroom. Beringer's view of the car park was more than compensated for by its spaciousness and attractive photos of the famous winery. Trompe l'oeil plasterwork is an interesting feature of the spacious drawing room. Continental breakfast is available in the privacy of your room. The bistro is central to the operation and its menu is fun and varied. *Directions:* Turn off the M3 at Junction 11 to Winchester and follow signposts for the city center. The Hotel du Vin is on the left with lots of parking to the rear.

HOTEL DU VIN
Manager: Mark Jones
14 Southgate Street
Winchester SO23 9EF, England
Tel: 01962 841414, Fax: 01962 842458
24 Rooms, Double: £140–£240*
*Breakfast not included: £9.95–£13.50
Open: all year, Credit cards: all major

Just beside the cathedral in a maze of little streets in the oldest part of Winchester, you can find comfortable accommodation at The Wykeham Arms and, across the road, under the same ownership, at The Saint George. The 250 year old Wykeham Arms is an extraordinarily convivial and welcoming inn, with log fires, candles, over 600 pictures on the walls, and 1,500 tankards hanging from beams, walls, and windows. Food in the pub ranges from elaborate to tasty, traditional fare, while a more sophisticated menu is offered at quieter tables in the Bishop's Bar or the Jameson Room. I loved Hamilton, a twin with red walls above white paneling, dozens of pictures of royalty and all things military, and huge bathroom with brick fireplace. The Saint George was converted from two tiny row houses and has the quaint attraction of a traditional general store just off the parlor. Up the narrow staircase there are four large, immaculate bedrooms, with absolutely everything from a sumptuous bathroom to a modem port. Offering most space is the Old College Bakehouse, a little cottage in the garden, with a large sitting room and bathroom downstairs, bedroom upstairs, and tall arched, leaded windows opening up to rooftop views. *Directions:* Winchester is between junctions 9 and 10 on the M3. The hotel is located near the cathedral—the staff will be happy to send you a map so that you can navigate through the pedestrian zone to the pub's car park.

🍺 🏌 CREDIT ☎ P ⊩ 🚶 🚶‍♀️

THE WYKEHAM ARMS & THE SAINT GEORGE
Managers: Ann & Dennis Evans
75 Kingsgate Street
Winchester SO23 9PE, England
Tel: 01962 853834, Fax: 01962 854411
14 Rooms, Double: £115–£150
Closed: Christmas, Credit cards: all major

A lot of water has passed under the bridge since John C spent boyhood holidays with his grandma at Gilpin Lodge. What started out as a traditional country house hotel has been transformed into a sophisticated destination, while still keeping all the personal touches of family and long-term staff's hands-on involvement. Enjoy the conviviality of the bar, afternoon tea in the lounge, quiet repose in one of the sitting nooks and dine in one of four lovely rooms that make up the award winning restaurant. While we love all of the bedrooms, we are particularly impressed by the garden suites with their understated contemporary decor, spacious living room and doors opening to a deck with a private hot tub overlooking the garden and beyond to the peaceful countryside. Stroll through the gardens to visit the llamas or enjoy a massage or treatment in the privacy of your room. A stone's throw away is Windermere golf course. A ferry takes you across the lake to Near Sawrey and Beatrix Potter's home. Wordsworth fans head for Rydal House and Dove Cottage, while walkers head for the hills. Gilpin Lodge can arrange for a private car and driver to escort you on your sightseeing. *Directions:* Exit the M6 at junction 36, taking the A591 around Kendal towards Windermere. At the large roundabout, turn onto the B5284 through Crook Village to Gilpin Lodge on the right.

GILPIN LODGE
Owners: Christine, John, Zoë & Barney Cunliffe
Crook Road
Windermere LA23 3NE, England
Tel: 015394 88818, Fax: 015394 88058
20 Rooms, Double: £210–£360*
*Includes dinner, bed & breakfast
Open: all year, Credit cards: all major
Relais & Châteaux

Windermere is one of the most popular and busy Lake District towns. You'll find Holbeck Ghyll peacefully set high above Lake Windermere in a rhododendron-filled garden overlooking the water and the peaks of the Langdale fells—idyllic scenery that has made the Lake District such a magnet for visitors. Mellow, golden-oak paneling in the entrance hall extends up the staircase of Holbeck Ghyll and heavy beams create a nook large enough for chairs round a cozy log fire. In summer, guests prefer the sitting rooms whose window seats offer a magnificent view of the lake and the distant mountains. The restaurant has been awarded a Michelin star for nine consecutive years. There are lots of choices for each course and superlatives are the order of the day. Accommodations offer lots of opportunities for spectacular views: Renée Zellweger reputedly considers the luxurious Miss Potter suite (a cottage) her favorite; I loved the seclusion of the historic converted barn (four luxurious bedrooms and the opportunity to have the chef cook dinner for you) and the spaciousness of room 6—the long ago billiard room. Pamper yourself with a beauty treatment in the health spa, relax in the sauna and steam room, or work out in the gym. Nearby are Dove Cottage, Rydal Mount, and the villages of Hawkshead and Grasmere. *Directions:* From Windermere take the A591 (Ambleside) for 3 miles, turn right on Holbeck Lane. The hotel is on the left after .5 miles.

HOLBECK GHYLL
Owners: Patricia & David Nicholson
Holbeck Lane
Windermere LA23 1LU, England
Tel: 015394 32375, Fax: 015394 34743
23 Rooms, Double: £240–£550
4 Cottages: from £300 daily
Open: all year, Credit cards: all major

The Samling is set high in the seclusion of its own sixty-seven-acre estate with sweeping views down to Lake Windermere. Built in the late 1700s, the property consists of the main house and cottage-style outbuildings, all of which have been extensively, but aesthetically, renovated and converted into ten luxury suites, nine directly overlooking the lake. Tyan, reportedly the favorite of Tom Cruise, has a rich, blue décor. Manmire is a duplex cottage suite. Its large sitting room has a private terrace and large bathroom with rustic wood walls. Pym is a large junior suite set into an attic space with large roof windows. Our favorite was The Bothy, a cottage with split-level living accommodation, separate living room, and private south-facing terrace. Its bathroom features an antique shower believed to be owned by Winston Churchill. Wander the estate, woodlands, fields and gardens dotted with contemporary works by well-known artists including iron work by William Pym and a spire of slate and glass by Charles Bailey. Relax with your chosen drink in the drawing room or on the terrace with its view down Lake Windermere. Full English breakfast is delivered to your room. The dining room specializes in local produce supported by a reasonably priced international wine list. *Directions:* From Windermere, take A59 towards Ambleside for 3 miles. Turn right up the hotels steep driveway.

THE SAMLING
Owner: Von Essen Hotels
Manager: Claire Pollock
Ambleside Road
Windermere LA23 1LR, England
Tel: 015394 31922, Fax: 015394 30400
11 Rooms, Double: £200–£430
Open: all year, Credit cards: all major

Seven 17th-century townhouses at the very heart of this delightful Cotswold town have been cleverly interwoven to create this charming hotel. This accounts for the maze of little staircases seemingly going every-which-way up and around to the bedrooms. Several with high ceilings, all are different and are decorated in soft, muted colors in a smart modern style. Nightingale, Jay, Swan, and Robin are particularly attractive rooms. Equally delightful rooms (Barn Owl, Osprey, Skylark and Partridge) are found in an adjacent cottage, as is the expansive Peacock suite. The elegant dining room is enhanced by dramatic, large flower arrangements. As an alternative to formal dining you can enjoy a more casual meal in the delightful bistro whose central, log fireplace burns a cheery blaze. French windows open up to a small garden where tables, benches, and colorful hanging baskets are encircled by a high, stone wall—a lovely spot to enjoy lunch in the summer. Massages and facials available. The small town of Woodstock is at its best after the crowds have left. Walk through the grounds to visit Blenheim Palace. Oxford is 8 miles away and Stratford-upon-Avon is 32 miles. Cotswold villages are at your doorstep. *Directions:* Market Street is off Oxford Street, the A44 Oxford to Stratford Road.

THE FEATHERS
Manager: Luc Morel
Market Street
Woodstock OX20 1SX, England
Tel: 01993 812291, Fax: 01993 813158
20 Rooms, Double: £169–£279*
*Service: 10%
Minimum Stay Required: 2 nights on weekends
Open: all year, Credit cards: all major

Judges Country House started out in the 1880's as Kirklevington Hall, originally commissioned by the Richardson family of Hartlepool as their rural retreat. It remained a private residence for nearly one hundred years, until it was taken over by the local authorities to provide lodging for circuit judges on location in the northeast of the country. More recently it has been reborn as a privately owned traditional country house hotel. Many of the original architectural features, high ceilings, sash windows, dark wood paneling and the spacious conservatory coexist with comfortable furnishings, luxurious feather mattresses, four-poster beds and all electrical mod-cons. An interesting twist is the presence of a goldfish in a bowl in each of the rooms. Meals are served in the conservatory and feature local produce alongside an extensive wine list. A small stream meanders over waterfalls and under bridges throughout the extensive grounds. Natural woodlands provide guests with a network of pathways to stroll or jog among the flora and fauna native to North Yorkshire. It's a central location for exploring the North York Moors and visiting Rievaulx Abbey as well as exploring the coast where Whitby (one-time home of Captain Cook) is a must visit. *Directions:* Exit the A1(M) at Thirsk and take the A168 (A19) for 25 miles to the A67 which you take in the direction of Yarm. Judges Country House is on your left after 1 mile.

JUDGES COUNTRY HOUSE HOTEL
Owners: Shirley & Michael Downs
Manager: Tim Howard
Kirklevington
Yarm TS15 9LW, England
Tel: 01642 789000, Fax: 01642 782878
21 Rooms, Double: £179–£230
Open: all year, Credit cards: all major

From the outside, Alexander House looks just like the many other terraced houses that line the streets in this neighborhood, but inside it is delightfully different, showcasing top-of-the-line decor by Gillian and Dave Reynard. A sunny yellow hallway rises from the entry, setting the cheerful mood felt throughout the house. In the sitting room plump sofas flank the fireplace and a glass-fronted cabinet displays Gill's extensive collection of Royal Doulton china figurines. The bedrooms are airy, immaculate, and really well equipped. I particularly admired room 5 at the top of the house, a family room with both a queen and single bed. After a hearty breakfast it's time to get acquainted with the many delights of York, see the magnificent Minster, explore the Viking city of Jorvik, and experience times past in the Castle Museum. Guests often enjoy interesting stories in the evening when they join a guide on a "ghost walk" through the historic streets of this ancient city. *Directions:* Leave the A64 (which forms the southern part of the York Outer Ring Road) at the A1036, in the direction of York city center (signposted York West). Turn right (opposite the Quickfit garage) into Scarcroft Road. At the end of the road turn right into Bishopthorpe Road and Alexander House is on your left after 100 yards. Dave will take your car to the off-road parking at the rear of the house.

■ ✷ CREDIT @ W P 🚭 📷 🚶 🚶🚶 🐎

ALEXANDER HOUSE
Owners: Gill & Dave Reynard
94 Bishopthorpe Road
York YO23 1J5, England
Tel: 01904 625016
4 Rooms, Double: £69–£85
Minimum Stay Required: 2 nights
Closed: Christmas and New Year, Credit cards: MC, VS

York, where Romans walked, Vikings ruled, and Normans conquered, is a fascinating city, its historical center encircled by a massive stone wall. The Grange, a lovely townhouse hotel, lies just beyond the city walls and ten minutes' walk from the Minster (cathedral), making it an ideal spot for exploring this wonderful city. The morning room, which leads directly off the stone-flagged lobby, has a rich, traditional feel with its Turkish carpet and Victorian portrait hung over the fireplace. The Ivy Brasserie is more modern in style and serves modern British food. The Cellar Bar is a convivial place to meet for drinks, light meals and lunch. Each of the bedrooms—some with canopied four-poster or half-tester beds—has different decor: several are very dramatic. I was impressed by the number of ground floor rooms—handy for folks who have difficulty with stairs. York takes several days to explore: attractions include the Minster, the Jorvik Viking museum, the Treasurer's House, the medieval streets of The Shambles, the castle and its adjacent museum, walks along the walls, and a boat ride on the River Ouse. . *Directions:* The Grange is located along Bootham, which is the A19, York to Thirsk road.

THE GRANGE
Owners: Vivien & Jeremy Castle
Manager: Dominic Bishop
1 Clifton
York Y030 6AA, England
Tel: 01904 644744, Fax: 01904 612453
36 Rooms, Double: £140–£300
Open: all year, Credit cards: all major

Middlethorpe Hall is an imposing, red-brick William-and-Mary country house built in 1699 for Thomas Barlow, a successful cutler who wished to distance himself from his industrial success and establish himself as a country gentleman. It has been skillfully restored by Historic House Hotels and is now a very grand hotel, but without one iota of stuffiness. The two refined dining rooms have large windows overlooking the grounds. After enjoying elegant, country-house fare you retire to the enormous, graceful drawing room for coffee, chocolates and liqueurs round the fire watched over by the massive portraits of long-departed gentry. Up the magnificent carved-oak staircase, bedrooms enjoy high ceilings, tall windows (those at the back with views across the grounds), and small bathrooms. Additionally, very attractive bedrooms are found in the stable block across the courtyard. The spa contains a pool, steam room, sauna, fitness room, and three beauty-treatment rooms. York (a five-minute drive away) will keep you busy for at least two days—add Castle Howard, explorations of the dales, moorlands, and the coast, and you can justify staying for a week. *Directions:* The hotel is situated just outside the village of Bishopthorpe, next to York racecourse. Leave the A64 (which forms the southern part of the York Outer Ring Road) at the A1036, in the direction of York West or Racecourse and follow the hotel's map.

MIDDLETHORPE HALL & SPA
Manager: Lionel Chatard
Bishopthorpe Road
York YO23 2GB, England
Tel: 01904 641241, Fax: 01904 620176
29 Rooms, Double: £140–£450
Open: all year, Credit cards: all major

Places to Stay in Scotland

Fifteen miles of winding, single-track road lead you through land and sea lochs in some of Scotland's wildest scenery to Achiltibuie, a few cottages along the road overlooking a broad expanse of bay and the Summer Isles. These grassy little islands include the five tiny communities on the peninsula of which Achiltibuie is one. Just beyond the post office you find the Summer Isles Hotel. Guests come to enjoy solitude and wild scenery in the daytime and in the evening experience the outstanding cooking of Chris Firth-Bernard. His five course dinner offers no choices (except for dessert which comes on a trolley laden with temptations). Accommodation comes in a range of distinct categories: rooms in the main house (ask for one facing the sea); the turf-roofed log cabins (lots of country charm but no view and priced accordingly); cottage rooms (very attractively decorated in white on white with two rooms offering views of the sea across the fields); the boathouse suite (fireplace in the sitting room and spectacular view from the bedroom atop a spiral staircase); and cottage suites (with view, sitting areas, and amazing bathrooms with high-pressure showers). You can take a local boat round the islands to see seals and birds. *Directions:* Achiltibuie is 85 miles from Inverness. Take the A835 for 10 miles beyond Ullapool and turn left for Achiltibuie.

SUMMER ISLES HOTEL
Owner: Terry Mackay
Achiltibuie
Wester Ross IV26 2YG, Scotland
Tel: 01854 622282, Fax: 01854 622251
12 Rooms, Double: £140–£260
1 Cottage: £260 daily
Open: Easter to mid-Oct, Credit cards: MC, VS

Boath House is a real beauty—a Georgian mansion overlooking a lake with 20 acres of grounds with its own Victorian walled garden. The spectacular bedrooms are just the beginning. The two lake view rooms are divine: Number 3 has a grand bathroom with side-by-side free standing tubs, Number 4 a magnificent four poster. Woodland view rooms are on a smaller scale with features such as vivid collages and Robert Burns quotations on the bathroom walls. The contemporary style restaurant overlooks the lake—a perfect match to the chef's stylish cuisine—some of the very finest in Scotland. Take a break from sightseeing and arrange for spa treatments or simply take it easy. Contemporary works from local artists are displayed throughout the house and the Mathesons encourage guests to move selected items to their room on a "try before you buy" basis. A separate double-bedded guest cottage in the grounds provides a secluded hideaway. Golfers head to the championship courses at Nairn and Dunbar but are also urged not to overlook the local good-value-for-money courses. Just outside Nairn you can visit the massive sand dunes that swallowed the village of Culbin. Loch Ness and Cawdor Castle are great attractions. *Directions:* From Inverness take the A96 towards Aberdeen. Go through Nairn and Boath House is on your left after 2 miles.

BOATH HOUSE
Owners: Wendy & Don Matheson
Auldearn
Nairn IV12 STE, Scotland
Tel: 01667 454896, Fax: 01667 455469
8 Rooms, Double: £220–£320
Open: all year, Credit cards: all major

If your vacation plans take you anywhere near southwest Ayrshire (maybe while traveling between Scotland and the Lake District or Ireland), treat yourself to a stay—house party-style—at luxurious Glenapp Castle, an elegant 1870 mansion in 30 acres of delightful grounds overlooking the Irish Sea. Fay and Graham Cowan devoted six years to bringing the castle from dilapidation to perfection—walls glow with attractive tiger-stripe oak paneling, tall windows are beautifully dressed with rich fabrics, chandeliers sparkle, lovely antiques and original oil paintings are expertly placed, and comfortable, plump-cushioned sofas and chairs are grouped invitingly around open fires. There are two dining rooms, both overlooking the sea: one, in a golden-yellow decor, for breakfast and lunch, and the other, dramatically decorated in burgundy and with spectacular sunset views, for outstanding six-course dinners. Guestrooms offer every amenity and the two master bedrooms are particularly lavish and spacious. Nine rooms have gas fires, lit for guests' arrival, and many bathrooms have beautifully renovated original marble walls and floors. This is the Cowan family's home and they bring a very warm and personal touch to this absolutely irresistible hotel. Advance reservations are a must. *Directions:* Going south on the A77, pass through Ballantrae and turn right just after the bridge at the edge of the village. Drive 1 mile to the hotel gates on the left.

GLENAPP CASTLE
Owners: Fay & Graham Cowan
Ballantrae KA26 0NZ, Scotland
Tel: 01465 831212, Fax: 01465 831000
20 Rooms, Double: £375–£575
Open: end of Mar to Jan 2, Credit cards: all major
Relais & Châteaux

With lush lawns stretching beside the confluence of the Dee and Feugh rivers, Banchory Lodge has a magnificent setting. There has been a hostelry here since the 16th century when the mail coach halted at Banchory to change horses. Over the years it has evolved into a pleasing, rather rambling, old-fashioned country house hotel. The first thing I always notice at Banchory House is the abundance of flower arrangements, from little posies on coffee tables to grand floral arrangements alongside splendid oil paintings. Log fires and oversized chairs set the relaxed, comfortable atmosphere of the place. Dinner is served in the grand dining room, which has a comfortable formality, with guests both in jacket and tie and casual attire. Country-house fare is the order of the day here, but if you wish to dine more simply, just choose one or two courses from the menu. Bedrooms are delightfully old-fashioned: room 9 with its semi-circular window is as always a particular favorite —though I would settle for any of the rooms that face the tumbling river. Fishing, golfing, and walking are popular pastimes. Nearby Crathes Castle (an L-shaped tower house) has an early-18th-century formal garden, while Drum Castle has a magnificent rose garden. Farther away lie Fyvie and Craigievar. *Directions:* From Aberdeen take the A93 for 17 miles to Banchory. Turn left at the traffic lights and left just before you cross the river.

BANCHORY LODGE
Owner: Margaret Jaffray
Banchory AB31 5HS, Scotland
Tel: 01330 822625, Fax: 01330 825019
23 Rooms, Double: £170–£220
Open: all year, Credit cards: all major

Dun na Mara has a special undefinable magic: a loch-side location with a private beach and views across the water to the distant Island of Mull, delightful architecture—a stylish Edwardian home built in 1911, and pleasing contemporary minimalist décor with soft colors creating a sense of calm and order. It's the baby of Suzanne Pole and Mark Phillips, a couple of architects who escaped the rat race to open Dun na Mara after falling head over heels in love with the place, spending over four years in acquiring it. Design and attention to detail—in the rooms and in the overall feng shui—is so evident from the welcome note to the placement of your breakfast napkin that you just know that Suzanne and Mark have thought of everything. I found it a total escape from the clutter of my everyday life with glorious views—a complete oasis of calm. The onetime gardener's home is a detached self-catering cottage with its own private garden—an ideal weeklong escape for two, equipped and decorated to the highest standard complete with an open fire. Whether you are taking a day trip to the islands (Mull, Staffa, and Iona); visiting, castles, lochs and glens; or just relaxing and strolling along the beach, there is enough to keep you busy for a week. *Directions:* From Crianlarich take the A85 towards Oban. At Connel take the bridge towards Fort William (A828) for 3 miles where you find Dun na Mara beside the loch just before the village of Benderloch.

DUN NA MARA
Owners: Suzanne & Mark McPhillips
Benderloch PA37 1RT, Scotland
Tel: 01631 720233
7 Rooms, Double: £95–£115
1 Cottage: £340–£540 weekly
Open: all year, Credit cards: MC, VS

Callander is such an attractive, busy, little place. I selected Brook Linn for being the most welcoming of bed and breakfasts and its lovely location high above the town. Built as a private home for a wealthy wool merchant, this solid Victorian home is set high on the hill well away from the bustle of the town but close enough for a ten-minute walk to find you at its heart. A hearty Scottish breakfast is the only meal served but Fiona and Derek are happy to recommend local restaurants that you can walk to and an outstanding fish restaurant a short drive away. The old pine doors and stained glass window on the staircase are most attractive period features. I particularly like rooms four and two—rooms large enough to have a seating area by the window so you can sit and drink in the splendid view of the distant Trossachs. Handily these two rooms also sport larger bathrooms with showers over the tub. With two twin, one double, and one single room, Derek and Fiona can accommodate most combinations of travelers. The Trossachs with their rolling pasture and heather moors, mountains, and glens are on your doorstep. The Wallace Monument Museum and Stirling Castle are just a short drive away. *Directions:* Take the A84 into Callander going north through the town and turn right just beyond Pinewood Nursing Home into Leny Feus. Follow the road up the hill and right into Brook Linn's driveway.

BROOK LINN
Owners: Fiona & Derek House
Leny Feus
Callander FK17 8AU, Scotland
Tel: 01877 330103
4 Rooms, Double: £60–£80
Open: Easter to Oct, Credit cards: MC, VS

We defy you not to wax lyrical over the Three Chimneys and The House Over-By, an outstanding restaurant with rooms. Just the thought of the marvelous food served at the Three Chimneys sends us into raptures and the location, a historic croft packed with all the old-world charm of thick walls, low beams, and cozy dining nooks just cannot be overstated. The Spears have run the restaurant for over 20 years and in this time Shirley has gained a worldwide following for her food. Incorporating as much fresh local produce as possible from Skye and the Highlands, many of her dishes are based on traditional ideas but given her own modern slant. Accommodation in the adjacent House Over-By is stylishly chic. The large luxurious bedrooms are decorated in soft, earthy Highland colors, and each has a sparkling, state-of-the-art bathroom and views across Loch Dunvegan to the Outer Hebrides. In the mornings a generous buffet is served in the breakfast room. Substantially dicounted rates are available for dinner, bed and breakfast for stays of 2 nights or longer. For sightseeing, you are just 5 miles from Dunvegan Castle. Narrow lanes wind you round the north of Skye, with its bays, clifftops, and spectacular views. *Directions:* From the outskirts of Dunvegan take the B884 towards Glendale for 4 miles to Colbost where you find Three Chimneys and The House Over-By on the left beside the Croft Museum.

THE THREE CHIMNEYS & THE HOUSE OVER-BY
Owners: Shirley & Eddie Spear
Colbost IV55 8ZT, Scotland
Tel: 01470 511258, Fax: 01470 511358
6 Rooms, Double: £275–£285
Closed: Jan 4 to Jan 29, Credit cards: all major

Beyond a vast expanse of immaculately mown lawn stands Culloden House, a beautiful Georgian mansion built to incorporate the ruins of Culloden Castle, Bonnie Prince Charlie's headquarters before the fateful battle of 1746. Culloden House has always had a reputation for hospitality, a tradition that is continued today. After canapés in the clubby bar, dine in the massive dining room with its lofty ceiling, faux-marble columns, and original plaster medallions. Finish the evening with coffee and homemade chocolates in the enormous drawing room. Bedrooms and suites in the main house vary in size from vast to snug, with bathrooms that run the gamut from small and rather ordinary to large and luxurious. Several of the most elegant rooms have smaller bathrooms, so be sure to discuss your choice of room when you make reservations. Parties of friends traveling together may wish to stay in the luxurious Adam-style pavilion with its large bedrooms and bathrooms. Culloden battlefield, just down the road, is a "must visit" as are nearby Cawdor Castle and Loch Ness. *Directions:* Take the A9 south from Inverness to the A96 Aberdeen and Nairn turnoff. Go straight over the first roundabout and take the next right to Culloden. Go through two sets of traffic lights and take the next road left to the hotel.

CULLODEN HOUSE
Manager: Stephen Davies
Culloden IV2 7BZ, Scotland
Tel: 01463 790461, Fax: 01463 792181
33 Rooms, Double: £240–£375
Open: all year, Credit cards: all major

The tree-lined drive winds through a vast estate to the parklike lawns surrounding Cromlix House. Little rabbits hop gaily around—they're so tame that you can approach within a few yards of them before they disappear into the surrounding woodlands. The heavy Victorian exterior of the building hides an absolute jewel of an interior. Cromlix House, converted in from what was the Eden family home, now is a very lovely country house hotel. It retains much of the original furniture designed for the house, along with family paintings and porcelain and old fittings dating back to when this grand house teemed with servants. The tone of this elegant Victorian home is set by the stately front hall with its wooden ceiling and richly paneled walls and is carried through into the inviting morning room, peaceful, well-stocked library, and garden conservatory. There is a private chapel with its organ pipes along one of the staircases. Upstairs are six luxurious rooms and eight very spacious, beautifully decorated and furnished suites. Serene countryside walks to little lochs or a visit to the family and pet cemeteries offer the chance for utter peace and quiet. Stirling Castle and the Trossachs with their lovely lakes are close by. Golf at Gleneagles is a 20-minute drive away. *Directions:* Take the A9 out of Dunblane, turn left onto B8033, go through Kinbuck village, and take the second left turn after a small bridge.

CROMLIX HOUSE
Manager: Alan Fry
Kinbuck
Dunblane FK15 9JT, Scotland
Tel: 01786 822125, Fax: 01786 825450
14 Rooms, Double: £180–£280
Open: all year, Credit cards: all major

Drumsheugh Gardens is a quiet square of Victorian townhouses grouped round a leafy garden just three minutes' walk from Princes Street. Three of these spacious townhouses have been beautifully restored as The Bonham hotel, which offers the elegance of an old exterior, a spacious interior, a tongue-in-cheek modern decor, and the most up-to-date of everything. You feel like Alice standing before the enormous looking glasses in the dining room, while in the sitting room there's the Cheshire cat sculpture sitting beside the fire, inviting you to sit on the circular cherry-red couch that swirls upward to an enormous light fixture. Bedrooms range in size from petite to grand suites and range in their decor from sedate to vibrant. Several enjoy lovely views over the Firth of Forth. A great many have whimsical touches such as a mural of a parrot in a porthole in a room with a nautical theme and an ornate chimney pot painted on the bedhead in a spacious room overlooking the rooftops. Bedrooms are in the forefront of technology, with an integrated system that turns the TV into a computer screen and provides CD audio, DVD, and full Internet access. Beds are large, bathrooms gleamingly modern. *Directions:* From the south the A1 brings you right into Edinburgh's City Center. Drive to the end of Queen St and bear right down St. Colme St. Turn right after following the road Randolph Crescent into Queensferry St. Turn left into Drumsheugh Gardens.

THE BONHAM
Owner: Peter Taylor
General Manager: Jeremy Hope
35 Drumsheugh Gardens
Edinburgh EH3 7RN, Scotland
Tel: 0131 274 7400, Fax: 0131 274 7405
48 Rooms, Double: £135–£400
Minimum Stay Required: 2 on weekends
Open: all year, Credit cards: all major

A brisk, fifteen-minute walk from Princes Street brings you to Channings, a delightful hotel encompassing five large Edwardian townhouses whose front parlors are now quiet sitting rooms with log burning fireplaces. Bedrooms are well equipped with DVD players, internet access, music system, and multiple television channels. They come in a range of styles, the suites at the top of the house having the most contemporary of décor (they are in a building that was once home to explorer Ernest Shackleton) and the most stylish of modern bathrooms. We stayed in a more traditional room (46) with two comfy chairs in the bay window where we sat on a summer evening overlooking gardens, chimneytops and a distant view of the hills of Fife. A little elevator runs between the floors. French cuisine is the forte of the restaurant. Breakfast is served in the conservatory. *Directions:* Take Queen Street (parallel to Princes Street) along to Randolph crescent, following the road left, then turning right onto Queensferry Road. Cross the river, take the second right (beside Learmonth Hotel) and follow South Learmonth Gardens to Channings. Double-park on arrival. Longer term parking is on nearby streets.

CHANNINGS
Owner: Peter Taylor
Manager: Ngaire Abbott
15 South Learmonth Gardens
Edinburgh EH4 1EZ, Scotland
Tel: 0131 274 7401, Fax: 0131 274 7405
41 Rooms, Double: £140–£390
Minimum Stay Required: 2 nights on weekends
Open: all year, Credit cards: all major

This conversion of three grand Victorian townhouses into an apartment hotel sits on a quiet square in Edinburgh's west end, retaining their elegant features of mellow paneling, ornate plasterwork ceilings, original fireplaces and grand staircases. Rooms are spacious, no two are the same, and three have their own private front door. Those at the back have excellent views of Edinburgh. You may stay in a mahogany-paneled bedroom (room 12) or have a vast sitting room (like 18). Bathrooms, all with separate shower and tub, are a feature: some have roll top baths, others Jacuzzi tubs for two, and a couple large enough to hold a party in. Suites come in three sizes: Classic—spacious room with sitting area and dining nook; Grand—larger than Classic; Townhouse Apartment—separate bedroom, sitting room with hidden "Murphy" beds, and two bathrooms. The butler brings breakfast (continental to hot breakfast with haggis, bacon and egg) and offers 24-hour room service (everything up to an elaborate three-course dinner). There's also a "cupboard" kitchen with microwave, kettle, crockery, cutlery, and cafetiere. For an in-town pied-à-terre, consider a "time ownership" for weeklong stays. *Directions:* From the south take the A1 into Edinburgh's City Center. Continue to the end of Queen St, bear right down St Colme St and turn right after into Randolph Cres. Continue into Queensferry Street, turn left into Drumsheugh Gardens and on into Rothesay Terrace.

THE EDINBURGH RESIDENCE
Owner: Peter Taylor
Manager: Ngaire Abbott
7 Rothesay Terrace
Edinburgh EH37RY, Scotland
Tel: 0131 556 5556, Fax: 0131 652 3652
29 Rooms, Double: £125–£5000
Minimum Stay Required: 2 nights on weekends
Closed: Jan 11 to Jan 24, Credit cards: all major

The location is absolutely perfect—just a ten-minute stroll from Princes Street in the heart of Georgian Edinburgh. Three townhouses have been combined to form this luxury hotel, which has the air of a private club. No expense has been spared to create the look and feel of a sumptuous home. Beautiful fabrics, antiques, gorgeous furniture, and an abundance of flowers set an elegant mood. The drawing room centers on an elaborate crystal chandelier. There is no bar: guests order from the butler. Each bedroom has a different decor and color scheme. A great many of the bathrooms are especially grand, several with claw-foot tubs, others with a bath and separate shower, and the suites have luxurious steam showers. Three suites have their own private terrace and entrance to Great King Street. The Howard has its own fine restaurant, The Atholl, specializing in traditional Scottish fare, and there are many more, from formal to funky, within easy walking distance. *Directions:* From the west end of Princes Street (with the castle on your right) turn left into Charlotte Square then turn right into Queen Street. Turn third left into Queen Street Gardens East, which becomes Dundas Street, then take the third right onto Great King Street. The Howard is on the right with a car park to the rear.

THE HOWARD
Owner: Peter Taylor
Manager: Fiona McInroy
34 Great King Street
Edinburgh EH3 6QH, Scotland
Tel: 0131 274 7402, Fax: 0131 274 7405
13 Rooms, Double: £165–£300
5 Suites: £220–£475
Minimum Stay Required: 2 nights on weekends
Open: all year, Credit cards: all major

The Scotsman has an ideal Edinburgh location just one minute's walk from Princes Street and the Royal Mile. Formerly baronial offices of the Scotsman newspaper, this 1905 building has received a complete revamp to stylish hotel. The grandeur of the building with its ornate plasterwork, marble floors, and paneling gives a traditional feel while the décor is totally modern chic. Bedrooms are high tech (DTV, broadband internet, CD-DVD players) with lovely bed linens and excellent lighting. There's a hatch so you do not have to open your door for room service and an Edinburgh monopoly board. Choose the red-bedecked Vermilion restaurant for fine dining or the more casual North Bridge Brasserie. Set in the former grand entrance lobby the brasserie sports an elliptical bar with illuminated glass counter between marble pillars giving a modern look to this traditional paneled room. A steel staircase zigzags up to the gallery whose tables have a birds-eye-view of the action. The health club extends over three levels and has lots of wow factors: a magnificent stainless steel swimming pool, a state-of-the-art gymnasium, and the Cowshed spa—offering all manner of pampering treatments from "pummeled cow" deep-tissue massage to "rawhide" sea salt exfoliation. You could not be more centrally located for exploring Edinburgh. *Directions:* Adjacent to Waverly train station. Arriving by car pull up in front to unload—valet parking at nearby garage.

THE SCOTSMAN
Manager: Daniel Pereira
20 North Bridge
Edinburgh EH1 1YT, Scotland
Tel: 0131 556 5565, Fax: 0131 652 3652
69 Rooms, Double: £115–£1300
Open: all year, Credit cards: all major

Windmill House has the feel of a country estate with a city address. There's a family of resident badgers by the tree stump, an ancient windmill, and acres of grounds stretching down to the Water of Leith—all just a mile as the crow flies from the center of Edinburgh. A remarkable setting with an equally remarkable home that looks hundreds of years old, though it was actually built just a few years ago—Michael is a builder and Georgian home restorer. It's a home so lovely that you are thrilled to stay there—or is it just that the Scotts put you in a euphoric mood? Sip tea in the drawing room or put your feet up and watch the television in the sitting room. Climb the elegant staircase to the spacious bedrooms, each beautifully decorated in sunny Georgian colors and accompanied by a top-of-the-line bathroom. One bedroom has an adjacent room for a child. Through the garden gate are the grounds of the Museum of Modern Art from whence a path leads you along the river and into the heart of the city. Those who prefer to ride will find the bus stop an eight-minute walk away. There are plenty of local restaurants for dinner. *Directions:* Going down Princes Street (castle on left) follow signs for Glasgow (go straight at the end of Princes Street). Follow the road for a mile until just before the BMW showroom (on left)—turn right into Murrayfield Avenue and immediately right into Coltbridge Avenue, leading to Coltbridge Gardens.

WINDMILL HOUSE
Owners: Vivien & Michael Scott
Coltbridge Gardens
Edinburgh EH12 6AQ, Scotland
Tel: 0131 346 0024
3 Rooms, Double: £110–£150
Minimum Stay Required: 2 nights in Aug
Closed: Christmas & New Year, Credit cards: none

Set on a quiet road high above Loch Linnhe with its gardens terracing down to a terrific view across the loch to the hills, The Grange has a countryside feel yet is just a few minutes' walk from the center of Fort William. Built in 1884 for a wealthy lady, The Grange, with gracefully sloping roofs and curved turrets, has a feminine feel that is continued indoors in the tasteful way Joan has decorated her home. The sitting room and the dining room, where breakfast with a great variety of choices is served, are comfortable, enjoyable spaces. The gorgeous bedrooms each have a loch view. I loved Rob Roy (where Jessica Lange stayed during the movie shoot), a lovely room with a luxurious bathroom with tub and shower, but for style and view, the Garden Room surpassed it. If you don't fancy carrying your luggage up stairs, opt for the ground floor Terrace room with its own patio and bathroom with claw-foot tub and shower. Guests often walk to the pier to enjoy a seafood dinner at the Cranogg Restaurant. Countless possibilities exist for touring by car, but a favorite non-car excursion is the steam train ride from Fort William to Mallaig through some of Scotland's most fabulous scenery (summer only). *Directions:* Arriving in Fort William from the south with the loch on your left, turn second right into Ashburn Lane and left into Grange Road. The Grange is on the corner of Ashburn Lane and Grange road.

THE GRANGE
Owners: Joan & John Campbell
Grange Road
Fort William PH33 6JF, Scotland
Tel: 01397 705516
3 Rooms, Double: £110–£118
Minimum Stay Required: 2 nights during high season
Open: Mar to mid-Nov, Credit cards: MC, VS

Nestling in the foothills of the mighty Ben Nevis, Inverlochy Castle sits amongst some of Scotland's finest scenery. Its magnificence does not appear to have altered since Queen Victoria visited in 1873. In her diaries she wrote, "I never saw a lovelier nor more romantic spot." Surrounded by landscaped gardens overlooking its own private loch, the turreted and gabled house was built to resemble a castle. Central heating and modern plumbing appear to be the only 21st-century additions. The two-storied Grand Hall with its frescoed ceiling sets the tone of this memorable hotel and the furnishings and decor throughout are luxurious. Dinner is an experience to savor in either of the dining rooms, each decorated with elaborate period furniture given as gifts by the King of Norway. The staff outnumbers the guests and attention to detail ensures that things are done properly. Inverlochy Castle is a very grand, very expensive, and most outstanding hotel. The small number of rooms and the hotel's popularity mean that early reservations are necessary. There are various outdoor activities available to guests including fly fishing for brown trout in the private loch, clay-pigeon shooting, guided walks, and grouse stalking. You can take the Road to the Isles, a lovely drive that brings you to Mallaig where you can board ferries to the isles of Skye, Rhum, Eigg, Canna, and Muck. *Directions:* The castle is on the A82, Inverness road, 3 miles north of Fort William.

INVERLOCHY CASTLE
Manager: Calum Milde
Torlundy
Fort William PH33 6SN, Scotland
Tel: 01397 702177, Fax: 01397 702953
17 Rooms, Double: £295–£640
Open: all year, Credit cards: all major
Relais & Châteaux

Just a stone's throw from Glamis and its famous castle (birthplace of the late Queen Mum) situated on the site of a medieval fortress, this Edwardian country house hotel is surrounded by a moat providing a tree-shaded country walk. Many things about the hotel are special, most importantly the warm, informal hospitality of David and Verity and their staff. Comfy sofas and a crackling log fire lend to the drawing room a warm coziness. Guests usually congregate in the convivial bar. The chef's food philosophy centers on using only the highest quality local ingredients—a great deal of the fruit and veggies come from the garden and orchard. The conservatory is an especially attractive place to dine on a summer evening and is kept toasty in winter with underfloor heating. The warm color scheme downstairs extends to the bedrooms, all neat as a pin with pretty flower arrangements, good bed linens, and tomorrow's weather forecast. Know that you deserve the best and opt for room 1 or room 5 (a four poster) both extra-large rooms with large bathrooms with separate shower and bath. Tamworth pigs, a rare porcine breed, root around in the orchard and welcome visits. Twenty golf courses are within striking distance. Glamis Castle, Scone Palace (coronation site of Scotland's kings), and the J.M. Barrie museum in Kirriemuir are popular venues. *Directions:* The hotel is beside A94 (Perth to Forfar road) three miles south of Glamis.

CASTLETON HOUSE HOTEL
Owners: Verity & David Webster
Glamis DD8 1SJ, Scotland
Tel: 01307 840340, Fax: 01307 840506
6 Rooms, Double: £160–£190
Closed: Christmas & New Year, Credit cards: all major

The Isle of Eriska is a 300-acre private island off the west coast of Scotland linked to the mainland by a decorative wrought-iron bridge. In 1884 the splendidly named Hippolyte Blanc designed this grand baronial mansion, now a destination hotel with so many things to keep you occupied that you'll have a hard time persuading yourself to leave the island. There's a spa with a vast range of treatments, a magnificent indoor swimming pool, a six-hole golf course, a tennis court, clay-pigeon shooting, and simply tramping round the island. You can stay in lovely country house rooms in the main house, in one of two cottages or opt for sheer indulgence and choose one of the spa suites each with a hot tub, conservatory, living room, bedroom and luxurious bathroom all tucked into its own walled garden. You may be tempted to hide away in your retreat but it would be a shame to miss the nightly ritual of badgers coming to the library steps to be fed, oblivious to guests enjoying a drink—perhaps one of the hotel's excellent assortment of single malts. Dinner is served in the dining room or can be enjoyed in your own room. Eriska is a splendid base for exploring the Western Highlands, visiting Glencoe, and making day trips to the islands of Mull, Staffa, and Iona. *Directions:* From Crianlarich take the A85 towards Oban. At Connel take the bridge towards Fort William (A825) for 4 miles to the village of Benderloch. Turn left and left again following signposts to the Isle of Eriska.

ISLE OF ERISKA
Owner: Buchanan-Smith family
Manager: Beppo Buchanan-Smith
Isle of Eriska PA37 1SD, Scotland
Tel: 01631 720371, Fax: 01631 720531
23 Rooms, Double: £325–£450
Closed: Jan, Credit cards: all major

Overlooking the romantic ruins of Kildrummy Castle and surrounded by acres of lovely gardens and woodlands, Kildrummy Castle Hotel is a grand mansion house. The richly paneled and tapestried walls and ornately carved staircase give a baronial feel to this grand house, a feel that is echoed in the lounge and bar whose large windows overlook the romantic castle ruins and the gardens. Yet this is not a stuffy, formal hotel: the smiling, friendly staff does a splendid job, offering people a really warm welcome. Dinner in the richly furnished dining room is a delight. The bedrooms (named after various pools in the hotel's trout stream) are tastefully decorated and traditionally furnished. Their size ranges from a snug attic bedroom with a private balcony to a grand corner room with enormous windows framing the countryside. Guests often visit the adjacent Kildrummy Castle Gardens which present an idyllic picture at all times of the year. From Kildrummy you can join the Speyside Whisky Trail and enjoy a "wee dram" or two. At Alford lies Craigiever, a fairy-tale castle unchanged since it was built in 1626. Between Kildrummy and Braemar, home of the September Royal Highland Gathering, lies Balmoral Castle whose grounds are open in June and July when the Royal Family is not in residence. *Directions:* From Aberdeen take the A944 through Alford to the A97 where you turn right for the castle.

KILDRUMMY CASTLE HOTEL
Owners: Frans & Jayne Faber
Kildrummy
Kildrummy AB33 8RA, Scotland
Tel: 019755 71288, Fax: 019755 71345
16 Rooms, Double: £95–£213
Closed: Jan 3 to Jan 25, Credit cards: all major

Ballathie House is a large turreted, Victorian, Scottish country estate home on the banks of the River Tay, surrounded by lawns, fields and woodlands. While the house is imposing, it has a wonderfully warm atmosphere and a homey feel as well as glorious views over the rushing River Tay. A grand sweep of staircase leads up from the enormous hallway where sofas and chairs are grouped around a blazing fire. The drawing room, with its tall windows framing views across the lawn to the river, is made more intimate by cozy groupings of tables and chairs. My favorite accommodations are the spacious bedrooms with turret bathrooms and the smaller bedrooms with river views. Beyond the kitchen there is a ground-floor suite equipped for the handicapped. For complete peace and quiet request a riverside room in the adjacent building—upstairs rooms have balconies. The bar is a lively place, and dinner is delicious. Red squirrels are found on the Ballathie estate, and you may be fortunate and catch a glimpse of one of these rarely-seen animals. Nearby is Dunkeld, a delightful town with a ruined cathedral set in expansive lawns. Scone Palace, where Scottish kings were once crowned, has fine furniture, clocks, porcelain, and needlework. *Directions:* From Perth take the A9 towards Inverness for about five minutes to the B9099, Stanley road. Go through Stanley and take a right-hand fork towards Blairgowrie, following signs for Ballathie House.

BALLATHIE HOUSE
Manager: Christopher Longden
Kinclaven PH1 4QN, Scotland
Tel: 01250 883268, Fax: 01250 883396
42 Rooms, Double: £196–£270
Open: all year, Credit cards: all major

Set at the foot of the Black Isle (a sheltered spit of land just north of Inverness), The Dower House was built as the retirement home for the owners of baronial Highfield House. While Highfield fell into disrepair, The Dower House flourished and was remodeled into a cottage orné, an adorable, single-story doll's house. The cute exterior belies a more spacious interior. The dining room and sitting room open up from the entrance hall. Mena has played on the interesting architecture and decorated the house in a most appealing, flowery, feminine way, adding attractive Victorian furniture and all the special touches that make you feel you are staying with friends. Robyn's delectable food has earned him a two AA Rosettes. An enjoyable day trip is to explore the villages of the Black Isle of which the historic port of Cromarty is a highlight. You can enjoy magnificent Highland scenery on the train journey from nearby Dingwall to Kyle of Lochalsh. The local distillery at Glen Ord offers tours and samples. Traditional Scottish tweeds and woolens are available in nearby Beauly. *Directions:* Take the A862 from Inverness through Beauly to Muir of Ord. The Dower House is on the left, 1 mile beyond the town on the Dingwall road.

THE DOWER HOUSE
Owners: Mena & Robyn Aitchison
Highfield
Muir of Ord IV6 7XN, Scotland
Tel & Fax: 01463 870090
5 Rooms, Double: £120–£175
1 Cottage: £450 weekly
Closed: Christmas, Credit cards: MC, VS

This 1780s former manse sits surrounded by acres of lawns and trees in the heart of the picturesque seaside town of North Berwick, not far from Edinburgh. The Scotts' furniture complements their lovely home perfectly. Gwen has a real eye for design and color and has done the most stylish job of decorating. From the front hallway a door opens to the downstairs wing, a suite of rooms with two bedrooms, one bathroom, and a cozy sitting room—absolutely perfect for families or friends traveling together. Upstairs are two more lovely bedrooms and bathrooms. Breakfast is the only meal served round the long dining-room table but there is no shortage of restaurants and pubs to walk to for dinner. Golfers are in heaven staying here for there are 18 courses within a 20-minute drive, including those at Gullane and Muirfield. A half-hour train ride finds you at the base of Edinburgh Castle, which makes for hassle-free day trips to all the shopping and historic sights. North Berwick's beach is a two-minute walk away as is the High Street with its shops and restaurants. Bass Rock, an important nesting site for sea birds can be visited. There are castles, museums, and a whisky distillery nearby. *Directions:* From Edinburgh take the A1 towards Berwick-upon-Tweed for 10 miles. Exit onto the A198 for North Berwick, keeping to the A198 through the town. Turn left on Law Road and The Glebe House is on your left after 100 yards.

THE GLEBE HOUSE
Owners: Gwen & Jake Scott
Law Road
North Berwick EH39 4PL, Scotland
Tel: 01620 892608, Fax: 01620 893588
4 Rooms, Double: £90–£100
Closed: Christmas & New Year, Credit cards: none

Oban, with its broad sweep of sheltered harbor, is the gateway to the islands—from here ferries ply their way to the isles of Mull, Iona, Coll, Staffa, Tiree, Colonsay, and Lismore. On a quiet street right on the bay, just beyond the bustling ferry terminal, sits The Manor House, built in 1780 as the principal home of the Duke of Argyll's Oban estate. Today this very nice traditional hotel is the perfect place to stay to enjoy various day trips to the Western Isles. Bedrooms are not large but each is accompanied by a snug bath or shower room, and all are most attractively decorated. It is well worth the few extra pounds to secure a room with a sweeping water view across to Mull, Lismore, and the hills of Morvern. The most popular day trips are to Mull, Staffa, and Iona. Walk to the nearby ferry terminal for the 10 am boat to Mull and pick up a scenic bus tour of the island in Craignure. Alternatively, venture onwards to Iona, the historic cradle of Christianity and burial place of many Scottish kings, including the infamous Macbeth, or to Staffa to explore Fingal's Cave, immortalized by Mendelssohn. Remember to wear sensible footwear and waterproof clothing for trips to Iona and Staffa. On the mainland Glencoe is a popular destination. *Directions:* Arriving in Oban, enter the one-way system following signposts for the ferry and Gallanach. Do not turn for the ferry but continue towards Gallanach—The Manor House is on the right after 300 yards.

THE MANOR HOUSE
Manager: Ann Maceachen
Gallanach Road
Oban PA34 4LS, Scotland
Tel: 01631 562087, Fax: 01631 563053
11 Rooms, Double: £150–£190
Closed: Christmas, Credit cards: all major

Dunmurray Lodge was built over 100 years ago and for over 50 years served as home to the town doctor. Irene believes in getting you off to a good start with a hearty breakfast. Muesli, fruit salad, yogurt, cheese and oatcakes are set out on the buffet and guests order their cooked breakfast the night before with choices ranging from a full-cooked breakfast with Mr. Macdonalds sausages to waffles with maple syrup and bacon. The airy, neat-as-a-new-pin bedrooms are named after local clans. Murray, a spacious room at the front of the house, enjoys a large bay window and zip-and-link beds that can be either king or twins. Combined with an adjacent twin-bedded room, it makes an ideal family suite. Robertson also has zip and link twin beds and overlooks the town's bowling green. Kerr and Stewart, both doubles, are decorated to the same high standard. Make yourself at home in the sitting rooms, all outfitted in shades of white. It's an excellent place to sit and plan your sightseeing forays. Blair Castle with its period furnishings and grand estate should not be missed. Perth and Scone Palace, where the kings of Scotland were crowned makes an excellent daytrip. There are local distilleries to visit, walks to take and the theatre to enjoy. It's a short walk into town for dinner. *Directions:* Arriving in Pitlochry on the A9 from Perth turn right on Bonnethill Road and the house is on your right. Park in front to unload and you will be directed to parking.

DUNMURRAY LODGE
Owners: Irene & Tony Willmore
72 Bonnethill Road
Pitlochry PH165ED, Scotland
Tel & Fax: 01796 473624
5 Rooms, Double: £60–£112
Minimum Stay Required: 2 nights Jul-Aug
Closed: Christmas & Jan, Credit cards: none

Pitlochry developed in the latter half of the 19th century as a Highland health resort, following a visit from Queen Victoria herself. It remains today an attractive town of beautiful, stone built Victorian houses standing back from the wooded shores of Loch Faskally. Knockendarroch House sits above the rooftops of the town on its own little hill and gardens, affording views of the surrounding hills and countryside. Liz runs the hotel with great enthusiasm and warmth, and pays utmost attention to ensuring that her guests enjoy their stay. Dinner guests take in the splendid views as they peruse the four-course menu. The ornate stained-glass windows filter sunlight on to the staircase leading up to the bedrooms–two of the attic bedrooms have little balconies overlooking the town and the hills beyond. All the rooms are en-suite and are equipped with telephones, flat screen TVs, and coffee and tea making facilities. WiFi is available in the public areas. If you have difficulty with stairs, request the ground floor bedroom. Pitlochry has a year-round events calendar, ranging from major cycle events to horse trials. Don't miss the repertoire of plays at the Pitlochry Festival Theatre, which makes it possible for you to see as many as four plays in a three-night stay. *Directions:* Enter Pitlochry from the south (A9). Pass under the railway bridge, turn right on East Moulin Road and take the second turning left onto Higher Oakfield (the hotel is on your left).

KNOCKENDARROCH HOUSE
Owner: Liz Martin
Higher Oakfield
Pitlochry PH16 5HT, Scotland
Tel: 01796 473473, Fax: 01796 474056
12 Rooms, Double: £120–£180*
*Includes dinner, bed & breakfast
Open: Jan to Dec, Credit cards: all major

This former ferry inn on the shore of Loch Linne continues to offer a level of hospitality rare in today's world. While traditional features are the priority this hotel manages to combine them with up to the minute services more usually associated with the modern boutique hotel. This rare combination is achieved through the personal involvement of the owners Shaun and Jenny McKivragan. Paul Burns, Scottish National Hotel Chef of the Year 2004 and 2007, continues to create culinary masterpieces with an emphasis on local produce, taking advantage of the abundance of fresh fish. Shaun and Jenny wrote to say that several of the smaller bedrooms have recently been enlarged. All are beautifully appointed with lovely fabrics, quality furniture, and very nice bathrooms. My favorites are the snug attic rooms that look out over the loch. The attentive staff ensures you do not have to haul your luggage up the narrow stairs. Alternatively you may want to request a main-floor room with a loch view. The loch suite also enjoys loch views both from the bedroom and the sitting room and has an immaculate, large bathroom. For more privacy opt for Bramble Cottage, a luxurious two bedroom cottage in the grounds. Culinary courses, gourmet nights and mushroom-picking weekends are offered. Enjoy the putting green, the croquet lawn and the utter tranquility of this picturesque spot. *Directions:* Port Appin is 2 miles off the A828, 20 miles north of Oban.

THE AIRDS HOTEL & RESTAURANT
Owners: Jenny & Shaun McKivragan
General Manager: Robert McKay
Port Appin PA38 4DF, Scotland
Tel: 01631 730236, Fax: 01631 730535
11 Rooms, Double: £255–£445
1 Cottage: £640–£1740 weekly
Open: all year, Credit cards: MC, VS
Relais & Châteaux

If you are looking to unwind completely, book a room at Knockinaam Lodge, a gray-stone Victorian country house set beside the Irish Sea amidst 30 acres of sheltering wooded hills and pretty gardens. The private beach is perfect for contemplative strolls—such as Churchill and Eisenhower might have taken when they stayed here during World War II. Inside, furnishings and decor respect the house's heritage while white-painted woodwork and pastel-colored walls create a light and cheerful atmosphere. Guests relax in the attractive sitting room or drawing room with their comfortable armchairs, tall windows, and decorative moldings. Delicious, innovative dinners, an important feature of the Knockinaam Lodge experience, are accompanied by wines from a 30-page list. After dinner, guests often repair to the cozy wood-paneled bar with its log fire, mounted stags' heads, and extensive collection of single-malt whiskies. There are nine individually decorated bedrooms of various sizes, all with en suite bathrooms, TVs, VCRs, and direct-dial phones. The most luxurious room (original master bedroom) has a king bed, a huge bathroom, and partial sea views. One of the three rooms with unobstructed sea views has a canopied queen-sized bed. *Directions:* From the A77 follow signs to Portpatrick, then 2 miles west of Lochans, turn left for the Colfin smokehouse and drive about 3 miles. (Best to arrive in daylight.)

KNOCKINAAM LODGE
Owners: Sian & David Ibbotson
Portpatrick DG9 9AD, Scotland
Tel: 01776 810471, Fax: 01776 810435
10 Rooms, Double: £250–£410
Open: all year, Credit cards: all major

Viewfield House has always been home to the Macdonald family and there have always been Macdonalds on Skye. At the end of the 19th century this prosperous family remodeled Viewfield House adding a huge extension of large, grand rooms and completing the refurbishment with a baronial tower. Continuing a tradition begun by his grandmother, Hugh welcomes guests to his home—while there are caring staff who will carry your bag, pour you a drink and bring you afternoon tea this is very much a home stay at a very special house. There's an elephant's foot umbrella stand and wellies in the entrance hall, trophies of hunts and safaris (along with a smattering of British wildlife specimens) in the entrance hall, and a welcoming fire in the living room. (If you want to watch telly ask for directions to the library.) Bedrooms come in all sizes from vast to cozy depending on whether you are in the Victorian or Georgian wing of the house—several have zip and link beds that can be king or twin. Two single rooms are available at half the price of a double. There are washers and dryers for the use of guests. Portree is an interesting town. Viewfield is a perfect base for your explorations of Skye. *Directions:* From Kyle of Lochalsh take the bridge to Skye, then the A87 to Portree. Just as you enter the town, Viewfield House is on your left-hand side.

VIEWFIELD HOUSE
Owner: Hugh Macdonald
Portree IV51 9EU, Scotland
Tel: 01478 612217, Fax: 01478 613517
11 Rooms, Double: £96–£140
1 Cottage: £450–£600 weekly
Open: Easter to mid-Oct, Credit cards: MC, VS

Shieldaig has an overwhelmingly beautiful location facing a small, tree-covered island on the shores of Loch Torridon. Here single-track roads wind you through spectacular, rugged scenery of mountains rising straight from the sea and sea lochs penetrating far inland. A wonderful place to stay in Shieldaig is Tigh an Eilean, an 18th-century house converted to a hotel and personally run by Cathryn and Christopher Field. The decor is quiet and soothing with soft beiges and warm pastels. Dinner is taken in the airy dining room overlooking the loch and there are snug little lounges and an honesty bar. Bedrooms are cozy and very comfortable—you absolutely have to have a room with a loch view! The hotel will pack you a picnic lunch or you can obtain supplies from the Fields' little shop next door. Walking, birdwatching, and fishing are popular pastimes with the Beinn Eighe Nature Reserve and the 15,000-acre National Trust estate nearby. Guests often drive around the Applecross Peninsula with its awesome, twisting pass of Bealach-na-Ba and its views of Skye and the Outer Hebrides. Tigh An Eilean is an excellent place to stop if you are traveling between Skye and Ullapool and do not want to rush through all this magnificent scenery in a day. *Directions:* Shieldaig is 68 miles from Inverness. Take the A832 (Ullapool road) to Garve and then on to Kinlochewe where you turn left on the A896 to Shieldaig. The hotel is on the waterfront.

TIGH AN EILEAN (HOUSE BY THE ISLAND)
Owners: Cathryn & Christopher Field
Shieldaig IV54 8XN, Scotland
Tel: 01520 755251, Fax: 01520 755321
11 Rooms, Double: £160
Open: mid-Mar to Nov, Credit cards: MC, VS

On a rocky spit of land almost surrounded by water, the whitewashed Eilean Iarmain hotel, a Harris Tweed shop and a huddle of cottages face Isle Ornsay, a tiny island whose lighthouse was built by Robert Louis Stephenson's grandfather. Across the sound mountains tumble directly into the sea, adding a wild, end-of-the-earth feel. The Eilean Iarmain (pronounced "Ellen Earman") is quite delightful. Chintz chairs add a homey touch to the cozy parlor and in the dining room you find that the menu is in Gaelic, thankfully with an English translation (the staff speak Gaelic and English). A tartan-patterned carpet leads up the pine stairs to six bedrooms. They have varied tariffs to match the great variety of size and decor: room 2 has a canopied half-tester bed that once resided in Armadale Castle; the turret room is paneled in mellow pine and has a seating area in the turret. More rooms are found in the cottage across the road. In addition there are four luxurious suites with sitting room and bathroom downstairs and bedroom upstairs. Step out of the front door of the hotel and round the side and you find yourself in the old-fashioned pub (bar meals are served) where locals gather—on Thursday evenings they often bring their instruments. Be sure to visit Armadale Castle. *Directions:* From Kyle of Lochalsh take the bridge to Skye, then the A850 to the A851 towards Armadale: turn left to Eilean Iarmain.

HOTEL EILEAN IARMAIN AT ISLE ORNSAY
Owners: Sir Iain & Lady Noble
Manager: Flora Maclean
Sleat IV43 8QR, Scotland
Tel: 01471 833332, Fax: 01471 833275
16 Rooms, Double: £100–£250
Open: all year, Credit cards: all major

The Creggans Inn stands next to the shore of Loch Fyne on the doorstep of some of the most remote and unspoiled countryside in Scotland. Previously owned by Sir Fitzroy McLean (thought to have been the role model for Ian Fleming's James Bond, otherwise known as "007"), the property is now in the hands of the Robertson family who continue to upgrade the property and keep the place up to snuff. There's a quiet upstairs sitting room with lovely loch view and spacious ground floor lounges where you enjoy drinks before dinner or coffee afterwards. A small but lively public bar at the end of the inn is popular with locals and lunch and simpler dinner fare is served here and in the casual dining rooms. Of course there's lots of opportunity to take a "wee dram" or sample some fine Scottish ale in the company of the locals. Be sure to request a room with a loch view—while none of the bedrooms are grand or particularly spacious they are simply furnished and well appointed. Strachur is easily accessible and well located as a base for touring and walking on the west coast. Nearby sights include castles (Inverary is home to the Duke of Argyll) and gardens (Younger botanical gardens benefit from the milder climate). *Directions:* From Glasgow take the M8 to Gourock, cross the Clyde by ferry to Dunoon, and take the A815 to Strachur where you find The Creggans Inn across the road from the loch.

THE CREGGANS INN
Owners: Gill & Archie Maclellan
Strachur PA27 8BX, Scotland
Tel: 01369 860279, Fax: 01369 860637
14 Rooms, Double: £100–£180
Open: all year, Credit cards: all major

Quite the most impressive building that you see for many a mile along the breathtakingly beautiful, rugged coast of Wester Ross is The Torridon Hotel, a grand shooting lodge built by the Earl of Lovelace in 1887. The Earl picked an isolated spot where the mountains descend almost to the lochside, leaving just enough room for this imposing building and its sweep of lawn to the water's edge. The public rooms are huge: an enormous bay window frames the idyllic view of loch and mountains. The bar stocks a vast number of single malts—which gives you lots of room for choice when selecting a dram. The large pine-paneled entry and the dining room have a tribute to the 50th anniversary of Queen Victoria's reign painted just below the ceiling as a border encircling the rooms. The Gregorys (Rohaise's parents) added theirs around the dining room celebrating the restoration of the house. The principal bedrooms are very large and enjoy grand bathrooms. Smaller bedrooms are tucked cozily under the eaves. Be sure to request a room with a loch view. The area is renowned for its beautiful Highland scenery—a spectacular drive takes you over the hair-raising Pass of the Cattle and back to Torridon. An activities manager is on hand to arrange Kayaking, falconry, hiking or rock climbing. *Directions:* Torridon is 64 miles from Inverness. Take the A832 (Ullapool road) to Kinlochewe where you turn left on the A896 to Torridon.

THE TORRIDON HOTEL
Owners: Rohaise & Daniel Rose-Bristow
Torridon IV22 2EY, Scotland
Tel: 01445 791242, Fax: 01445 712253
19 Rooms, Double: £146–£395
Closed: Jan, Credit cards: all major

Roses climb up the walls of what was once a row of fishermen's cottages in Ullapool a popular holiday resort, ferry terminal and fishing port on the shores of Loch Broom, a broad sea loch. Now it's known as the Ceilidh Place. Ceilidh (pronounced "kaylee") is Gaelic for meeting socially and you certainly have lots of opportunities to do that here for you'll find locals and visitors alike about the place: selecting a book in the book store, enjoying a drink at the bar, dinner at the restaurant, or an evening's musical entertainment. The restaurant serves food all day and evening so you'll have lots of opportunities to sample the specials posted on the board and no excuse not to try a slice or two of Laurie and Alison's homemade cakes. Upstairs the bedrooms are contemporary in their décor, often with a built-in desk and fitted furniture—each contains a selection of books recommended by folks who work at or frequent the Ceilidh Place (but no TV). The bookstore carries all the recommended selections. Guests have a spacious upstairs sitting room with its homey mix of furniture arranged in cozy seating areas, tea- and coffee-makings, and honor bar. Possible day trips include Inchnadamph Caves, Ardvreck Castle, and Lochinver with its heart-stopping views. *Directions:* Ullapool is 60 miles northwest of Inverness on the A835. West Argyle Street parallels the harbor one street back from the water.

≝ ✕ 🅲🆁🅴🅳🅸🆃 ☎ 🏠@ P ⫴ ⚔ ⟰ 🧍 👯

THE CEILIDH PLACE
Owner: Jean Urquhart
14 West Argyle Street
Ullapool IV26 2TY, Scotland
Tel: 01854 612103, Fax: 01854 613773
13 Rooms, Double: £96–£140
Open: all year, Credit cards: all major

320

Places to Stay in Wales

The Olde Bull's Head has a long and interesting history. Established in 1472 and rebuilt in 1617, the walls of its traditional beamed bar are decorated with antique weaponry, brass and copper knick knacks and the town's ancient ducking chair—all enticingly olde worlde Dickensian. Charles Dickens actually did stay here and the rooms, found up creaking staircases are named after characters in his books. Each bedroom is individually decorated and nicely appointed with either antique or contemporary furniture. All have modern bathrooms, television, and phone and some have lovely antique brass or iron beds. Additional bedrooms are found in an adjacent 300 year old townhouse. Bedrooms here sport every modern convenience and contemporary decor. Room names (such as Clemantine, Plum, Scarlet and Pearl) give you an indication of the bedrooms signature color. Dine in the lively brasserie or enjoy modern French style food in the restaurant situated upstairs in the former hayloft. Castle Street leads to Beaumaris Castle, a squat, concentric fortification commissioned by Edward I, now a world heritage site. Nearby, the Marquis of Anglesey's house and gardens are open to the public. Past Bangor, on the mainland, is Caernarfon Castle where Prince Charles was invested as Prince of Wales. *Directions:* From Chester take the A55, coast road, to Anglesey and cross on the Britannia Road Bridge, then follow the A545 to Beaumaris.

THE OLDE BULL'S HEAD
Owners: David Robertson & Keith Rothwell
Castle Street
Beaumaris LL58 8AP, Wales
Tel: 01248 810329, Fax: 01248 811294
26 Rooms, Double: £105–£160
Closed: Christmas & New Year, Credit cards: all major

Tan-y-Foel, "the house under the hillside," sits high above the Conwy Valley, just outside Betws-y-Coed, within 6 acres of rugged woodland and pasture on the edge of the Snowdonia National Park. This small 5 star country house, owned and run by Janet and Peter Pitman and their daughter Kelly has fabulous views of the Conwy valley. In contrast to the traditional exterior the interior is modern, lots of creams and buttermilk colors have replaced the brighter modern décor that the Pitmans previously favored. Janet, a Master Chef of Great Britain, uses organic and fine local produce and takes pride in her modern cooking with Oriental and Asian influences. Dinner is served in a delightful little beamed dining room that in former times was the farm's dairy. Rooms 4, 5, and 6 enjoy spectacular views. Rooms 1 and 9 (an especially lovely converted hayloft) have separate entrances. The rugged grandeur of the Snowdonia mountain passes is in complete contrast to the pretty countryside around Tan-y-Foel. Castle lovers head for Conwy and Caernarfon. *Directions:* From the Llandudno roundabout on the A55 take the A470 towards Betws-y-Coed through Llanrwst and continue for 2 miles. Turn left at the signpost for Capel Garmon and Nebo (do not take the single-track road) and Tan-y-Foel is on your left after 1½ miles. Manchester airport is about an hour and a half's drive away.

TAN-Y-FOEL
Owners: Kelly Jeeves, Janet & Peter Pitman
near Betws-y-Coed
Capel Garmon LL26 0RE, Wales
Tel: 01690 710507, Fax: 01690 710681
5 Rooms, Double: £150–£225
Minimum Stay Required: 2 nights on weekends
Closed: Dec & Jan, Credit cards: MC, VS

The Castle Hotel stands on the site of a former Cistercian abbey, the latest incarnation of a 14th Century coaching inn. The impressive granite and brick façade was "recently" added at the turn of the 19th Century. Once inside exposed beams, antiques, collectibles nooks and crannies bear testament to the building's fascinating heritage. Over its life the hotel has played host to a variety of celebrities including, most notably, William Wordsworth, Samuel Johnson and Charlotte Bronte. A particularly grand old hand carved four-poster bed, dated 1570, was reputedly used by none other than King Charles I during the Civil War. All the rooms have been recently renovated and provide comfortable, contemporary style, accommodations come in a variety of shapes and sizes ranging up to the grandly spacious Wynn and Caer Rhun suites, the latter with a two person spa bathtub. Dawson's Bar and restaurant feature extensive use of local Welsh produce. The town of Conwy, an important gateway to North Wales for centuries, is dominated by its magnificent Edwardian Castle. It is also home to what is reputedly the "smallest house in Britain" on the waterfront, a few minutes walk from the hotel. *Directions:* Exit the A55 westbound at J18 for Conwy. Follow the one way system through the town. High Street is the main road on the right, parking is behind the hotel.

🛏️ 🏃 💳 @ W P 🍽️ ⚖️ 🚶 🚶‍♀️

CASTLE HOTEL
Owners: Graham Tinsley & The Lavin family
High Street
Conwy LL32 8DB, Wales
Tel: 01492 582800, Fax: 01492 582300
28 Rooms, Double: £120–£260
Open: all year, Credit cards: all major

Ynyshir Hall shares its location on the Dovey river estuary with a 1,000-acre bird reserve, home to herons, oystercatchers, curlews, and cormorants. Nestled in acres of gardens full of azaleas and rhododendrons, the hall was built in the 16th century, its most illustrious owner being Queen Victoria. Now it is home to professional artist Rob Reen and his wife Joan who have done the most wonderful job of decorating their country house hotel in rich colors, with each room accented by Rob's oils, acrylics, and watercolors. Relax round the fire in the elegant blue drawing room, enjoy a drink in the richly decorated bar, and dine on country-house fare in the turquoise-blue dining room. Bedrooms are named after famous artists. Monet, a ground-floor suite has a conservatory sitting room. A frieze of wispy clouds adds whimsy to the bathroom in the Renoir suite, which has particularly lovely views of the garden. Ynyshir Hall's central location makes it an ideal base for exploring the rugged Snowdonia National Park to the north and coastal paths to the south. Outstanding castles in the vicinity include Harlech, Powys, and Chirk. In nearby Machynlleth a traditional Welsh street market is held every Wednesday. *Directions:* From Aberystwyth take the A487 for 11 miles (towards Machynlleth) to Eglwysfach. Turn left in the village and Ynyshir Hall is on your right after half a mile.

YNYSHIR HALL
Manager: Gian Luca Rizzo
Eglwysfach SY20 8TA, Wales
Tel: 01654 781209, Fax: 01654 781366
11 Rooms, Double: £275–£375
Closed: Jan 5 to 25, Credit cards: all major
Relais & Châteaux

The Felin Fach Griffin's bright terra cotta exterior contrasts with the lush green Welsh countryside and immediately sparks your curiosity. Step inside and experience the refreshing simplicity and comfort of this one of a kind country pub cum restaurant. Upstairs the bedrooms are decorated simply, with soft-pastel-painted walls, white ceilings, and stripped wooden floors accented by an eclectic collection of antique furnishings and beds including some four-posters, goosedown pillows, Irish linens, and Welsh blankets. Modern bathrooms feature deep tubs to soak your bones after walking the surrounding hills. Downstairs, as befits the local pub, the public rooms are truly public. Flagstone floors, painted-stone walls, exposed wood beams, natural-slate-topped bars, and leather sofas round the fireplace all contribute to a very relaxed atmosphere. Food and drink and the enjoyment thereof are a major part of "the Griffin experience". Local ales are available and an excellent selection of wines by the glass and small carafe. Dinner is served by candlelight and breakfast enjoyed at a communal table in the Old Back Kitchen. Make your own toast, from excellent bread, on the cream-colored Aga. Go walking in the Brecon Beacons, fishing on the Wye and Usk and exploring southern Wales. *Directions:* The Griffin is located beside the A470 a little over 4 miles north of Brecon.

THE FELIN FACH GRIFFIN
Manager: Julie Bell
Felin Fach LD3 0UB, Wales
Tel: 01874 620111, Fax: 01874 620120
7 Rooms, Double: £105–£150
Closed: Christmas, Credit cards: MC, VS

The Cawdor is centrally located on the high street of Llandeilo in the heart of Carmarthenshire. Starting life as a coaching inn in 1796 it was recently completely refurbished and transformed into a contemporary boutique hotel. The striking pink and black external décor gives a clear first indication that this is "something different". Bold use of color continues inside. Lilacs, mauves purples and maroon drapes, carpets and bed covers accentuate the cool beige and white walls. Dark grey slate floors and cherrywood furnishings complete the picture. The jazz themed bar and residents' lounge with its large fireplace beckon as places to enjoy a glass of wine or afternoon tea. The stylish restaurant features local produce, Welsh meats and cheese, fresh seafood from the Pembrokeshire coast, vegetables from the Cawdor's own five acre kitchen garden. Bedrooms are all named after local castles and towns. All are decorated, furnished and equipped to the same exacting standards with extra large beds, sumptuous white linens, spectacular modern bathrooms amenities. We were particularly taken by the two huge suites on the top floor. The Cawdor is conveniently located for visits to the Welsh Botanical Gardens, and three famous castles, Diefwr, Carreg Cennen and Llansteffan. *Directions:* Llandeilo is on the A40 between Carmarthen and Brecon. The Cawdor is on the main street, unload in the courtyard and you will be directed to the nearby car park.

THE CAWDOR
Owners: Louisa & Martin Morgan
Manager: Gareth Davies
2 Rhosmean Street
Llandeilo SA19 6EN, Wales
Tel: 01558 823500, Fax: 01558 822399
23 Rooms, Double: £65–£200
2 Apartments: £250 daily
Open: all year, Credit cards: all major

Tyddyn Llan is a delightful gray-stone country house set in the peaceful Vale of Edeyrnion at the eastern gateway to Snowdonia. A onetime shooting lodge for the Dukes of Westminster it is now a foodie haven and delightful country house hotel owned by the Webbs. Susan runs the front of house while Bryan produces culinary magic in the kitchen. Enjoy a seven course tasting menu or dine a la carte. At the time of our visit the menu included: griddled scallops with vegetable relish and rocket, loin of lamb with braised peppers and pannacotta with blood oranges. There are comfortable lounges with cozy nooks and a snug bar to relax in and enjoy before and after dinner drinks. Accommodation, decorated in restful colors, range in size from cozy to spacious. We were particularly impressed by the impressive ground floor suite with its large luxurious bathroom (handicap equipped) and french windows opening to a secluded garden patio. Between meals you can hike the old drovers' roads and tramp into the nearby Berwyn Mountains. Steam trains run on a narrow track down one side of the lake. A more scenic train ride is from Blaenau Ffestiniog, a mining town where slate crags overhang the houses, to Porthmadog on the coast. On the way to the train visit Llechwedd slate caverns. Visit the walled city of Chester with its half-timbered shops. *Directions:* Tyddyn Llan is near Llandrillo, on the B4401 between Corwen (A5) and Bala.

TYDDYN LLAN
Owners: Susan & Bryan Webb
Llandrillo LL21 0ST, Wales
Tel: 01490 440264, Fax: 01490 440414
12 Rooms, Double: £130–£280
Open: all year, Credit cards: all major

Snowdonia is home to the most beautiful Welsh scenery and Bodysgallen Hall, the most beautiful of Welsh hotels. Built around a 13th-century watchtower with Conwy Castle in the distance, this rambling hotel looks surprisingly uniform, considering eight centuries of additions, alterations, and restorations. The mellow elegance and character of the house are beautifully preserved. The spacious, dark-oak-paneled Jacobean entrance hall and the drawing room on the first floor have large fireplaces, mullioned windows, and comfortable furniture that create a tremendously luxurios old fashioned feel. Fifteen beautiful bedrooms are found in the main house: including four absolutely decadent suites each with two bathrooms—I particularly enjoyed my stay in room 8, which has a sitting nook and the loveliest of views of the garden. Sixteen suites are located in adjoining little cottages. Food is modern British. The grounds are an absolute delight and include a 17th-century knot garden, an 18th-century walled rose garden, and a woodland walk that offers spectacular views. Work out in the gym, swim in the indoor pool, laze on the terrace, or enjoy a pampering treatment. Snowdonia and historic Conwy are just down the road. *Directions:* Take the A55 from Chester to Junction 19 on the outskirts of Conwy where you turn right on the A470. The hotel entrance is on your right after 2 miles.

BODYSGALLEN HALL AND SPA
Manager: Matthew Johnson
Llandudno LL30 1RS, Wales
Tel: 01492 584466, Fax: 01492 582519
31 Rooms, Double: £175–£450
Open: all year, Credit cards: all major

This grand and dignified house was designed by Sir Clough Williams-Ellis (of fanciful Portmeirion) and rescued from ruin by Sir Bernard Ashley (of Laura Ashley fame). The lounges are a delight: a great hall with an open fire, antiques, huge sofas, and interesting original artwork; a beautiful sitting room; and a book-filled library with leather chairs and a snooker table. Each bedroom or suite is individually planned and quite different from the next—some are very flowery, others very masculine. The suites are up two long flights of stairs under the eaves. The smaller rooms of the north wing are most attractive—several have small four-poster beds and Welsh mineral water, sherry, homemade biscuits, and fluffy robes are provided. The Wye river valley offers several places of interest and nearby are the ruins of Tintern Abbey, celebrated by Wordsworth. You can visit Hereford, a lovely, sleepy, medieval city astride the River Wye, its cathedral built in several styles from the 11th century, and Hay-on-Wye with its many bookstores. There is an abundance of pretty countryside, from the stark beauty of the Brecon Beacons to the soft prettiness of the Wye valley. *Directions:* Llangoed Hall is on the A470, midway between Builth Wells and Brecon.

LLANGOED HALL
Owner: The Ashley Family
Manager: David Howe
Brecon
Llyswen LD3 0YP, Wales
Tel: 01874 754525, Fax: 01874 754545
23 Rooms, Double: £225–£400
Open: all year, Credit cards: all major

A soft pink colorwash brightens the exterior of this spacious onetime-doctors home in the village of Newport. You will love the welcoming, free-and-easy atmosphere that pervades this home where Judith and Michael Cooper extend the warmest of welcomes. It's the kind of place where you pop your head round the kitchen door with questions. Enjoy before-dinner drinks in either the sitting room or the bar, both snug characterful rooms filled with country antiques. Welsh beef and local organic veg are on the dinner menu along with a tempting selection of starters and desserts (vegetarian dishes are available). There are three zip and link twin/king rooms and two queen bedrooms all artfully decorated in a light, airy style and immaculately furnished, with every nook and cranny filled with old family treasures. One guestroom is a family room with a small adjoining bunk-bedroom for children. An absolutely adorable 3 bedroom, two bath, cottage is available for one week lets. Just down the lane you find Newport's pretty beach and a particularly lovely section of the Welsh coastal path. *Directions:* Newport is on the A487 11 miles west of Cardigan and 7 miles east of Fishguard (not to be confused with the other Newport near Cardiff).

CNAPAN HOUSE
Owners: Lloyd & Cooper Families
East Street
Newport SA42 0WF, Wales
Tel: 01239 820575, Fax: 01239 820878
5 Rooms, Double: £88
1 Cottage: from £300 weekly
Closed: Jan & Feb, Credit cards: MC, VS

Penmaenuchaf Hall is a lovely country house hotel with a quite unpronounceable name. According to owners Lorraine Fielding and Mark Watson, "pen mine ich av" is a somewhat accurate pronunciation. Lorraine, Mark, and daughter Lara moved here in 1989 and spent two years converting this beautiful old home into a hotel. Lorraine says the most enjoyable part was deciding upon the color schemes and choosing the fabrics—you'll be pleased with her choices: the decor throughout is absolutely delightful. From the log fire that warms the hallway sitting room through the comfortable lounge to the cozy dining room, the house exudes a welcoming ambiance. The principal bedroom, Leigh Taylor, is named after the wealthy Lancashire cotton magnate who built Penmaenuchaf as a grand holiday home. Today it can be your holiday home in northern Wales. Venture to explore Snowdonia National Park and the central Welsh coast and return in the evening to enjoy an excellent dinner. Of particular interest are the rugged scenery of Snowdonia, Portmeirion village with its Italianate houses, the narrow-gauge Ffestiniog railway, 13th-century Harlech Castle, Llechwedd Slate Caverns, and Bodnant, one of the world's finest gardens. *Directions:* From the Dollgellau bypass (A470) take the A493 towards Tywyn and Fairbourne. The entrance to Penmaenuchaf Hall is on the left after ¾ mile.

PENMAENUCHAF HALL
Owners: Lorraine Fielding & Mark Watson
Dolgellau
Penmaenpool LL40 1YB, Wales
Tel: 01341 422129, Fax: 01341 422787
15 Rooms, Double: £150–£230
Open: all year, Credit cards: all major

Maes-y-Neuadd, solidly built of granite and slate, is set at the edge of the spectacular scenery of the Snowdonia National Park with views of the mountains and sweeping vistas down to Cardigan Bay. Furnished and equipped to a high standard, the bedrooms reflect the various periods during which the house was built dating back to the 14th-century four-poster rooms, 16th-cenutury beams and dormer windows, and high ceilings and period furniture of the Georgian era. The sunny conservatory is perfect for morning coffee. Enjoy afternoon tea in the cozy lounge and watch the sun set over the Llyn peninsula from the terrace while sipping a glass of chilled champagne. The restaurant uses only fresh local produce with much of the fruit, herbs and vegetables coming from the extensive kitchen gardens. Apart from exploring castles, visiting Portmerion (of The Prisoner fame), playing golf (Royal St Davids is 10 minutes away), admiring gardens (Bodnant Gardens is a gem), and the attractions of Snowdonia National Park, one of the delights of staying here is to ride on the nearby Ffestiniog Railway with its steam train that takes you through spectacular countryside. *Directions:* Maes-y-Neuadd is off the B4573, 3 miles north of Harlech.

MAES-Y-NEUADD
Owners: Lynn & Peter Jackson, Doreen & Peter Payne
Talsarnau LL47 6YA, Wales
Tel: 01766 780200, Fax: 01766 780211
16 Rooms, Double: £119–£200
Open: all year, Credit cards: all major

Index

A

Abbey Hotel, The, Penzance, 228
Abbotsbury
  Abbey House, 134
Abney, 67
  Barrel Inn, 67
Achiltibuie
  Summer Isles Hotel, 286
Airds Hotel & Restaurant, Port Appin, 312
Airfare, 2
Aldeburgh, 50
  Moot Hall, 50
Alexander House, York, 282
Alfriston, 42
  Clergy House, 42
Alstonfield, 62
  Post Office Tea Shop, 62
Ambleside, 56
  Rothay Manor, 135
Anchorage House, St. Austell, 253
Anglesey, Isle of, 108
Applecross, 97
Arbor Low, 63
Ardehslaig, 97
Arisaig, 95
Armadale, 95
  Castle, 94
Arundel, 43
  Castle, 43
Arundell Arms, Lifton, 210
Ashbourne, 61
  Gingerbread Shop, 61

Ashford-in-the-Water, 64
Ashwater
  Blagdon Manor Hotel, 136
At the Sign of the Angel, Lacock, 28, 204
Augill Castle, Brough-in-Westmorland, 159
Auldearn
  Boath House, 287
Austwick
  Austwick Hall, 137
Avebury, 28
Aylesbury
  Hartwell House, 138
Aysgarth, 77
  Falls, 77

B

Bakewell, 63
  Bakewell Pudding Factory, 63
  Market Hall, 63
  Old House Museum, The, 63
  Ye Olde Original Pudding Shop, 63
Ballantrae
  Glenapp Castle, 288
Ballater, 87
Ballathie Castle, 88
Ballathie House, Kinclaven, 306
Ballindalloch Castle, 89
Balmoral Castle, 86
Banchory
  Banchory Lodge, 289
Barngates
  Drunken Duck, The, 139

Culloden, 89
  Culloden House, 293
Currency, 3

D

Dale Head Hall, Thirlmere, 261
Dannah Farm, Shottle, 248
Dartmoor, 36
  Haytor Crags, 36
  Lydford Gorge, 36
Dedham, 50
  Castle House, 51
Derwent Water, 57
Devonshire Arms, The, Bolton Abbey, 151
Devonshire Fell, The, Burnsall, 163
Dolwyddlan Castle, 111
Dorset Square Hotel, London, 119
Dovedale, 61
Dower House, The, Muir of Ord, 307
Driving, 3
Drumnadrochit, 90
  Loch Ness Monster Exhibition, 90
Drunken Duck, The, Barngates, 139
Dufftown, 88
  Glenfiddich Distillery, 88
Dukes Hotel, Bath, 144
Dukes Hotel, London, 120
Dun na Mara, Benderloch, 290
Dunblane
  Cromlix House, 294
Dunkeld, 85
  Cathedral, 85
Dunmurray Lodge, Pitlochry, 310

Dunster, 30
  Castle, 30
  Watermill, 31
Duntulm Castle, 93
Dunvegan, 93
  Castle, 93
Dunwich, 49
  Flora Tea Rooms, 49
Durley House, London, 121

E

Eagle House, Bathford, 148
East Bergholt, 51
East Grinstead
  Gravetye Manor, 178
East Hoathly
  Old Whyly, 179
East Lodge, Rowsley, 240
Eastbourne, 42
Edale, 67
Eden Project, The, 35
Edensor, 64
Edinburgh, 81
  Bonham, The, 295
  Britannia, 84
  Castle, 82
  Channings, 296
  Edinburgh Residence, The, 297
  Festival, 81
  Gladstone's Land, 82
  Howard, The, 298
  John Knox House, 83
  Museum of Childhood, 83
  Museum of Scotland, 82

338   *Index*

KAREN BROWN wrote her first travel guide in 1976. Her personalized travel series has grown to 17 titles, which Karen and her small staff work diligently to keep updated. Karen and her husband, Rick, live in a small town on the coast south of San Francisco.

JUNE EVELEIGH BROWN hails from Sheffield, England and lived in Zambia and Canada before moving to northern California where she lives in San Mateo with her husband, Tony, and their German Shepherd.

BARBARA MACLURCAN TAPP, the talented artist who produces all of the hotel sketches and delightful illustrations in this guide, was raised in Sydney, Australia where she studied interior design. Although Barbara continues with architectural rendering and watercolor painting, she devotes much of her time to illustrating the Karen Brown guides. Barbara lives in Kensington, California, with her husband, Richard, and is Mum to Jono, Alex and Georgia. For more information about her work visit *www.barbaratapp.com*.

JANN POLLARD, the artist of the cover painting has studied art since childhood, and is well known for her outstanding impressionistic-style watercolors. Jann's works are in private and corporate collections internationally and she has become a popular workshop teacher in the States, Mexico and Europe. *www.jannpollard.com*. Fine art giclée prints of her paintings are available at *www.karenbrown.com*.

Karen Brown's World of Travel

**A FREE KAREN BROWN WEBSITE MEMBERSHIP
IS INCLUDED WITH THE PURCHASE OF THIS GUIDE**

$20 Value – Equal to the cover price of this book!

In appreciation for purchasing our guide, we offer a free membership that includes:

• The ability to custom plan and build unlimited itineraries
• 15% discount on all purchases made in the Karen Brown website store
• One free downloadable Karen Brown Itinerary from over 100 choices
• Karen Brown's World of Travel Newsletter—includes special offers & updates
    Membership valid through December 31, 2010

To take advantage of this free offer go to the Karen Brown website shown below and create a login profile so we can recognize you as a Preferred Customer; then you can utilize the unrestricted trip planning and take advantage of the 15% store discount. Once you set up an account you will receive by email a coupon code to order the free itinerary.

Go to ***www.karenbrown.com/preferred.php*** to create your profile!

Karen Brown's
2010 Readers' Choice Awards

Most Romantic
Viewfield House
Portree, Scotland

Warmest Welcome
Dukes Hotel
London, England

Greatest Value
Hall End
Ledbury, England

Splendid Splurge
Hambleton Hall
Hambleton, England

Be sure to vote for next year's winners by visiting
www.karenbrown.com